A Year in Hell

A Year in Hell

*Memoir of an Army Foot Soldier
Turned Reporter in Vietnam,
1965–1966*

RAY PEZZOLI, JR.

McFarland & Company, Inc., Publishers
Jefferson, North Carolina, and London

LIBRARY OF CONGRESS CATALOGUING-IN-PUBLICATION DATA

Pezzoli, Ray, Jr., 1940–
    A year in hell : memoir of an army foot soldier turned reporter
in Vietnam, 1965–1966 / Ray Pezzoli, Jr.
        p.   cm.
    Includes index.

    ISBN-13: 978-0-7864-2396-5
    ISBN-10: 0-7864-2396-X
    (softcover : 50# alkaline paper) ∞

    1. Vietnam War, 1961–1975—Personal narratives, American.
2. Pezzoli, Ray, 1940–   I. Title.
DS559.5.P444   2006
959.704'3092—dc22   2006018558
    [B]

British Library cataloguing data are available

On the cover: The author climbing a typical perpendicular stream bank

Manufactured in the United States of America

McFarland & Company, Inc., Publishers
    Box 611, Jefferson, North Carolina 28640
        www.mcfarlandpub.com

To the troops of Vietnam,
that they are not forgotton

Acknowledgments

Thanks to Joe Margiotta of Santa Barbara, California, for his computer assistance. Tolerance is a virtue.

Thanks to John Cabassi of Manhattan Beach, California, who was responsible for the tedious task of assembling my maze of information into a recognizable form of literature.

My very special friend, Maryann Russo, provided excellent support in developing the manuscript into a marketable book.

Table of Contents

Preface

The people of the former free-enterprise, democratic country of South Vietnam fell victim to the adage, "The pen is mightier than the sword." The lives of its citizens were tools to fashion sensationalistic, profitable news stories, regardless of how the outcome would affect their lives, under the guise of the First Amendment, a unique feature prevalent in our media.

Tragedy in Vietnam always meant great copy. People were interested in the ghoulish, real-live TV coverage of the war. Its battles produced our first authentic, true action flick of a war accompanied with all its blood and gore, emptied into secure American living rooms.

The enemy didn't need spies; they merely had to read our news and watch TV to be familiar with our military objectives. Not only did U.S. troops have to fight an evasive enemy, their combat included a struggle for appreciation from fellow Americans. All they asked for was a sensible, righteous, and sincere representation from our media.

The motto of the *New York Times* is, "All the news that's fit to print." Today, as we've seen how a people were sold out by our news industry, it might be altered to read, "All the news that's fit and profitable enough to print."

This book does not have an agenda or vendetta against the media. It is a vehicle to provide an understanding for Vietnam vets, showing fellow Americans aspects of that conflict never deemed "newsworthy enough" for national distribution.

I endured the first three months in Vietnam as a perspiration-saturated infantryman, nesting in the 125-degree sand dunes of Cam Ranh Bay where my squad washed in the South China Sea each morning and nursed one tepid canteen of army-purified water each day, while attempting to find epicurean satisfaction out of the 12 kinds of mundane, air temperature C rations.

Later my battalion was assigned responsibility for the "Iron Triangle," the contested jungles between Cambodia and Saigon, the Communists' main infiltration route to the capital. I became the reporter and photographer for my battalion there, continuing to accompany troops into the "boonies" out of respect and admiration for the guys "out there." I felt compelled by the integrity of my job to portray the troops in my unit, the 1st Battalion, 18th Infantry, 1st Infantry Division, as the proficient warriors they were. Consequently, more combat photos and stories were published of them in military papers than any other unit in Vietnam at the time. Soldiers mentioned numerous times of their parents seeing their photo or a story about their unit in major papers—credit being "U.S. Army Photo or Story." My quest never interfered with my main objective: to continue looking and acting as a U.S. infantryman whose job it was to kill Communists with a habit which later became aloof, analogous to swatting a fly. I was proud to snuff out at least a dozen.

As one of these troops, I lived closer to being an animal than I had ever conceived. This included tolerating 18 days without washing, shaving, and brushing my teeth, sleeping one night in the blood of one of my men, killing a person with my bare hands, being involved in a friendly air strike, and a chopper firing at us one night, while managing to recognize God for the first time in my life.

Columnist Len Morgan of *Flying* magazine, June 1991, mentioned what I believe to be the seat of evil with our media. "Think money," he states. "The media's professed aims are to report events, record history, and present both sides of important issues but the bottom line is none of the above. The media primarily exists to earn profits for their stockholders. Success is measured by circulation and ratings, which in turn determine advertising rates. Audit Bureau of Circulation's [ABC] and Nielsen numbers add up to black ink or red.

"A thrill a minute approach is the result. There must be exciting stories to tell, even when nothing exciting has happened. Unless headlines and newscasts rivet attention, ratings slip. Non news is often dramatized beyond recognition and many Americans ask, 'Is much of that stuff necessary?'"

William K. Lane Jr.'s article, "Vietnam Vets: Ambushed in Hollywood," was condensed from the *Wall Street Journal* (July 28, 1988) and later appeared in the *Reader's Digest*. He thought that the hundreds of brave Americans who fought in Southeast Asia deserved a better caricature than that of a legion of losers as depicted by Hollywood.

Also, in another *Reader's Digest* article (July 1992), condensed from *Image,* journalist Ginger Casey states, "Some reporters will do anything to get a story. Have they no shame?" she asks. "A kind of feeding frenzy takes over at highly charged events, and reporters don't necessarily act, but react."

Especially applicable to Vietnam, she states, "We journalists rarely consider the consequences of our presence at an event."

"Of course," she continues, "limiting press access can lead to censorship, which would violate the First Amendment."

In closing she reaches the crux of this argument of press restrictions: "We have a moral and ethical responsibility that goes beyond objective reporting. It's the responsibility to be gentle and compassionate to those in pain. It's the responsibility to know when we have overstepped our bounds. Ultimately, it's the responsibility to hold the mirror up, not just to the news event, but also to us."

Dan Rather, a pioneer of network TV news and recently defrocked CBS anchorman for his debacle of an expose during the 2004 presidential election regarding President George W. Bush's National Guard service, expressed in an article for the "My Turn" column in *Newsweek,* July 17, 1989, that what really appeals to the media is profitability and the value of foreign news. He said that contrary to what some people in the news industry believe, Americans are really interested in world affairs and news. "Alas, the business of selling copy. Vietnam, especially anti–Vietnam, was a guaranteed 'print.'"

According to Rather in "My Turn," that was it in a nutshell, to "make news profitable."

Peter Arnett was another leading correspondent who covered succulent assignments the past 30 years. He received the hatchet from NBC recently for his fiasco in Iraq with erroneous remarks, speciously claiming during an interview with Iraqi state television that Washington's "first war plan has just failed because of Iraqi resistance.... Clearly the American war planners misjudged the determination of the Iraqi forces."

I met him during a search-and-destroy mission in the jungles of the "Iron Triangle" in November 1966 when he arrived on a chopper to evacuate captured equipment and prisoners.

Enthusiastically I greeted him with the news that we had killed five Viet Cong and injured two others, and that eight rifles, ammunition, a stone rice mill, and 26 50-pound bags of rice had been seized.

"How many Americans killed?" he demanded.

"None," I eagerly replied. "Nobody even got hurt!"

"No one killed!" He sniffed and stomped back to the chopper about to depart with enemy prisoners and equipment for a location where American soldiers might have been killed.

Is it polite to laugh at a corpse during a funeral because of its disfigured physical appearance?

The men loading the prisoners did not appreciate his rude and despicable attitude, suggesting a course of action contrary to the Code of Military Justice.

A soldier's view of journalists interfering with troops in combat is nothing new. General Sherman's view during the Civil War was that newspapermen were worse than spies.

Names have been changed to protect privacy.

Chapter 1

"Hi, My Name Is Ray"

I crooned to Marty in June 1965 at Falmouth Heights Beach, while on leave at my home in the Massachusetts resort of Cape Cod. She was an attractive brunette sitting at the beach with intriguing dark eyes; protecting her body from the morning fog was a "Hartford" sweatshirt. Hartford was the nursing school she had recently graduated from, 50 miles from my alma mater of two years previous, the University of Bridgeport. We had a common denominator to begin our brief courtship, each familiar with both southern Connecticut cities.

Marty said she was waiting for results from numerous job applications throughout the U.S.; her most desired locations were the warmer climes of California.

I majored in industrial relations, graduating in 1963, but never worked in that capacity because the draft board banged down my door shortly after. If I was drafted, I would spend two years assigned to a less-demanding capacity; yet, by enlisting I could request my assignment, though I would have to spend another year in the Army. I always wanted to be someone of consequence so I passed tests for qualification in the demanding Army Officer Candidate School (OCS). Unfortunately, or maybe for my fortune later, I didn't last the 24 weeks and was "paneled out" in my 12th week because of an "attitude problem": I was not aggressive enough. Unfortunately, I did a 180-degree turn later as an infantryman, 111.10 MOS, frequently acting cool, impersonal, and ambivalent toward other enlisted men. I wasn't very popular with the troops in my barracks; most felt I was still playing the role. My few friends where the half dozen ex-candidates who were paneled out with me in OCS Class 51.

Marty became intrigued, especially after I showed my independence by exhibiting a disdain for the authority of the Army hierarchy.

The sun burned through and "Hartford" slid off, exhibiting a firm

5

body with tight-stretched, light olive Italian skin. Marty took on a different perspective as I continued my dissertation.

I was staying with my folks at another Cape Cod town before being shipped, as rumor had it, "Some place in Southeast Asia," and apprehensive about the destination. I had spent the previous summer rotting through three months of jungle training at Eglin Air Force Base, Florida, with the First Infantry Division. In addition to acting as guinea pigs for the Army, testing the best manner in which to assault an enemy in the jungle either via C-130 aircraft or UH-1B (Huey) helicopter, we participated in Ranger patrolling tactics for evasive enemy guerrillas.

No way did we sleep in beds! The troops spent those three summer months in the vines and ferns of jungle, no cover over their heads, continuously outside, lying and sleeping on the ground amongst the indigenous creatures, conducting patrols, war games, and jungle familiarization exercises. The heat was intense in that humid, damp jungle with mosquitoes feasting each night. Also, I was christened two different times by scorpions, one managing to crawl inside my shirtsleeve to sting me six times.

There was an exciting week of intense Ranger training where we learned to kill and prepare animals in the jungle, differentiate between poisonous and nonpoisonous fruits, and slaughter or maim a person with our bare hands. Everyone found this exhilarating but hoped never to be a position to have to utilize these tools.

We were issued two sets of jungle fatigues on which we sewed name tags, insignia, and patches, suggesting garrison duty in a secure location some place.

The sun was getting hot, prompting an excuse for a few beers and a salad at the Casino by the Sea, adjacent to the beach.

Although my primary duty was Infantry, during most of my last assignment with the 1st Infantry Division at Fort Riley, Kansas, I was editor of the 1st Battalion, 28th Infantry "Black Lions" weekly mimeographed newspaper, *The Rimrock Register*. Each week I assembled news of the pending week's training agenda and activities, whatever trivia I could discover, and a weekly message from each of our chaplains.

This was a lot of fun because I was completely independent of any authority supervising my actions, providing the battalion commander was satisfied with the paper.

Johnnie Mack, mess sergeant of Alpha Company, invited me to a sumptuous Sunday lunch, about which I wrote exclusively. This initiated a rivalry between the cooks of the four mess halls, each vying for me join them the following Sunday. Soon the reputation spread throughout the "Big Red One" that the Black Lions ate better than anyone else in the division.

Suffice it to say, all the men began to benefit from Army chow that was steps above what was expected.

Also, there was a subtle award program in my battalion where the soldier who excelled that week in inspections, target practice, motivation, and general overall conduct was awarded the distinction "Black Lion Extraordinaire." This ostentatious plaque was positioned on the recipient's footlocker for the week. I twisted the battalion commander's arm to grant each recipient a weekend pass while exclusively mentioning him in an article with a distinction that made other troops envious.

Marty was a liberal free spirit of New England in the Boston venue, who purred that my considerations for the little man were a noble gesture.

By then it was time to hit Zack's, the craziest bar in town, for happy hour. After our moderate wait at the front door, we entered this converted barn, showcasing a rock band, and found the patrons swinging from the rafters upside down and gyrating to and fro with the music, per usual. I scooped up some of the loose change that had fallen on the floor before squeezing to the bar. Pitchers of Narragansett draft beer went down quickly and easily that night.

The next morning, following an interesting evening, Marty gathered her belongings before returning to Hartford while I showered at her motel room. I didn't want to look disheveled when I returned to my mother, waiting expectantly in her kitchen in Wareham, 45 minutes away.

We enjoyed breakfast together at the Coffee Kart, a local breakfast place serving the largest omelets in town, swapped addresses, promised to write, and I vowed not to get shot wherever I was sent because we had a date when I returned.

Chapter 2

"Make Sure You Say Good-Bye to All the Neighbors"

"For crying out loud, Ma, I'm only going to be gone for a year."

"Things happen. Say bye to Father Chandler; I'm sure he will keep you in his prayers."

It felt like my last supper as my parents drove me back to Fort Riley, Kansas.

My dad, who had been exempt from serving in World War II, was accomplishing what he'd always felt guilty about, his obligation to America, through me. He proudly told friends I was with the 1st Infantry Division going to Asia to help folks.

In case I did see combat, I'd have to look and act tough as in the movies. I bought several boxes of Parodi cigars, figuring the smell from these short, black, crooked, branch-looking stogies was foul enough to incapacitate the hardiest enemy soldier.

Newspapers showed military activity increasing in Vietnam with more Special Forces involvement.

Our deployment for Vietnam, its date, and locations were already decided upon, but remained secret to us.

We arrived at Fort Riley, George Custer's old cavalry post. My folks were entertained by its historical significance while I was troubled by the coincidence of Custer's last stand.

The folks watched reveille. Ma remarked how straight and tall I looked standing at attention. They returned to Massachusetts with this vision and wondered if this would be their last.

Brigade was a ghost town now. All our heavy equipment had been shipped to San Francisco. The 5,000 men of 3rd Brigade had their equipment packed. The two other brigades conducted normal garrison duties, seemingly oblivious to our departure plans.

Three days before our flight to San Francisco, the headlines from a neighboring town's newspaper screamed, "Big Red One to Vietnam." The secret destination and location of our three infantry battalions was splattered across the front page, every intricacy of our secret operation printed for all to see. The men in my barracks were stunned, feeling that we had been betrayed. A lower-echelon person in Operations could have made this secret information available to this local rag.

The disgust of the guys in my barracks wasn't a vendetta toward the paper for its lack of consideration. Their anger reflected the emotions of men whose heads were placed on the chopping block by fellow Americans for a few bucks. They felt it commensurate with announcing the Normandy invasion on the front page of the *New York Times*. Since, I have discussed this incident with people showing ambivalence toward the men's disdain for the paper. I told them to discuss this with me the next time someone tried to kill them.

Our troops felt it inconceivable that we were going into combat and the paper didn't have the civility and gravity to wait until we landed and established our defenses to broadcast this news.

Three thousand of the 2nd Brigade's infantry were flown to Oakland Army Terminal on June 21. The remainder of the brigade's more than 5,000 men were the support compliment in transit on railroads or loading two of the three transport ships.

The infantry sailed on the U.S.S. *Gordon* the next day.

"We've been asked by the Republic of Vietnam to help with the Communists," our company commander, Capt. Philip Pope said, briefing us three miles out to sea.

After the first day, the ocean was calm for the remainder of our 17-day voyage. A small storm would have been a welcome diversion after several days of tedious boredom.

Activities included fire watch, cleaning weapons, physical training (PT), briefings, inspections, G.I. duties, lifeboat and evacuation drills, and mostly standing and griping wherever we could find a spot.

We were never "brainwashed" about duty in Vietnam; we were told only their government invited us and our location would be Cam Ranh Bay. Our assignment was protecting the engineers constructing the deepwater port.

Cam Ranh Peninsula ran parallel to the mainland, attaching near the resort town of Na Trang. Our peninsula was 15 miles long and one mile wide. A string of sand dunes rose 400 yards behind a 200-yard wide beach of coarse sand. The inside of the peninsula was plain, mostly soft, powdery beach sand on slowly rolling dunes and scrub brush.

Alpha Company occupied a narrow, shallow crossing point three quarters of the way down the peninsula to stop Viet Cong infiltration. My company, Bravo, would spread across to further discourage infiltration. Charlie and Headquarters Companies were adjacent to the harbor, securing it.

The remaining infantry battalions continued to Saigon, convoying to Bien Hoa, 30 miles northeast, defending the Air Force complex there.

The troops studied Vietnam's history, people, enemy, jungle combat, and our locations. The country was a democracy; its citizens enjoyed civil rights, freedom of choice, different religions, elections, and capitalism with private ownership, not a totalitarian government like the Communist North. The men learned the Vietnamese words: "halt, kill Cong, and surrender" and counting to 10.

The Viet Cong didn't wear uniforms, merely their trademark black silk "pajamas" during night combat. During the day they wore peasant clothes, looking like civilians, discouraging us from killing any person seen in the jungle. Troops were supposed to capture whoever was found and transport them to the Command Post (CP) for interrogation. If a man was seen with a rifle, he couldn't be fired upon because he might be a Popular Force trooper, much like our Minutemen, in the jungle trying to zap a few VC. If a VC shot from Cambodia, troops couldn't fire back because it was neutral. Captured VC thought this was a joke.

Before a search-and-destroy mission, leaflets were dropped warning everyone about the impending invasion and to vacate for their safety. Unfortunately they didn't; they merely established ambushes for troops.

When a VC was killed, we had to verify he was actually dead and not wounded, capable of crawling away. The infamous body count had to be accurate; unfortunately, discovered bloated bodies couldn't be tallied.

The topic of conversation during the voyage was what we might find at our destination and the ridiculous way to fight a war with restrictions.

Soldiers felt friendships shouldn't materialize. The most important obsession was our own life; the death of a buddy shouldn't dull our senses. Consequently, many remained aloof, a poignant lesson for replacements in the future.

Eventually we ran out of things to talk about. I needed something to fill this void, so I began my 10-year dependency on cigarettes. They may have prevented me from cracking up. I eventually smoked four packs a day.

My excessive energy and boredom encouraged my mind to run rampant. I wrote to Marty saying I was fed up with our government, that we were mere pawns for the aspirations, whims, and follies of politicians. We had no business interfering with another country's internal affairs and this was probably the objective of big business stimulating our economy.

The first two weeks dragged. Our only highlights were the meals, the best for a year, and a nightly movie. At the end of the second week everyone apprehensively counted, "16, 17 days, we'll be there." The Lord only knew what to expect, though it was possible we would be in combat soon.

Chapter 3

Vietnam, July 11, 1965, 0700 hours

My gear for the landing was stacked in a corner of our crowded hold. I assembled early, but many waited until the last minute. I knew I'd be nervous and apprehensive so I lay down early; at least I would rest my body.

My equipment consisted of a steel helmet, dress baseball cap worn for news cameras when we came ashore, 40mm grenade launcher, three days C rations, three canteens of water, a deadly looking bone-handle knife which rusted in a month, .45 automatic pistol, two hand grenades, an entrenching tool, a backpack, and a poncho. Everyone had a meager basic load of ammo; mine consisted of one .45 magazine in the weapon, three in each of my two ammo pouches, a bandolier of six 40mm rounds around my neck, and a spare in my pocket.

This was all the ammo troops would have stretched across sand dunes; supplied with food and water every three days and cautioned, "Be careful with the ammo and water; there's no more."

I remembered my combat training, lugging different types of military paraphernalia, "armed to the teeth." Now, involved in the real thing, we were cautioned about ammo, food, and water.

Troops were also cautioned about temperatures over 100 degrees, sun reflecting on the dunes, and 90-percent humidity. Rain several times a day, caught in steel pots, would provide supplemental water.

To wash, the ocean would help with a rinse. Salt tablets were available and every Friday the medic would supply malaria tablets.

Some of the men showered. I showered in the morning, not knowing my next chance.

The lights were on at 0300 hours. My shower was the last hot water to touch my body for a year.

The whine of the ship's engines slowed, then went quiet during breakfast, and we were lying motionless. Within the confines of the *Gordon*'s hull, we sensed the ominous feeling—we were there!

The platoon was assembled in our hold at 0500 hours, gear on and duffel bag ready. I made sure my cigars were accessible, Winstons next to them and two books of matches.

Troops filed out of the semi ventilated hold to the deck at 0530, feeling the intensity of Vietnam's heat and moisture for the first time. Dim lights illuminated the outside deck, though hardly sufficient to see pipes and tubes which hooked and blocked. Each man gingerly shuffled to the gangplanks to board the LCM, landing crafts. While shuffling and squeezing forward, my harness became entangled. It was difficult to reach behind to undo it and the guy next to me was too close to raise his hands. Some toe stands, wiggles, and small hops worked. I turned toward the railing. The sun was rising.

The Republic of South Vietnam.

Chapter 4

Cam Ranh Bay, the Republic of Vietnam, on the Other Side of America's World

The *Gordon* proceeded into this dark blue bay, one of the deepest bays in the world, at early morning light. Black green pinnacles of rock rose from the sandy white beaches through a green scrub brush-lined bay.

Two steep hills stood on each side of the two harbors, resembling sentinels.

This country had more striking geography than imagined.

The VC harassed a hamlet in the northern province of Binh Dinh, demanding rice and supplies from a farmer. When he refused, he was shot. His son's hand was cut off for not helping. In another part of that province, a woman reported VC dragged away her husband and sons.

Further north in Quang Nam province, VC indiscriminately fired into a village, killing two girls.

Two days after a recent mortar attack on Da Nang Air Base, the bodies of two men and a woman were found floating in a nearby stream, their hands tied behind their backs and the woman's feet chopped off.

A grenade was tossed into a market in Gia Dinh province with one person killed and several wounded.

A 14-year-old boy had recently been shot by VC because he would not cooperate, refusing to give his rice to a passing squad of guerrillas as a "protection tax."

In all these cases, the VC were trying to undercut the government, striking at local officials. Many village chiefs spent nights in different huts, keeping a step ahead of their pursuers. Our work was set out for us.

Disembarking the U.S.S. Gordon at Cam Ranh Bay into an LCM on July 12, 1965.

We became a feast for flies and mosquitoes immediately after the ship entered the harbor. As the sun rose higher, the intensity of the heat and humidity increased with everyone sweating profusely.

The harbor facilities consisted of only one pier. The *Gordon* anchored midchannel, lowered the gangplank, and began loading the LCM.

I wrestled aboard the craft and lit my first Parodi stogie—landing on the beaches of Normandy.

I took that black, crooked thing out of its metal box, placed the foul little sucker in the corner of my mouth, and lit up. The first puff of smoke was so intense I lost my breath, making me increasingly lightheaded after each subsequent puff. I became dizzy, while the motion of the rocking craft made my stomach sick. The Parodis received an immediate burial at sea.

An officer for the 35th Engineers greeted us on the shore; they were happy to see us because of enemy activity.

Also waiting ashore were 40 press and TV correspondents and a force of Montagnard troops on patrol with U.S. advisors. A sign sarcastically proclaimed, "Welcome Big Red 1! This Beach Secured by 123rd Transportation Company."

I'm in the middle of these troops, wearing the V-shaped visor (see arrow), nervous and apprehensive like the rest of the men while we prepared to disembark this landing.

We remained assembled on the beach an hour while Transportation prepared vehicles to convoy two of our three rifle companies to locations in the sand dunes. Everyone noticed how fine the sand was, like talcum powder. This was bizarre because our lightly oiled weapons didn't accumulate grains of sand as anticipated; instead, they acquired a thin film of sandy dust. The men immediately began dusting weapons while waiting for rides.

I sat perplexed with my company, looking in wonderment. "Is this real combat?" Seagulls dove for bait, fishing junks cast nets, and merchants dawdled at stands on packed, puttering, polluting mopeds.

Charlie Company began to hump the dunes to a rocky mount a mile away surrounded a small, deep, scenic pond nestled between towers of stone that plates of earth had formed ages ago. The water was onyx, the blackest of shiny black.

Charlie formed a perimeter from the base of these rocks halfway down that side toward the harbor. After they established defenses, Headquarters Company joined, establishing camp along the bank of the pond.

Alpha Company had to straddle the bay on its isolated, narrow crossing point 10 miles away. The constant rains had deposited silt in the channel; consequently the bay rapidly became shallow shortly after entering. After several miles in, it looked more like a river than a harbor.

Finally, by midmorning, Transportation arrived after depositing Alpha. We climbed into the trucks, took off our baseball hats, put on steel pots, and "lock and load," locked the weapon and loaded a round.

The road was actually two wheel tracks in soft, white sand, following parallel to and a few feet from the shore along the inside of Cam Ranh. Low scrub brush and clumps of grass were the only vegetation. Everyone apprehensively strained his eyes searching the road ahead for the small three prongs of a Bouncing Betty mine, trip wires, or a whole platoon of VC waiting to ambush us.

The dust our convoy kicked up made the road appear to enter a fog bank. It was hopeless trying to keep weapons clean; everything, including the troops, was covered with powdered yellow dust. Perspiration-drenched shirts absorbed it; everyone looked like yellow snowmen.

We reached our departure point in 20 minutes. Trucks stopped, men departed, trucks left, and Bravo was by itself. I was lonesome with nothing for cover but sand dunes and scrub brush. Platoon defensive stations were established. Men broke out a C ration lunch while our commanding officer (CO), Captain Pope, and his staff decided how to deploy our company across the peninsula. A C meal is three cans, a beef, pork, or chicken main meal, bread or crackers, and dessert.

Also there's an aluminum foil pouch with five cigarettes, toilet paper, matches, gum, a plastic spoon, and P–38 can opener.

The 110° temperature had heated the meals so they were tastier. Unfortunately, this had the reverse effect on the purified canteen water, which tasted putrid.

G.I.s attempted to enjoy eating on the edge of soft sand dunes while harassed by hungry flies and mosquitoes. This peninsula was void of anything of nutritional value; the flies were on the verge of starving to death. We had to literally fight them for our rations, scrutinizing the spoon, preventing the fly that landed from entering the mouth. Men wiped the food off their lips after each bite otherwise the flies would snack.

A fly landed on the back of my hand. The other hand was holding food so I couldn't swat it. I watched him, puzzled at first as to what he doing before realizing he was drinking my sweat.

The CO discovered no fresh water here. There were monsoon rains three or four times a day, but this desert-like sand was porous; rain was immediately absorbed and puddles never formed.

Black monsoon clouds dumped rain, a relief, cooling and washing troops while keeping bugs away. The rain stopped in 15 minutes; the sun came out and dried our clothes immediately.

Our company of 150 men was strategically placed in groups of two across the peninsula so every position could see the other.

Everyone was oriented with a map to know where he was in relationship to the geography. Our company was a mile from Alpha at the bay crossing point and a half-mile from the small, friendly village of My Ca. It was supposedly friendly, giving all the more reason to be cautious.

Troops from 1st Platoon were placed on the shore by the road and extended east toward the ocean. Second Platoon would be next, and mine the last.

Three-quarters of a mile from the Command Post (CP) and bordering on the beach was a ridge of steep sand dunes extending parallel to the coast the entire 15 miles of Cam Ranh. This ridge stood 500 or 600 feet above the rest of the plateau-like top of the peninsula. My six-man squad would establish defensive positions on top of the dune constituting the ridge.

This defensive line across had to be absolutely straight; consequently it took time to get a fire team into the proper position, move the companies down that dune, and up the next. By 1700 hours all of First Platoon was dug in and Staff was certain where the remainder of our company would be placed. It stopped raining for the third time while the temperature finally cooled off. We were at the midpoint across this desert-like strip of small, rolling dunes.

I was glad I had a spare pair of socks in my pack; my boots and socks were wet and wouldn't dry before night. I took the boots off, wrung out the socks, hung them on my harness to dry, and propped the boots and feet up to the sun while I ate. I was thirsty but cautious about drinking too much because I had only a quarter of my first canteen left. Both of the others were supposed to last another two days.

By 1800 an evening defensive perimeter was established; my boots dried so I put them back on. The new socks felt like down, while the flies and mosquitoes were as persistent.

Platoon Sgt. Jay Smith called me, saying to get two men for an outpost (OP). We were to patrol 300 yards outside our perimeter, utilize two-thirds alert (two awake all the time), and if we saw any VC, kill them and try to make it to the lines without being shot either by the enemy or our own troops. The OP is basically an expendable position, the initial warning system for the rest of the troops.

The other two guys, Pfcs. Jerry Taylor and John Howard, were in my platoon also, but from different squads. The password was "tea cup."

The sun set behind the rugged, mystic blue hills at 1900. As we left we told the guys on line we were OP and if we saw any VC we would kill them all. If we didn't, we would be running back, yelling the password all the way and "please do not shoot."

These guys were as nervous as we; our chances of getting back without being shot was next to zero.

I took the patrol out 300 yards. It was imperative that we stayed within this zone; it was restricted from indiscriminate firing by artillery and mortars. If we made contact and pulled back, Artillery would send in a walking barrage saturating our position.

We left the perimeter at 1930 hrs., dusk. I was very afraid now; we were cutting our umbilical cord to life, leaving the security of the rest of our unit behind.

Sand dunes were the small, rolling type: six feet high and five feet wide, and six feet down the other side. The last monsoon shower washed the perspiration off my body and clothes. Even though the sunset, the temperature was still in the mid–80s and humidity above 90 percent. The patrol began perspiring immediately after climbing and descending a few dunes.

There wasn't a moon, yet we were surprised how bright the terrain was. The dunes had a bright steel-gray appearance, reflecting the light of the stars, so brilliant they seemed closer. Taylor whispered that we shouldn't have a problem seeing VC tonight. I said I hoped we wouldn't see any regardless.

We climbed a dune taller than the rest, offering an unobstructed 360-degree view. Four clumps of grass provided minimal concealment. The clear sky made the dunes looked surrealistic, like a dream. I had a flashback to beach parties at the dunes by my home in Cape Cod, trying to think positive, remembering the good times.

Howard, Taylor, and Pezzoli—here we were, in some foreign country, outside, at night, sitting on beach sand, wearing sweaty clothes, looking for some guys to kill, and eaten alive by mosquitoes that outlasted the flies. We stretched our ponchos on the ground and wrapped them around like mummies, trying to keep the heat in and the mosquitoes and sand out. I had the M-79, Taylor an M-14, and Howard the fully auto M-14.

Our artillery consisted of three hand grenades each and two strategically placed Claymore antipersonnel mines capable of scattering steel pellets in a 90-degree arc. We waited, lying under the stars, to kill someone before they killed us. The guys told me to have first sleep.

I was too wound up and excited to sleep immediately. My clothes were wet, my poncho smelled of stale rubber, dried perspiration, and C ration dribble. Sand dusted my face while mosquitoes made a whirring sound, dive-bombing my partially covered head.

I sprayed insect repellent on my hands and face, pulled my sleeves down, buttoned them and my top collar, and pulled my head back inside the poncho. I felt I had just fallen to sleep when Taylor got me up for my watch. Howard and I sat and looked in front. Absolutely nothing was happening; we had been apprehensive, expecting something to happen, but it never occurred. Of course, we weren't disappointed.

Howard was getting tired; he woke Taylor for his break. I hadn't slept much since 0300 the previous morning and was falling asleep, trying everything possible to keep awake.

We looked west and saw the bay illuminated by stars and behind it the dark outline of the mainland.

I whispered to Taylor how beautiful it was. We could see all the stars including the Big Dipper, reminding me of those beach parties.

As soon as I said that, automatic weapon fire erupted from several locations on the hills of the mainland, raining tracers down their sides. Howard woke up immediately; we snapped our safeties off. Everyone was alert now, precisely aware of everything around us, shocked as if by jolts of electricity. I glanced at those other guys and laugh now, reflecting upon it. Their eyes were wide with eyeballs darting back and forth like an owl. I'm sure mine were similar.

We didn't discuss the firing as frequently seen in war movies. Any idiot realized the 173rd Airborne was in the hills across the bay, that the gunfire came from three weapons next to each other, and they were firing down. Also it came from outgoing U.S. weapons.

Alpha was by the base of the hill, yet they were quiet. Whoever provoked the firing would have to get through Alpha to reach us. Some conciliation, we thought; we'll probably get shot anyway.

The firing stopped later as quickly as it started, then absolute silence. The 173rd was there a month before we arrived. We realized later this was their modus operandi each night: trigger-happy fingers squeezing off rounds, warding off various sounds. The 1st Infantry Division philosophy was "hold the fire till you see the whites of their eyes; don't give away your positions." The 173rd's idea was scare the enemy away—with firepower.

It was my turn to sleep; I was still wired from the firing and had a difficult time sleeping. I finally managed to fall asleep, then it was my turn for watch again. At home you lie down, fall asleep, and wake up in what appears to be a short time but actually was for the night. Nights like these never seem to end.

Taylor touched me and I was awake, fully cognizant of my surroundings, not a customary daze. Infantrymen were light switches: switch turned off, the light is off; flicked on, the light immediately bright.

At 0500 Howard was sleeping, I could hardly keep my eyes open. Taylor's scan included a glance at me to ensure my eyes were still open. I longed for a method to prop my eyelids open.

A slow, solemn bell—gong-gong-gong—eliminated this problem for the rest of the night as it rang in front.

We thought VC had infiltrated Alpha, probably killed them all, and were signaling to attack us.

I trembled, holding us still to kill a few before running back to our lines.

This unintentional bravado saved our lives. Later we discovered the bell was from the chapel in a local village signaling the parishioners to mass. If we had run back everybody was so jumpy, they would have shot even Commanding General Westmoreland.

The sun lit the sky at 0530 and we began seeing things like the bell tower of a chapel rising above the dunes, only a quarter of a mile from the village of My Ca.

We headed back to the perimeter at 0600, opened a can of rations and tried to eat them while cradling the weapons and stumbling along the dunes. Shortly the sun rose above the ridge of dunes by the ocean, flicking on the switch to the sweat machine.

Voices came from behind a dune; I assumed they were our lines and called out to alert everyone we were friendlies returning from our Listening Post (LP).

"Ya, what's the password?"

"Tea."

"Cup."

"OK. What are you guys doing out there?"

We were the LP. They shrugged their shoulders, saying they thought we were closer to the beach, and then asked about the deal with the bell.

Our bravado now showed; we laughed that they were jumpy over a church bell, trigger-happy like the 173rd, and were candy arses. After 30 hours in country, we got cocky (confidence is the key to survival) because we had been "out there" by ourselves last night.

At 0800 the defensive line continued to be formed across the dunes with a nip here and a tuck there. Our line of defenses was seen each time we reached the top of a dune, depositing another fire team there.

By noon, we reached a gully, 3rd Platoon's command post. Second Lt. Mike La Fontaine, Staff Sergeant Smith, and radio telephone operator (RTO) Pfc. Billy Jones would stay there. A two-trail lane was large enough to facilitate a three-quarter-ton truck with our duffel bags and supplies. Also there would be served hot chow for lunch each day and fresh water for a rinse once a week, with rations and canteens of water each day. Extra ammo was a joke.

My squad leader was Sgt. Billy "Combat" Cooper, a gung-ho lifer who saw combat in Korea at our age. The squad stocked up canteens of water and C rations for three days. My friend Pfc. Harry Kerry was point man as we began the torturous climb, taking half an hour at midday, lugging our equipment up the dunes to positions on the last, highest dune adjacent to the beach, two football fields away and one above the CP.

The sun was hotter because the dunes comprising the ridge were void of vegetation, reflecting the sun like a mirror, although it had redeeming features: a sea breeze off the ocean—our washroom six days a week for the next three months, and only 15 minutes away. Walking there was easy on coarse gravel.

I dug a prone shelter on the edge of the dune overlooking the peninsula below.

A .50-caliber machine gun team carved a niche out of the ramp used to ascend the ridge. Harry scooped a shelter behind me and knocked the top off to see the ocean. Taylor, "Combat," Howard, and two other guys completed our semicircle. This was our new home for the next two and a half weeks. Everybody felt anxious here by ourselves, isolated from the rest of the platoon. If a force attacked the ridgeline or from the ocean, they would not have much battle; our ammo supply was limited.

There were six Claymores in front, which wouldn't last during an assault. If we started to get overrun and ran down the dune to join the rest of the platoon, we would have made excellent targets for both the VC and our jumpy troops below.

Our shallow positions were dug by mid–afternoon. One of the guys asked Sarge when we'd be able to wash off.

"Better get used to it; you ain't seen nothin' yet." His prophecy came true.

It didn't seem logical placing a .50-caliber gun along the ramp in a static position against a mobile, fluid enemy force like VC guerrillas; it was the beginning of many things that would seem illogical.

We shaped up our desperate situation. If it appeared we were on the verge of being overrun, we would run about the dunes, playing cowboys and Indians with the VC as we did as kids.

This was our little world; isolated from civilization, like the kids in Golding's *Lord of the Flies*, writing our own rules.

Each three defensive positions demanded a person awake 24 hours a day. Harry and I shared one location. When one of us wanted to leave the spot, sleep, or nap, he had to check with the other.

We had a magnificent view. "Look, Harry," I said during the first sunset; the South China Sea was on our right and the dark hills of the Vietnamese mainland on the left with a bright orange sun glowing behind. Soon the sun set for the troops on the black plateau below. Most of the flies had retired, the mosquitoes' bellies were full, and our clothes were finally dried by the sun, not smelling sour anymore.

Harry told me to sleep first. I wanted to brush my teeth, but was afraid to use precious water. Later I realized if my mouth was clean I wouldn't be so thirsty.

It didn't seem I slept long before Harry whispered it was my watch. I sat on the edge of my prone shelter watching the rolling dunes in front, then peered over the side of a dune, watching the plateau below for VC trying to infiltrate the gullies. My seat became uncomfortable, so I stretched out with my chin resting on the top of my helmet.

I was shocked awake; I had just been asleep! It wasn't long though, only a half hour, yet I had been asleep. I shuddered when I realized bad guys could have cut my throat.

I wanted Harry to sleep for another hour so I walked around our defenses to keep awake. I took sneakers with me. While in the States, I put thick, heavy tractor soles on my boots, looking combat macho. Now that I was involved in the real thing I regretted it because they retained rainwater, making them heavy. My sneakers felt better walking the dunes so I wore them each day until they eventually rotted off three weeks later.

I whispered to Taylor I was coming over. He was 20 yards in front and on the side of us. I sat with him whispering for five minutes before returning to my position.

Then I woke Harry, wrapped myself inside my poncho, and immediately sank into a deep sleep to be awakened by the 173rd firing again. Harry and I spoke in normal tones because the commotion across the bay was so loud it was difficult to hear. We marveled, commenting the VC had better not mess with us, while envious they had surplus ammo to play with. It was difficult to sleep right away; soon it would be Harry's turn to sleep. I watched, we alternated, and finally I finished the night.

Everybody on our dune stirred once the sky lightened.

A C ration breakfast, holes dug for bodily wastes, into the second canteen, and discussion of the procedure for beach wash. We needed permission for our first trip.

Harry, Taylor, and I were the first to wash the third day. Sgt. Cooper said it was OK to take our shirts off in the dunes, providing we wore flak vests. They were thick and heavy, but a little cooler than our shirts, allowing air to circulate. We were elated walking to the shore, experiencing sea breezes, smells, the roar of the surf, and prospects of cooling off. Everyone stripped and waded into clear ocean water with a clean sandy bottom.

The peninsula was attached to the mainland eight miles away. The resort town of Na Trang, population 80,000, was on the coast at the base of steep dark green brush covered hills. It was the commercial hub with fishing, shipping of local agriculture and fish, and mostly tourist oriented businesses, its restaurants lining the coast.

In the opposite direction we could see this ridge of tall sand dunes leading to the mouth of Cam Ranh Bay 10 miles away, punctuated at the entrance by a black, rocky hill behind Battalion CP. The beach rose gradually for the first 100 yards, and then abruptly blended into the ridge of dunes, creating a most picturesque beach. The sound of gunfire yanked everyone back into the reality of warfare.

After the 173rd firing stopped, Taylor placed our weapons on a log at the water's edge; we waded into the water and began washing.

Taylor and I could not make suds. This was frustrating because Harry was covered with bubbles from Zest, the only soap that could be used in the ocean. Fortunately, our supply officer, Capt. Bill Million, found several cases at the PX, which he requisitioned for us. We used it to wash, shave, shampoo, and launder our clothes. The sun was so hot that our clothes dried immediately while sterilizing them.

We finished shaving and were rinsing when Taylor saw two A-1 Skyraiders with bombs and rockets on the horizon.

"Wow. Are they ours or Vietnamese?"

They circled once, flew out to sea, did a 180-degree turn, and began a strafing run.

We stood waist deep in water, gawking at this semicircle, when reality lifted its ugly head—we were about to be strafed and blown up; the pilots didn't know who we were. This was the first time Americans had been at Cam Ranh and couldn't be identified by uniform because we were naked.

We dove underwater. I had swam since I was four, always feeling comfortable in water. Unfortunately at this moment, I could not get my big butt underwater, frantically splashing and kicking, but to no avail. The pilots must have noticed others across the dunes because they pulled up before firing.

We ran out of the water and looked at each other meekly grunting, "Wow!"

After wiping off and dressing, we returned to the dunes. The guys at our post were laughing because it looked as though we were about to get bombed.

We boasted we weren't worried about the planes dive-bombing us; we knew they wouldn't. Now it was funny.

Harry had an afternoon patrol and Taylor one that night. I sat on the edge of my prone shelter at 1100, ate my lunch, said good-bye to Harry at

My home for a month on top of this desolate ridgeline at Cam Ranh Bay. All my "comforts of home" are shown at the left.

1230, and briefed different groups hiking to wash. I informed them to use Zest and that we would cover them with our weapons.

By 1500 it had rained twice, washing off new sweat, helping me feel clean, while perspiring continuously even though only sitting. Our weapons continuously had sand blown on them, necessitating nonstop maintenance.

I found a pulpy, plant-type vegetation the size of a small bush, hacked it down and planted it next to my hole. This was a stand on which to hang my pistol belt, harness, M-79, and ammo, ready for use and above the sand. It also facilitated hanging my towel after the morning wash. Showers each day were an excellent wash for clothes that couldn't be cleaned at the beach while the log was a dryer for after showers.

Harry returned from patrol at 1700. He was exhausted walking these dunes of soft sand. His patrol struggled to three different locations, establishing ambush sites for an hour. I told him to sleep but he couldn't because it was too hot.

I ate some rations; he said he was too tired for them also. Everyone was out of shape because of our month of inactivity prior to arriving.

Taylor prepared for his night ambush patrol at 1900. He managed to take a nap in the shadow of the dune while Harry was still wound up and

The .50 cal machine gun position nestled below my sand dune with the hills of Vietnam mainland silhouetted in the background.

suffering from a headache. He had me sleep and took first watch. What a bonus; he couldn't unwind until 2330.

Day four was like three as was six like five. We had the routine of wash in the ocean, eating rations (after day four, hot chow was served at the CP for lunch but nobody felt like walking there at midday for something hot), afternoon and evening patrols, and boredom. No TV, books, papers, shade, chairs, music, beer, women, or ice cubes. The constant mosquitoes and flies and the boring one out of 12 possible C ration choices soon beleaguered us. After the first week we ran out of things to talk about and tempers flared. Every Friday the medic gave us a malaria tablet and we received a rinse of fresh water barely washing off six days' accumulation of salt. Everyone's skin was dry and scaled. Some guys had sunburn problems initially, especially the Africans who weren't used to direct sun on their skin like white guys. My Italian skin turned red the first day, but olive oil in my system moistened it, turning it brown.

By the start of the second week, I commanded a night patrol. We dispensed with excessive gear, taking only a basic load of ammo, patrol cap, one grenade, claymores, a radio, and knives. One guy was from another platoon; Spec 4 Ron Milan was a Cuban officer for Castro. After Castro made his Communist intentions known, Ron escaped to Florida.

Our six-man patrol left at dusk; Ron insisted on being permanent point. I was reluctant because I didn't know him. Later, after I saw how capable he was, I became thrilled.

He was alert, prowling around the sand dunes like a cougar, creeping through dry underbrush, walking a 100 yards and stopping poised and taut, ready to spring. I learned more about guerrilla patrolling during those few hours than I had from two years in the Army.

I continued admiring him from a military aspect, seeing him periodically, but never had time to express how I respected him. I lost my chance two months later when he was killed in the largest ambush of American troops to that date.

After two and a half weeks the defense line was rearranged with positions a mile closer to the mainland. The terrain was smoother, though dunes with deep shafts ran along each side and the tall ridge of dunes running along the coast diminished. We, the ridge people, were broken up. I would share a foxhole with Pfc. John Canders; a platoon member I had seen but never spoken to. He appeared like a pretty good guy—not a big mouth, loser, or a dud. Shortly he joined me on our dune as I figured its layout.

"Hi," I said, reaching for his hand. "We're going to be seeing a lot of each the next few months. My name is Ray."

He refused to shake hands.

"We black people don't use first names with whites. White people never showed us respect; they've always used our first names." Things were different now and I was to call him Canders or not talk at all.

I was shocked, never experiencing dialogue like this. I was raised in Wareham, Massachusetts; a third of the population was Cape Verdians, immigrating from the Portuguese islands off Africa. They were leaders in different aspects of our town—political, religious, athletic, educational, etc. The other two-thirds of my classmates were first or second generation from Europe. We understood differences in physical appearances of peoples, but that never concerned us.

Many of my friends in college were African as were some guys in OCS. I always realized there were color differences in people, but it never made a difference until today.

I shrugged my shoulders and suggested we start digging, taking turns, one digging and filling a sandbag while the other holds, ties, and stands it.

"You don't tell me what to do; if you had made it through OCS, you could order me, but you didn't and can't."

I didn't know what to say; we needed our hole for protection before nightfall. He sat down on the sand and looked at me. I wondered who or what had gotten to him. He had always seemed like a decent guy. Actually I didn't think he meant what he said; speaking with trepidation, reciting a programmed mind.

I pleaded, "We've got to dig a foxhole. I'm going to start because I want protection tonight."

I dug sand, emptied it in a bag, then tossed it out of the hole. Canders started digging next to me; he would shovel the sand outside the hole, climb out, and scoop his dig into bags.

Two o' clock was the hottest part of the day, the sun almost directly overhead, the air still, and bugs abundant. We were soon exhausted; today's ration of water was mostly gone.

Canders stopped digging because he was too hot. I became furious because we needed this by night; we were excellent targets on top of the dune. I was frightened, like skydiving without a 'chute. I told him I was hot and tired also, that maybe if he took his shirt off he'd feel cooler.

This brought the standard response that black people's skin is sensitive to the sun, etc., and he needed protection from his shirt. I tried to reason that once the skin, anybody's skin, got exposed and used to the sun, it wouldn't bother.

I continued digging and filling bags until 1700 when much of the hole was complete and lined with sandbags. Most of the other foxholes had been completed also. Several troops visited the beach, which was closer now, rinsing off.

"Why wash in the ocean if it leaves a film of salt?"

Salt was salt and sweat was sweat; we chose the lesser of two evils, desperately trying to keep clean.

By the time I returned at 1830, Canders had filled more bags and placed a low wall with firing ports around the front and side.

I felt better with the sun setting and being doused. He fell asleep immediately; I ate dinner and took first watch.

I finally relaxed; by 2130 my eyes were heavy and unable to keep open. We got into an argument when I woke him for his watch; he felt he should be able to sleep longer. I was lost for words. An hour later I could not keep my eyes open any longer and told him if I fell asleep a VC could slit both of our throats. This seemed to make sense.

I couldn't say a thing to this guy that seemed right. Others in our platoon noticed the animosity. I was moved to Sergeant Lopez's foxhole in two days. Later I learned Canders boasted he was going to shoot me. I wasn't worried; he was too harmless to shoot me—if he tried, I would kill him first.

Every evening we set two Claymore mines at a different location than the night before because of indications the VC had been scouting. Patrols had discovered bushes with chalk marks pointing to our positions.

Three factors remained constant each night: mosquitoes, the 173rd Airborne firing, and boredom. After two months, the battalion commander, Lt. Col. Norman Salisbury, decided on a military venture—an impromptu inspection of my company's combat readiness. He was a career officer holding desk jobs, never infantry qualified, and lacked leadership capacity and ability.

I was one of 10 selected for the inspection. The threads attaching the tractor soles to my boots had rotted while the soles flopped open, exposing my toes like a hobo. Most of the canvas of my sneakers had rotted, leaving my dress boots as the only other shoes to wear.

The engineers building the harbor facilities had jungle boots already. I wanted to make a point to the colonel, so I wore my boots with floppy soles. Most didn't have a chance to wash and shave; their faces and clothing were weathered from the night's dust and the morning's sweat. Washing clothes in the ocean caused a buildup of white, streaking salt, much not washed out by afternoon monsoons. Two of the men had skin eruptions, one ripped his pants, while two others cut themselves hastily shaving. This assemblage definitely appeared like combat soldiers even though we hadn't seen action yet.

The crowd stood at attention by the base of the dunes for the colonel's inspection. Weapons had already collected a fine film of sand. By 1300 our clothes were saturated with sweat. Flies and mosquitoes dined while we tried to stand at attention.

The colonel took one step, left face, and inspected the weapon. "Dusty." Gave it back.

"How's it going out there, trooper?"

"OK, sir."

Right face, one step forward, left face. "And how about you, son?"

I had a difficult time not giggling when he approached me. Every man was disheveled in different degrees, looking like he had just stepped out of an advertisement for a gung-ho combat flick.

"Do you feel competent with that weapon, Specialist?" he meowed, motioning to my M-79 grenade launcher.

"Yes, sir," I barked back like I was taught in OCS, "and I wish you'd give me a chance to kill someone with it."

OCS taught to us stare directly into a person's eyeballs and not flinch or blink. "Be intense, show no emotion." After sitting on those dunes, washing in the ocean, and sleeping in and on sand every night, I had a lot of intensity to show.

The colonel's fatigues were starched and pressed, probably by a maid. His camouflaged helmet liner appeared just out of the box, never rained upon or bleached by the sun. His jungle boots had their original shine. He didn't have a drop of sweat on him, and I even smelled after-shave lotion.

He was barely able to keep his poise after my retort, but attempted a, "Well, son, you'll have a chance in a week."

I slew him with my ace in the hole slowly lowering my eyes from his, past his waist, and to the jungle boots. His eyes followed mine down to my boots where my toes wiggled outside for the world to see. He saw them, lost his composure, gagged, and sputtered something innocuous like, "Be getting jungle boots here soon trooper."

The men in formation began elbowing each other and almost lost it seeing my white toes flapping in the breeze.

The inspection ended immediately.

I became one of the first to get jungle boots.

The guy sharing the hole with Howard had patrol that night so I covered for him. Howard said he heard that I fall asleep on watch and wondered if I could stay awake.

"Of course," I assured him, "no problem. I'll take first watch."

Howard slept like an owl, waking several times to assure I was still awake.

The silence, exhaustion, heat, humidity, and boredom of having to sit in one spot, looking at the same dune, and watching nondescript stars in the sky started to affect me. I finally got him for his watch at 2300. He awoke me up at 0230. I was still very tired but felt better after a drink of water, which had finally cooled. If I could only have a cigarette, I'd be more alert; unfortunately, I had no way to light one without alerting everybody. Almost five weeks of sitting in the same spot and looking at the same black outline of rugged hills on the mainland became monotonous, routine, and redundant. Even the 173rd's gunfire finally lacked luster.

I sat with my back resting on a sandbag, knees pushed against my chest by arms, feeling snug when Howard grabbed me.

"Man, you fell asleep again. I don't trust you, I'm going to have to stay awake for the rest of the night."

I pleaded with him to let me continue the watch.

"You can if want, but I can't sleep with you in the same foxhole. I don't trust you."

The next day several guys suggested I stay on my feet during the watch. They said they had the same problem and this helped.

Several nights later I heard the innocuous "pop-fizz" sound of a trip flare ignite while sleeping. I jumped up, my mind exploding: "Here they come!"

The flare on the dune to our left had tripped. I searched—nothing but the dune.

"Pop-fizz," on the position next to me.

The world's most delicious wild boar thrilled us.

"Kill it, fresh meat!"

Every machine gun, automatic rifle, and grenade launcher opened up. The boar bounded from the dune and between two others, managing to detonate another flair.

He sprang to the top, illuminated by tracers, explosions from M-79s, and claymores. Nobody, including myself, hit it.

The 173rd thought this was finally the real thing. They opened up with all their weapons and continued firing well after we quit. The rest of the night was spent stringing new mines and flares. One lucky boar had left many G.I.s still ravenous for fresh meat.

Several days later I heard guys from the next two dunes yelling excitedly while running behind with weapons and pistol belts on.

Three things told me there was an emergency: 1. Troops shouting. 2. Troops running. 3. Several didn't have time to put shirts and helmets on.

I grabbed my M-79 and pistol belt, following them to the top of the first dune to my rear. Several men were lying on top with their weapons aimed below by the time I puffed to the top.

"What's going on?"

They aimed at two Vietnamese civilians with a transit who hastily informed us, in broken English, they were surveyors taking measurements for an Air Force runway.

The Army's engineers had completed most of the work intended for the harbor and defensive positions without seeing a VC. Consequently our defenses relaxed.

Several days later our company had to obtain supplies from Alpha at the crossing point. I rode "shotgun" in our three fourths-ton truck with another guy in the back. This was civilization for me, my first time out of the dunes in 10 weeks. The crossing point was a few 100 yards past the village of My Ca where the chapel was located. A couple of old Mediterranean-style villas, which probably belonged to the French, were located on a bluff above town. Some of the local kids ran to us as we drove by.

"Watch them," our NCO said. "These kids might be loaded."

"Di-di-mau—get out of here."

"Here they come, the desert rats," Alpha called while we crossed the shallow bay in hubcap-deep water. They cheered us because we had become legendary living in the dunes, invisible until now.

We parked the truck on the mainland at Supply. The Alphas asked us how we survived the harsh environment of the dunes. The three months in Florida swamps were just as harsh. They wanted to know about the firing a week ago.

"VC," we smiled and left before they asked any more questions, which might have incriminated us in this lie.

"Wow!"

Three of us walked down the dirt road running adjacent to the bay. There were numerous Vietnamese merchants trying to sell anything from La Ve "Tiger Beer," to Cokes, American cigarettes, and fruit—all at exorbitant prices. We saw everything, including strumpets; a merchant said he had "boom-boom" in one of the bushes for 200 piasters, roughly two bucks.

The Alpha guys said the merchants were safe. They hated the VC because the VC were hoods that would come into the merchants' village and take their property, claiming it as a tax. Many of these people were Catholics who didn't like Communists because of their disbelief in God or intolerance of religion.

We walked into the bush with a middle-aged Vietnamese to see his merchandise. A sweaty G.I. passed us, trying not to look us in the eye. The pimp reached a clear spot between scruffy brushes where a blanket lay across a rocky, dried riverbed. Stretched out on the blanket and trying to look sexy after already screwing a number of guys was a middle-aged Vietnamese woman who had fallen into the twilight of her life. Her black silk pajamas were wrinkled and white silk blouse unbuttoned. She gave us a feeble smile, opening the blouse to two droopy, wrinkled, sweaty breasts, while the blanket was permeated with a smell that would defuse any erection.

We bid a rapid adieu and continued to walk down the road to see the 173rd Airborne's defenses.

They began asking if we were from the sand dunes and did the firing recently.

"We kill beaucoup VC," meaning "many" in French.

They scoffed at us.

We were talking with these paratroopers when one with his shirt off asked if I was Pezzoli.

I recognized him as a guy in my class at OCS who had made it. I asked his status.

This is the real pits, he replied, saying he was no better off as an officer.

Later, after I saw combat, I realized it was an act of God that I didn't make it through officer's school. Judging by the danger I would voluntarily have been involved with and having responsibilities and people to impress, I would have shortly ended up in a field of poppies.

The driver, loader, and I returned to Supply after our supplies were collected. This short trip had been therapeutic; caged birds released for a day's flight before returning to the roost.

I grasped the nature of the primitive living conditions we endured upon our return. Civilization again and meeting Vietnamese people for the first time helped assert this feeling.

Meals of heated canned chow, sprinkled with local vegetables, were available now.

Salt tablets were washed down with warm water five or six times daily and Friday was fresh water rinse and malaria tablet.

Helicopters frequently patrolled the dunes, flying like "hot rodders," swerving between them at 70–90 mph. We were envious; the gunners kept cool by the rotor blast while the pilots looked like kids playing on bumper cars. We waved to them while sitting on our helmets or a sand bag in the dunes. There it goes, real civilization, "Hi guys—wish we were with you."

Boredom and monotony were taking their toll again with quick tempers and low morale. We had run out of things to talk about a long time ago.

I was one of seven guys to receive jungle boots in my platoon. These, along with my later acquisitions, an M-16 and a VC hammock, were my most valued possessions. The boots were lighter with tractor soles, canvas from the ankles up, and two holes above the arch designed to pump water out of the boot like a bilge pump. Later, while in the swamps, I was impressed by how well they worked and how indestructable they appeared.

August 17 we had a meeting with platoon leader 2nd Lt. Mike La Fontaine. "Operation Barracuda" was slated in two days. B Company would stretch across a plain at the base of steep hills at Dien Khonh, three miles south of where Cam Ranh peninsula attached to the mainland. Our company would "be in the blocking position while A and C Companies drove the enemy towards us."

My squad looked at each other in disbelief, questioning if this battle plan was for real. Drive VC straight back to us after stalking them through five miles of hill and dale in their back yards? The VC weren't dumb and would merely slide out the sides.

Some of the battle plans initially were ludicrous, designed by people without the slightest conception of the kind of combat we would be involved in. I'm sure the battalion commander, Lieutenant Colonel Salisbury, designed these plans. Most of the rest of the Headquarters Section, as I was to discover later, were competent.

During this briefing we were reminded of the infamous body count which became notoriously ridiculous; significantly adhered to by lower echelons and abused by the upper.

My "uniform for the day" included a steel pot, baseball cap, flak vest, three days' chow (28 C ration cans and three canteens of water), an entrenching tool (shovel), pistol belt and harness, backpack, poncho, water purification tablets, insect repellent, med packet, and 12 packs of Winstons.

In addition to my weapons were minuscule amounts of ammo, one hand and white phosphorus grenade, and a bayonet. Other guys carried different colored smoke grenades and that fantastic putty-like C-4 plastic explosive.

My gear wasn't that heavy yet, approximately 60 pounds. Later, with the M-14 and double basic load of ammo and grenades, it approached 90 pounds.

We split watches the night before. At 0400 everybody assembled at the CP for transportation. Some ate while others napped, but most were too excited to nap. Trucks arrived at 0500.

We crossed the bay at My Ca and noted A Company had left. Our convoy of 11 trucks kicked up fine dust, coating our weapons.

Bravo proceeded south on the mainland where Cam Ranh peninsula merged into it. The company disembarked from the trucks and assembled at 0530 as the sky lightened. Staff coordinated the marching order while waiting for daylight. Everyone cleaned his weapon again. Local roosters began crowing at sunrise. We heard native voices about us and were surprised they were not aware of us.

After sunrise, we approached the edge of the local market where farmers brought wares and merchants made purchases. All were busily carting and setting up displays for merchandise, scuttling from different points to secure their spots. We laughed; they reminded us of used-car salesmen.

Someone called to mount up and move out.

The men were in different degrees of disarray: unbuckled pistol belts hanging from the shoulder harness, helmets off, a few rifles partially disassembled, and rations snacked—one guy even had his boots off.

By 0615 the sun was climbing over the hills lining our route, a narrow dirt road along the left side of the delta. Our sweat switch was turned on by the sun and equipment. I felt clean earlier even though the convoy dusted us.

We began sweating profusely, especially from our heads; it flowed from the steel pot liner sweatband into our eyes, stinging them. Also it dripped down the back of the neck into the channel formed by the backbone, continuing to the waist where the pistol belt dammed it from further flow.

The company divided into two single files, each man 10 feet apart. We had to be reminded only once not to bunch up and to monitor the water and ammo.

Also we were reminded to keep our eyes open for mines and snipers.

I became so thirsty now I licked my sweat. Some of the men began taking sweat tablets. The dry, hard, dusty clay road reflected the sun.

We had no idea what we would be running into, though the VC had bothered the farmers. I was apprehensive about the unknown ahead, feeling like I was carrying 10 dozen eggs in my pack while walking down a hill of gravel. Each step was measured, each glance calculated. For one of the few times in my life, I was concentrating 100 percent, like when I played baseball and stepped up to the plate to bat, or caught a pop fly. My focusing began for a minute, then an hour, and finally lasting all day.

Everybody had the same alertness across their faces for snipers, mines, or any quick movement on our flanks; even flashes or reflections of light.

Cigarette taste is narcotic. It was almost impossible at night to wait until sunrise for my first. I often used this as an incentive to remain awake during watch.

I held the cigarette between the middle and fourth finger of my left hand so my trigger finger was always free. I wasn't aware of this; looking through some ot my Vietnam photos is amusing because it looks fruity, yet authentic. My consumption gradually increased in ratio to my action. What began as a pack a day increased to four. This was extraordinary, especially considering they were smoked during daylight. I don't know how I could have survived Vietnam without them.

We approached a hut of people that were supposedly friendly, yet we still scrutinized them. An old lady stood in front of her mud hut critically watching us. There was a well and a long pole with a bucket attached hung over it. I took my steel pot off and held it to her. "Mamma-san, mamma-san," I laughed, "give me some water please."

She broke out into a capacious, toothless smile, laughed something back in Vietnamese, filled the pot with water, splashed it on me, then filled another load into my helmet. I drank most of this as I walked, but it didn't seem to quench my thirst. I gave the remains to two guys behind me. The road followed the left side of the delta, continuing to form the dimensions of the peninsula as it extended three miles inland. The delta was U-shaped; the mouth was the peninsula base and its sides were formed by the rugged, abrupt hills. This terrain was mostly dried, flat clay, formed into squares half the size of a football field. They were rice paddies, formed by a "dike," a continuous one-foot-tall mound, circumscribing squares to be flooded.

Local farmers wouldn't support the VC's cause, the National Liberation Force (NLF); often they were either killed or their crops were destroyed. If they joined the Communist organization, their crops were taken for the war effort regardless. Most of these paddies had been abandoned a year before because the government didn't have sufficient police or soldiers to defend every parcel of property.

South Vietnam had a free-market economy and was struggling to attract foreign investments and business with its labor force.

North Vietnam was on the opposite end of the spectrum. It was a totalitarian, Communist government supported financially and militarily by Russia. The economy was military with available men in the military and women comprising the labor force.

Communism has finally died in Europe after half a century of terror. Liberals even acknowledged vices in that system.

At 1100 our company assembled and formed a defensive perimeter at the upper left corner of the inverted U formed by the delta. The clay was dry and baked hard, capturing mud footprints frozen in time.

We were briefed on our lines as we ate chow. First Platoon, then 2nd, and finally 3rd stretched their blocking line across dried rice paddies, 300 yards from a line of low mountains forming the base for the delta in the front.

One of the guys questioned how Alpha and Charlie were supposed to chase VC out of those hills in front.

Bravo's CO, Captain Pope, tried not to show his frustration with this battle scenario, saying to dig in and be alert upon arriving at our location.

All three platoons filed across this delta, the men 20 feet apart with several support trucks factored in. This clumsy, ponderous line stretched over a third of a mile.

Chapter 5

We Were Entering Battle and About to Get Our Feet Wet

Our long file of troops looked massive and imposing, giving a false sense of security. Despite this, the movement across this plain of dried rice paddies was a cumbersome, slow moving, awkward creature. The brass was experimenting with combat tactics. The World War II theory with moving troops was to spread apart, becoming a less-concentrated target.

The local VC cadre noticed us when we left the marketplace and began reconnoitering the dirt road to our destination. They noticed the other companies leave one hour earlier and projected they would be combing the hills five miles south and no threat from there.

They watched us deploy fire teams, walk a hundred yards, stop, deploy several fire teams 20 yards apart, then continue across the paddies another hundred yards before establish several more positions.

These VC had a .30-caliber machine gun hidden in a tunnel storage facility a mile away, with almost a full box of ammo and instructions on firing it. They had never fired a round from a machine gun before, but held it during simulated firings.

This was everybody's weapon, it belonged to "the people," consequently no one utilized the care and maintenance this complicated weapon demanded.

The dried mud in these paddies was solid clay bricks, yet enough moisture was left to emit offensive odors. This clay had clumps of weeds, which were rice stalks once. The sun reflecting off this shiny surface felt hotter than the dunes, which the troops didn't think possible. The hot dunes didn't seem so bad after all; missing here were showers and refreshing ocean breezes.

Our file followed an ox-cart trail running along the dikes, devoid of shade. We approached a clump of bushes, 20 yards in diameter and bisected by the trail, offering the relief of shade. Fortunately, my squad was in the middle when we stopped for lunch break. Unfortunately, the short stubby bushes didn't offer much help.

The pistol belt cut my side, so I unsnapped it. Now the harness irritated my shoulders; I took it off. The flak vest didn't allow body heat to escape; I unzipped it. My back was hot and sweating, I took the vest off. As I did this, I heard a bird of intuition whisper into my ear that this was combat.

It took an hour to deploy 1st Platoon, decide where the company's blocking line would be stretched, and for the troops to eat.

The VC scout watching returned to the men with the machine gun. It became evident we were stretching across the top of the delta and arranging positions into groups of two. It was difficult to figure out what we were up to, although it looked like we might stay awhile. Our movement was slow enough to allow time to establish an ambush.

I fired and saw live demonstrations of almost every infantry weapon in our arsenal. Also, I participated in the Confidence Course, crawling under barbed wire while TNT charges exploded next to me and machine gun bullets streaked overhead. The course was also held at night with every sixth round, a tracer, spitting fire directly at me.

A shot sounds different when you fire than it does when you are on the receiving end. When you fire the weapon, regardless of the type, the sound is a muted "boom." When it is fired at you, there's a "crack," the sound made by the explosion of the round when the bullet blasts out of the cartridge, through the barrel, and breaks the sound barrier. After we had been fired upon more, the men became proficient at knowing precisely where the bullet originated from by its sound. The clue was the intensity of the "crack." At times they could actually feel the shock waves emitted by the bullet slipping past their heads. The ears were radar antennae, honed in on a shot and transmitting a picture of the target in the brain of where it was just fired. If the initial shots failed to hit anyone, as was frequently the case, it often proved fatal for the shooter.

I opened the breech of my M-79, resembling a stubby, single-barrel shotgun, and took out and examined its 40-mm grenade projectile before replacing it. Then I lit another cigarette and was about to take a long drag.

"Crack, crack, crack, crack, crack!" Five shots were fired in our direction from an automatic weapon in the hill.

Everybody froze for a second, thinking it a mistake or a misfire, the first time someone shot in our direction intending to kill us. Instinctively my squad sprang up and ran along the trail through the brush to join the rest of the platoon in the rice paddy outside.

I awkwardly struggled to my feet, plopped on my helmet, and grabbed the flak vest, pistol belt harness, and backpack apparatus, slipping the vest and harness on as I ran. I carried the M-79 with one hand while struggling to secure the pistol belt with the other.

The rest of the squad had already reached the paddies when I finally burst out of the brush. My bayonet was upside down and stuck under the belt, preventing me from snapping it. The other gear hanging from the belt—the machete, pistol, entrenching tool, backpack, three canteens, two ammo pouches with a grenade on each, and first aid kit—were flopping as I ran. I stopped before leaving the concealment of the trees and shook the belt to untangle the mess. My efforts worked on the first try; I snapped the belt buckle together and ran into the paddy.

The machine gun was still firing as I entered. The last two members of my squad had just dropped behind the final strip of protective dike.

A three-quarters-ton truck was on the trail in front with a trooper slumped over. When the VC fired, two the men in the back jumped out, two others hit the floor, while the fifth froze and was killed. He made a good target, as I would if I didn't find cover immediately. My squad occupied the dike; the truck had men behind it and was currently in the enemy's sights, and the next empty dike was 50 yards away—in the direction of the enemy.

The troops concealed themselves, not distracting the shooter with return fire. The VC gunnery unit continued firing at something. A desolate feeling overwhelmed me when I realized I was running forward in the open, the only target left, and the machine gun was probably firing at me.

I didn't dawdle after this comprehension and struggled forward in a frenzy to the next dike. I had a flashback of G.I.s in John Wayne movies zigzagging against an enemy machine gun nest, so I zigzagged like a halfback running for a touchdown. Adrenaline was pumping and my breathing became erratic; I felt light-headed. The equipment hanging from my pistol belt impeded my zigzag. I don't recall seeing Hollywood's combat heroes burdened with flopping equipment like mine. When I played football and lacrosse, everything fit in place snugly. This equipment was sliding and bouncing, each piece completely out of harmony with the others.

I could feel the gun firing directly at me. Bullets didn't hit the dirt as they do in movies, yet I knew they were aimed directly at me because I felt the sharp "crack" from each individual shot of this machine gun fire. I glanced to the hill, looking for the location of flashes, and could feel exactly where the gun was fired from. Fortunately I made it to the dike before they could zero in on me.

I puffed heavily from the run, making it nearly impossible to set the nimble sight on my M-79 for 250 meters, the distance I estimated the VC. He was still firing at me while I aimed for his spot on the hill and squeezed off a round.

"Poop!"

A three-second wait.

"Crack!" The explosion came from precisely where I aimed.

"I got them!" I cheered myself on. "They're not firing anymore, I got 'em!"

Sergeant Lopez, my foxhole mate, was at the dike where I had just plopped myself. "Save your ammo," he growled.

I screamed I fired directly back at them where they were and they weren't firing anymore.

He reminded me we couldn't claim a kill until we find the body, and that I should go out there and find the bodies.

I reneged but knew I got them.

I accomplished these "heroics" because it was the only way out of that situation, not because I wanted to. Hollywood wants you to believe a hero, their hero, is superhuman, all macho, gung-ho, fearless, and brave. I'm sure there are a few like that, but most authentic heroes were like me: forced into the situation, scared stiff, with some smarts, and mostly lucky.

I congratulated the VC cadre for its ineffectiveness in training its recruits. This was the first of many times I was not killed because of poor marksmanship; actually I owe my life to them. I figure I zapped at least two here; you never find one person lugging a machine gun and ammo by himself. I didn't get credit for any kill. That gun did stop firing and did not fire again, and there were no more casualties.

All was quiet. My squad formed its defensive locations, digging positions. Third platoon continued stretching across the paddies to the hills forming the right flank, three-quarters of a mile away.

A helicopter arrived to evacuate the body. The battalion commander, Lieutenant Colonel Salisbury, was on it wearing his traditional starched, sweat-free fatigues, jungle boots spit-shined by a Vietnamese orderly, and full combat dress including flak vest. We attempted to figure out what he was doing here because it was dangerous—one of the guys was just killed.

One of the enlisted men (EM) muttered that the colonel wanted his CIB.

The prized possession for a career in the Army is the Combat Infantryman's Badge. Without it you'll remain in the lower echelon. You are authorized to wear it with laurel wreath if you had been in combat and acted appropriately. This badge, plus the Purple Heart, were two awards I was not anxious to receive.

Every trooper received the CIB for this operation, leaving us apprehensive about our remaining missions. The next time I saw the colonel he wore full combat gear festooned with CIB and laurel wreath.

Bravo strung across the top of the delta with two men at the top of each paddy. There was limited protection from the foot-tall dike; consequently, we had to dig a prone shelter behind it extending five feet, one foot deep and two feet wide. Digging here was different from the sand at Cam Ranh Bay. This clay mud had not seen rain and dried solid, having to be chipped with the pick on the opposite side of our shovel.   Everyone had their shirts off by 1300 and desperately tried to carve their shelter before dark. I imagined having more difficulty than others, their clay being softer or pick sharper. Everybody seemed to have shelters dug before me.

I sat down at 1500 feeling faint. My first canteen was less than a third full. I took clay chips in the hole and stacked them along the edge, creating a foot-tall ridge. Now I had my prone shelter, with marginal protection.

Platoon sergeant Smith was in the CP behind my position, a couple of paddies to the right. Included with him was the platoon officer, Second Lieutenant La Fontaine, RTO Howard, and an artillery forward observer (FO). They had at their disposal a three-quarters-ton truck with cases of rations and two five-gallon water cans. Water wasn't offered to us.

Sergeant Lopez was next to me and shared the watch. He asked for the first sleep. I didn't mind because I had a headache. After the sunset, the temperature began to cool off. I was drowsy at 2200 and woke Sarge half an hour later. Mosquitoes bothered me as I tried to sleep, even after I liberally applied repellent and pulled my head inside the poncho. Finally I became tired enough to sleep.

I was awakened for the next watch, swatted a few mosquitoes, looked at the bright stars, tried to remember college astronomy, and waited for the enemy to be driven out of those hills toward me.

The next day came and went with no rain, enemy, or relief. Ditto that night.

It was the third day now; A and C Companies would emerge from the hills, completing their sweeps this morning. They had been organized in platoon-sized units, arriving at different intervals. The 173rd Airborne had recon elements patrolling our flanks from VC who might have been flushed out. This was a surprise; we didn't think this method yielded results.

Elements of Alpha began trickling into the paddies when we heard M-60 machine gun and M-14 auto rifle fire by the base of the hills near the right flank of 3rd Platoon. Our RTO learned 173rd Recon saw some guy sitting on a rock at one of the hills and fired at him.

Troops heard "boom" sounds from the Navy in the bay. A few seconds later screeching sounds indicated artillery passing overhead. When they exploded on that hill, we heard the "crack" sound from their explosion, feeling the shock waves of concussion. The barrage stopped in a minute.

Seconds later, two F-101s arrived for a bombing run on the hill. They commenced with a steep dive over the bay then flat at 500 feet screaming up behind. Each released two 2,500-pound bombs and pulled up, sitting on their tails before disappearing over the hills. Bombs sailed directly over the troops to the target three-quarters of a mile away, astonishing everyone. They were experiencing real live bombing, no firepower display or movie. The bombs exploded with much more force than the Navy's big guns. The white flash of shock waves from concussions slapped men in their faces. Everybody sat on the edge of dikes, observing this show of artillery, bombing, and strafing jets as we would on our living room TV. This was authentic, though, actually happening right in front of us. Each man was part of the show; later we would play much more significant roles. The troops found this show exciting, like boys at a movie, delighted by all the action.

The troops were indoctrinated to the rules of combat: dirty bodies, hungry flies, exhaustion, time dragging endlessly, limited hygiene, thirst, hunger, and smelly clothes. Welcome to real war.

By noon, most of Alpha and Charlie filtered from the hills. They lay behind us completely exhausted. I asked if any had passed the spot in the hill where I had shot at the VC; none had. They didn't want to talk about what they did because they were too hot, though they wanted to know what the bombing and artillery barrages were about. I told them VC were spotted, shots fired, artillery dropped, and air strikes deployed, but didn't know the outcome.

An RTO staggered out of the bush by himself, 200 yards in front. He was obviously exhausted: his shirt, flak vest, and pistol belt were open with the rifle slung over his shoulder, helmet swinging in one hand and radio dragged by the other. He drudged to our positions and yelled, "You guys Charlie Company?"

"No, we're Bravo. Charlie's on the right there behind 3rd Platoon."

He tossed his helmet on the ground, cursed something, and then walked over booting it like soccer ball.

We thought it funny; somebody else had a rough time. Our heat was unbearable sitting in one spot all day, yet it was easier than slogging with heavy equipment through the hills.

The companies' defenses began to relax; we would convoy back to the dunes at 1400. Companies began assembling to account for all their personnel. Alpha still had a patrol out which should be returning shortly. My platoon gathered on the dirt service road, our convoy pick-up point. Most were eating and talking about their experiences the past three days. Our innocence had been lost, the sacred part of you that can never be returned once it's gone, like losing your virginity.

Two of the 173rd Recon jeeps passed along the service road from their positions in the hills. The first had a prize stretched spread-eagle across the hood resembling a recently shot deer.

When they got closer I could see it was human, probably the VC all the shooting and bombing was about. They confirmed it, stating he had been watching our positions, probably a scout. Stretching and lashing the body over the hood appeared overly dramatic; our men thought it completely unnecessary. The recon guys thought otherwise, saying they wanted to show the VC they "shouldn't mess around with the 173rd."

We arrived at our dunes and discovered Cam Ranh Bay had not been overrun. The engineers finally completed a water processing facility, so water wouldn't be a precious commodity anymore. My platoon had adequate water that evening, each man able to take a "whore's bath" (wash the face, underarm, and crotch). The next day everybody thoroughly washed themselves and their clothes for the first time in five days, although still in the ocean.

Military newspapers were delivered that afternoon. An article on the front page announced the Big Red One had killed 25 during "Operation Barracuda" at Cam Ranh Bay.

I couldn't claim the VC I killed; still a person in Headquarters thought we had blasted some 25. Let's say I did get three, the 173rd definitely zapped one, the bombs and artillery might have blown up a few more, and A and C Companies might have winged a couple, but that doesn't add up to 25.

Security was comfortable in the dunes after the operation. Staff was satisfied there weren't threatening VC around. A gigantic weight was lifted from our necks.

This new feeling of invulnerability was significant to an increase of traffic along the dirt road on Cam Ranh Peninsula. The harbor facilities were mostly completed; consequently the Transportation and Supply vehicles were driving it constantly, distributing material. Army engineers erected a pontoon bridge at the crossing point at My Ca, relieving the now-congested traffic movement from the harbor to the mainland and Na Trang.

Many were allowed on the beach the same time while washing, with only one man from each squad at their post. A trooper packed a football; we had touch games at the beach. Somebody left a Frisbee with my squad, which was shared with troops using the beach. The 100 percent alert at positions was relaxed, allowing men to visit different foxholes and remain most of the day.

The food became palatable again. Much of the hot chow served for lunch and dinner was prepared from heated canned food, laced by locally grown vegetables. Our bodies finally tolerated the heat, humidity, dusty sand, and bugs.

Several days after returning, passes were granted to the resort city of Na Trang. This would be perfect: relatively high living standard, medium sized, plenty of bars and restaurants, friendly people, and an hour away. Viet Cong activity declined because Vietnamese police secured most of the route.

"Passes to Na Trang, cold beer, fresh meat, and women!"

I lucked out, getting in with the first group. I finally unpacked civilian clothes from the duffel bag. Everyone ocean washed, dressed, and was ready to convoy by 0600.

This city looked typically Asian, with a plethora of identical shops lining crowded narrow streets of pedicabs, rickshaws, small cars, loose chickens flopping around seemingly belonging to nobody, and many bicycles. We left the trucks at a small square by the beach. Staff Sgt. Jerry Stand, Headquarters Company, the convoy commander, told us to be back by 1600.

While meandering through this maze, I attempted to communicate with locals for a special place to eat but none spoke English well. I said, "Chop-chop," eat. They merely pointed to the two-mile long waterfront lined with small restaurants, all appeared made from the same blueprint. I had a difficulty deciding where to go and what to eat.

I saw one that looked clean with a sign offering filet mignon and beer, my first beer in two months. La Ve came in a brown, liter-sized bottle with a growling panther on the front. The beer was flat but tasted good because it was cool and wet. I planned to have a steak and beer here, but noticed some girls in the bar next door. This might satisfy my sexual desires; I made a mental note of the filet place for steak later and its proximity to the convoy departure point. Unfortunately, the girls next door weren't whores, but it didn't stop me from having a few more beers, intensifying my forgotten sex drive.

My recollection began to get hazy. I went to a bar with Vietnamese soldiers and asked where I could get laid. Alcohol had its effect faster than normal because of my two-month abstinence. The soldiers laughed after my futile graphic references to sex.

"Oh," they laughed, "boom-boom."

"Yes, I want boom-boom."

They gave me directions in Vietnamese, which I couldn't comprehend. These took me in from the beach to a more shabby part of town. I became disoriented while becoming ravenous for fresh meat. Smoke and exotic smells emanated from a hut, with a beer sign. I went in, ordered a beer, and tried to explain I was hungry and wanted filet mignon, which I hoped they might have.

"Oh-h-h, chop-chop, velly good, velly good."

Whatever I ate was not filet and I doubt it was beef. It was thin slices of some type of meat, probably water buffalo. Still, it was hot with a spicy Oriental flavor, chewy, but delicious. I licked the plate and refused to wash it down with beer; afraid I'd wash away the taste.

I asked the waiter about boom-boom girls and ordered another beer.

"Oh yes, boom-boom, numba one boom-boom." He described a place a few blocks away.

By the time I finished this beer, I was crocked and couldn't find a needle in a haystack. The stores and streets all blended together; I couldn't understand street signs.

I glanced at my watch and panicked, it was almost 1600, time to leave. I found the coast by orienting myself with the sun. Once I found it, I couldn't grasp which square I wanted. One looked familiar but I couldn't find the filet mignon sign. A restaurant a block away looked familiar but didn't have the sign either. I was sure this was the place and assumed they ran out of steak and took the sign down.

By 1630 I couldn't find convoy trucks or my people. I realized I screwed up; they left because I was late. There was no U.S. military presence at night; it would be imperative to return before then. No U.S. vehicles were on the road from town, so I flagged down a pedicab driver, told him Cam Ranh, showed him money, and grabbed another beer.

We were out of the urban area and into the countryside. I was still pretty drunk, but thought rationally for the first time. "This Vietnamese is pedaling an American from Cape Cod, who is dressed like an American from Cape Cod with shorts and a college T-shirt, through a primal area of peasant farmers."

This wasn't very comforting, especially when I realized I was near the delta I where I was shot at earlier. Also, I was afraid this guy wouldn't be able to pedal this contraption to camp before sunset.

I started to have a lonely, empty feeling, like a person might feel jumping out of a plane and discovering the chute didn't have a ripcord.

There were truck sounds behind me; I turned to gratefully see three trucks returning to Cam Ranh with the pass people. Sergeant Stand was furious; I had showed up at the wrong square. He waited over an hour before departing. Nobody knew where I was; some were afraid I had been captured. When he saw me on this dirt road, in the middle of nowhere in a pedicab, still holding a beer, he became so furious he wanted to court-martial me. Fortunately he cooled down by the time we reached camp and never took action.

September 2, two days after payroll, I took out another night patrol. Unfortunately I didn't have the caliber of people as those on my first patrol. Most had experienced combat but life had become tame. It was difficult to be serious about defending a foxhole in the dunes because we hadn't seen a VC in two months. Most of these men had been to Na Trang on pass, some got laid, and everyone got drunk. Washing at the beach was like a beach party now; nobody on this ambush patrol took it seriously. The guys were joking with the troops on the perimeter before we left at dusk. Everybody thought the patrol was absurd, just like the "fire watches" we had in the States.

Nobody wanted to take the point because it meant harder work. I had to designate someone different each half hour. This was different than my previous patrol with a man like Ron the Cuban volunteering for point during the entire patrol.

Pfc. Jimmy Wilson resented my giving orders, even though I was patrol leader. He whispered constantly; most of the time making innuendoes about my psychological need to give orders and that I was no longer in OCS. My objective was only taking this patrol to achieve the mission and return without any complications. I established two ambush sites, didn't see anybody, and headed back to camp at first light.

Wilson returned with his rifle upside down, sling over his shoulder, and muzzle swinging inches above the sand. I told him to lift his rifle up.

"You can't order me to do anything. This is my gun!"

I told him I was in charge and responsible for the safety and performance of everybody in the patrol.

If we had become involved in a firefight, he would have been useless if the weapon had sand jammed into the muzzle. Having a man with an inoperative weapon would be comparable to running an obstacle course with a useless appendage.

The next day someone called for me from the next dune. I had to go the CP; Lieutenant La Fontaine, the platoon leader, wanted me.

He received a note from the 2nd Brigade's information officer, 1st Lt. Bill Angle; saying he wants me to be a reporter for the battalion.

It read, "Dear ex-candidate." Lt. Angle was in the OCS class ahead of me and graduated. "Need someone to write the news and take photos. The S-1, 1st Lt. George Kline, will review before you submit. You will be attached to Headquarters Company."

This was ideal, allowing independence and freedom, while using my creative writing experiences from college. Also I would have a chance to be imaginative while living in a better environment at Headquarters.

Headquarters Company was established adjacent to the picturesque deep pond near the entrance to the harbor. I would be sharing a platoon tent on a cliff 50 feet above the pond. The tents had a floor of wooden pallets and canvas cots enclosed inside mosquito nets, surrounded by a grove of trees. There was a gradual, one-mile descent from the tent to the harbor. Along the route were different logistical, transportation, medical, radio, and administration facilities for the 1st Battalion, 18th Infantry.

Headquarters Company didn't need defensive positions because C Company was security. The guys in my tent were either battalion clerks or drivers, the closest things to friends I would have in Vietnam. Each was associated with Staff and Administration; consequently they would not be going into the jungle on sweeps. Nevertheless, each would eventually see combat.

Pfc. Freddy Wadsworth and Spec 4 Bob Murphy were the Personnel clerks, claiming they ran Battalion.

Wadsworth was soft spoken, polite, and intelligent sounding and acting. He was good looking but never tried to get laid. I felt that he was gay, but he was probably just smart for not taking chances.

Murphy looked and sounded like a typical nerd: overweight, bifocals, dirty rifle that he didn't know how to fire, and bright. Unfortunately he lacked common sense. He immediately pulled out a photo of his girl when we met; they were a perfect match.

Mike Staton was assigned to another company like me and also attached. He was an excellent handyman. If anything broke or needed assembled, he fixed or made it. Not without compensation of course. He was permitted to constantly express his dislike for the Army and all it entailed without retribution from above because he was too valuable. Whenever he began on one of his tirades, the officers and NCOs let him rant and rave, completely ignoring him.

Hans Burg Baker was a mail clerk and the son of a German officer killed in World War II. His mother married a G.I. and moved to Michigan where he was raised. The first thing he told me was that he graduated from college majoring in industrial relations and that his dad was German, killed in WW II. He still had a pronounced German accent and shouted orders in German after a few beers. His features and mannerisms were so Nazi it was frightening. Later I wished he had Nazi will to kill.

Dick Peter drove the Headquarters three-quarter-ton truck, HQ 1. When we got disgusted with his indifferent attitude, he was called "Penis." His unique distinction was shaking hands with Secretary of Defense McNamara while reviewing the troops of Headquarters Company that summer. A photo appeared in a military paper with Peter nonchalantly standing by a truck, displaying his typical goofy expression on his face, while McNamara stretched out his hand.

Jim O'Riley was a little bifocal-wearing Irishman who had been in the U.S. less than a year before being drafted. He was the driver for S-4 Supply Officer Capt. Bill Million. Whenever Jimmy became excited, he stuttered.

Bobby Crow, the driver for the battalion commander, Lieutenant Colonel Salisbury, was handsome with brown curly hair and cocky to the point of being arrogant. The colonel appreciated that characteristic. He had reason to be that way; he was exempted from all duties and answered only to the colonel. I thought this air of confidence was all show; later he proved me wrong.

Staff Sgt. Robert Grassburg was the Personnel NCO responsible for keeping track of this group. He was a career man who went to Baptist services at home carrying the Bible. He never bought any of the ladies, and fortunately for us, he was a tolerant man.

I was living the good life now. Supply asked me what weapon I wanted; I took an automatic M-14. Vietnamese people picked up our laundry each day. What a paradox: now that I didn't get my clothes dirty, they were washed and pressed every day. There was a latrine with commodes and showers built by Mike. A wash and shower in fresh water each day was luxury.

Hot chow was served in a mess hall with a small PX nearby to get cold beer, soft drinks, and cigarettes. Our cooler was always filled.

Battalion bought me a camera out of the slush fund. Murphy and Sergeant Grassburg claimed to know cameras, discussing the type I needed for combat photography in the jungle. A Nikonos 35mm waterproof would have been ideal, but the local PX didn't have one. Murphy saw a Yashica Mat 66 with 120 film. "This is what you want because large film will print well."

The Yashica was large and bulky, ideal for taking pictures of a family reunion, not designed for the jungle during a combat operation. When it hung from my neck, the strap felt like the yoke of a wagon.

I asked if it wasn't too big, with trepidation, because I had never taken a picture before.

He said it was perfect.

I told him I would be accompanying the troops into the jungle but, "Murphy says ..." and you don't question him.

We heard Battalion would be soon joining the rest of Brigade outside Saigon. Military papers reported Brigade was finding action there and we would be joining them shortly.

The guys in my tent were happy to have me join them. I was one more body to split radio watch with at night, monitoring the situation reports (sit-reps) from the companies.

I tried to find something newsworthy to write about around the harbor. There wasn't much going on, mainly pencil-pushing clerk stories, sand dunes, dirt trails, and recently constructed harbor facilities. I took a few photos and brought them to the MAC-V Intelligence facility to be printed. I left them for a week and hoped when they were returned they would be cropped the way I requested.

One night a week later I heard loud music, laughter, and commotion from the officers' hut. Captain Weeks was now Maj. Roland Weeks, Bn S-3 Operations. I had never met him before I came to Headquarters; after I got to know him I respected this Special Forces officer more than any other.

There will be more about him later. He was a man's man—a natural leader whose attributes were evident without a sign hung around his neck.

Weeks had been a major once but was busted to captain after he slugged his commanding officer. Since he made field-grade officer again, Weeks began a magnificent red handle bar mustache. Once it filled out, he looked like the actor Keenan Wynn except more muscular.

With our camp moving shortly, everyone became restless. My tent had overheard conversations in the administration tents regarding supply, convoy security, air strikes, evacuating wounded, body bags, Cambodia, booby traps, and tunnels.

Battalion would be joining the rest of the Brigade outside Bien Hoa by the village of Ho Nai. The people were Catholics from North Vietnam led south in 1955 by a Canadian monk to practice their religion without interference from the Communist North's intolerance of religions.

The troops would be shipped south to Saigon on Navy LSTs. This would take two days, then convoy an hour to Ho Nai, 35 miles northeast on Highway #1. Our mission would be to patrol the 65-mile radius west of Saigon, later called the "Iron Triangle," with search-and-destroy missions. North Vietnamese troops were infiltrating the South at an alarming rate. Our task was to stymie this, discover enemy installations, and prepare and document everything for the coming arrival of the remaining 1st Division.

We had less to talk about now in apprehension of what lay ahead. The guys spent the last few nights silently sitting at the edge of the deep, black, crystal-clear pond beneath our tent. We sat in that serene, tranquil location drinking a few beers, eating popcorn, and essentially just thinking— thinking of what lay ahead in the new league we would be entering.

The calm ended September 21; we were leaving Cam Ranh Bay in two days.

Chapter 6

Entering the Major Leagues

The convoy from the port of Saigon traveled modern, avant-garde Highway #1 to Tan Heip, 15 miles away, next to 2nd Brigade Headquarters. Past the intersection to Bien Hoa and Vung Tau, the road narrowed to the more typical two lanes with scattered potholes, uneven surface, and mud puddles on the sides. We took a right in the center of the hamlet of Ho Nai to a dirt road leading behind, up a slight rise, and across a railroad crossing. Combat Engineers prepared the camp, bulldozing the scrub brush and six-foot mound clay anthills. Roads lined with drainage ditches laced the camp.

Ho Nai was a tidy town; a dim white plastered church and school were centrally located, while the rest of the village radiated out. The focal point was a 10-foot globe of the world with a statue of the Virgin Mother on top, hands outstretched, the first structure erected after arriving in freedom.

While at Cam Ranh, our battalion was spread over a 10-mile radius; now we were together in a clearing of two football fields side by side. The rest of Brigade was a few miles behind at Highway #1. Brigade was together now.

Our battalion was a tent city. All 1,000 men shared platoon tents; wooden pallets were a floor above the mud with canvas cots sheltered by mosquito nets. Latrines, wash racks for basins, and showers consisting of 50-gallon drums with faucets were erected. Mike began building our chapel from scrap lumber and tin sheets.

Each company had a mess hall where better meals were available because of the proximity to Saigon. The point of entry supplied us with meat and chicken in more flavorsome forms than canned. Everyone received several new sets of jungle fatigues; real combat clothes with no brass,

Statue of the Virgin Mary in front of the Catholic school in the village of Ho Nai, erected by North Vietnamese refugees to commemorate their newly found freedom here.

nametags, or insignia. The festooned pair we arrived with was for garrison duty, basically what we had experienced thus far. We finally had work clothes.

Finally we were blessed with American music from Armed Forces Radio in Saigon. One of the DJs played mostly current, hip sounds rather than the polkas, big band sound, and two-step ho-hum normally heard. The troops became too busy building and establishing base camp for time to sit, listen to the radio, and comprehend rumors.

While in the Personnel tent the fourth morning I heard "Good Morning, Vietnam!" on the radio, bellowed by that DJ always playing good music. I could tell whenever he was broadcasting because the attitude of the troops was more positive. Everyone went about their duties in a happier frame of mind, fingers snapping, laughing, and singing.

The weather and bugs were similar here, yet troops found another irritation—mud. This clay turned into a quagmire after a shower because it couldn't drain. Fortunately the engineers put gravel on top of the roads and ditches on the sides to catch runoff.

Whenever we left a tent after the afternoon monsoons, we contended with slippery mud. Tractor soles on jungle boots provided traction.

This was the slipperiest mud I ever experienced, like sheets of ice. While walking, one had to go slowly and cautiously, continuously maintaining balance.

Each time I ran into a tent next door or to and from a jeep, mud would cram inside the cleats, creating a mess on the pallets. Regardless, it was a minor inconvenience for the benefit of being at a location with a shelter over our heads. Everyone appreciated it immensely; unfortunately, the longest our troops would stay at base camp between operations would be four days. Work had been cut out for us.

Battalion was now amalgamated with civilization: movies each night, while news from the outside world was on the radio and in magazines and newspapers from the States. The men were surprised to see protests about our increased involvement. Most of us had been uptight when we learned our destination was Vietnam. My feelings had been changing since I arrived, met the people, and learned what the Communists had been doing. Nobody paid much attention to the protesters at first because these people's feelings were identical to ours initially. They, like us, didn't like to get shot either.

Lieutenant Angle briefed me on what was expected from the Information Office. He took me to Bien Hoa Air Force Base Photo Lab where I met Airman Martin who would show me how to develop and process my film. I could print, crop, and burn in whichever and how many I cared to, processing my photos immediately.

Our temporary chapel was completed Saturday. Sunday morning our brigade chaplain, Father Thomas Confroy, consecrated it while the Canadian monk from Ho Nai gave the sermon, thanking the Americans for coming and expecting more to settle around us because of the protection we provided from the Viet Cong.

Father Confroy was the brigade chaplain I knew when the 1st Division was at Fort Riley. This former Latin teacher was a Benedictine who owned nothing; his stipends went directly to the order which gave him a portion. I was surprised to see him in a combat area because he always seemed frail, speaking in a mild, hushed voice. He had a round frame, but not fat—just basically without muscle tone.

I wrote the weekly battalion newsletter, "The Black Lion Extraordinaire," in the States. Every week one of the chaplains would write a brief message. Father's always emphasized love, tolerance, understanding, and forgiveness.

He asked if I would serve mass today. I felt complimented and served each time he held mass and was grateful because it helped me find and appreciate God.

I didn't think Father Confroy would be able to cut the mustard offering mass to the infantry in combat conditions. A person had to be exceptional to be there. I didn't realize until later how outstanding Father really was.

The tents were up, latrines operating, supplies flowing in smoothly, and all equipment dusted off from the sand dunes.

We at Headquarters had been sampling the virtues of the local maidens. My section had to make frequent trips to Bien Hoa for administrative purposes. We found a shortcut past a rubber plantation next to a Vietnamese army post and surrounded by hookers. We did cursory looking and sampling of the product line, but seldom participated because most were marginal. The main road to Bien Hoa had better samples which we eagerly digested at a righteously priced 200 piasters or $2.

By the end of September we had an addition to Headquarters Staff, Sergeant Fong. This Vietnamese soldier, who had recently finished training as an interpreter, became a member of Staff and shared our tent. He didn't look like a typical Vietnamese because of Indian blood. The southern part of Vietnam was a melting pot of different nationalities. Fong joined our tent and became our friend.

The remaining two brigades of the 1st Division would be arriving in a month at the staging area for the North Vietnamese, Phuoc Vinh province. It was our job to search, destroy, and document enemy activity so new arrivals would know what to expect and where to find it. Also, the VC had been plundering it extensively.

Chapter 7

A Bloody Nose Doesn't Hurt as Bad as It Looks

A bloody nose is common among athletes. The first time is traumatic, remembered for every detail. The same happened to us here in the major leagues.

Battalion's Headquarters Staff was told everyone was going "out there" during the next operation and make sure all combat gear had been serviced. The crew at Headquarters was infantry qualified and would soon earn their combat pay.

I would join the three infantry companies in the jungle yet remain under the jurisdiction of Headquarters. Operation officer Major Weeks verified my intentions with each of the company COs. They granted permission—providing they wouldn't be responsible for my safety.

Battalion CP Staff would be the Forward CP, established near the area of operation. This facility consisted of the hundred men from Headquarters, Supply, Medical, Operations, Artillery, and Transportation, assisting the infantry sweeping neighboring jungles.

In two days, October 4, "Operation Hopscotch" started. I informed the Air Force Photo Lab, which had instructed me in the rudiments of photo processing. The Air Force chided me saying I'd better bring back good stories and photos if I wanted continued access to their facilities; they were expecting enemy memorabilia. My primary objective was to have material newsworthy to be printed. The paradox was it would be dangerous where newsworthy events occurred.

October 4, 0300 Battalion was awake and preparing for convoy. I finished my last shower for two and a half weeks, ate chow, and helped Peter and Sergeant Grassburg load Headquarters' three-quarter-ton Personnel truck. Hans needed someone to ride shotgun on his mail truck. I volunteered and also helped him load providing I wouldn't have to take orders. There was always friction between us which was never resolved. It infuriated me when he barked at me in German. I couldn't understand him and knew he was insulting me. Our interpreter, Fong, and Murphy the clerk rode in the back.

All the vehicles had their canvas tops off and windshields down allowing an unobstructed view and fields of fire. Big .50-caliber machine guns were used on the 2½-ton troop-carrying trucks. They were necessary in past wars to fire at planes, tanks, and armored personnel carriers. Troops couldn't understand how .50's would be effective against guerrilla-type forces, but we carried them anyway. Six of the 15 trucks in the convoy had them mounted.

The convoy left shortly after sunrise; Phuoc Vinh was 60 miles away. Our movement would take two hours. Huey gunships escorted us most of the way.

Air power, big .50s, 500 heavily armed troops, and flak vests rendered the men a sense of security and confidence. We questioned who would dare attack now.

The trip was uneventful. Phuoc Vinh was modest of 50,000 people, with much of the income from rice, bananas, lumber, and sugar. There were rubber plantations also, but Communist interference made operating them impractical. The convoy threaded through the nicer part of town with many of its structures built of clay. Most of the people were well dressed, with many military men from the local Vietnamese post. The streets in this part of town weren't paved, however the businesses and residences appeared tidy and neat.

The route took us down a hill and over a small bridge to "the other part of town." Scraps of wood with tin sheet roofs tacked and rope tied together composed many structures. These shanties were mostly teahouses, restaurants, and bars. The men wore peasant-type dark, silky pajama tops and bottoms, giving cold stares as we passed. I called to Fong and said I thought they looked like bad guys. He said they probably were.

"Why don't we go back and kill a few?"

He asked what kind of an American I was. That we believed in human rights, due process of law, and innocent until proven guilty. "You still have freedom of speech in America, don't you?"

Excessive freedom of speech and press led to the demise of his country because a VC couldn't be killed simply because he was a Communist. The country was a democracy with different parties.

I told Fong he couldn't prevent me from returning their nasty stares.

He laughed and said it was OK if it made me feel better.

I gave each a mean John Wayne scowl, flicked my cigarette butt at one, and felt much better.

The road meandered past rice paddies and swamps, leading toward the jungle. Our convoy assembled in a field of elephant grass by 0930, just before the heat became unbearable, one of the many locations established as CP during this operation. The three rifle companies got off the trucks, immediately deploying into the jungle on a search-and-destroy mission. This was a coordinated brigade effort with six rifle companies of the other battalions here also. Troops at the CP conducted their duties, erecting this little post, while I helped with the Battalion Administration tent; cots were erected in the rear section while the front was an office with two portable desks, one typewriter, and a field radio. The facilities were for Personnel, mail, and my writing.

Jimmy O'Riley left a case of hand grenades and M-14 ammo, telling us to help ourselves; there was plenty here.

In the tent canvas cots, sleeping bags, and mosquito nets made sleeping comfy; Staff would be living like "fat cats."

Our lunch and dinner were C rations heated in their cans over a propane stove. A guy in the next tent had some Tabasco sauce, which made rations tastier when added to heated cans.

By noon we heard shots. Alpha Company made first contact with VC sappers, who were testing them. Moments later, a report to Operations said they might have zapped a few sappers and were recovering their supplies.

Major Weeks was in a frenzy; he wanted to see the supplies and dead VC. The Battalion CO, Lieutenant Colonel Salisbury, wouldn't let him join Alpha; it would be too dangerous to walk through the jungle unescorted. Resupply was in two days; he would be able to get a lift to Alpha with the chopper. His RTO, Pfc. Sammy Thompson, gratefully agreed this sounded better.

Fortunately no Americans were hit during that exchange. A problem developed which was never clearly resolved. VC medical supplies and bags of rice were recovered; unfortunately there wasn't a plan to evacuate them. The men could carry the caches to the CP through the jungle, but this would place them behind schedule in the operations plan. This would also provide the VC opportunities to establish ambushes en route. The men felt that there were a lot of bad guys there waiting to kill them. The contributing factors to their anxiety were overall stillness in the jungle, intelligence reports, and considerable enemy supplies. A warrior from the Korean War advised the men to relax, that they were merely experiencing nervous anticipation. We had entered the major leagues and stepped up to the plate.

Staff's tent was near the center of Headquarters' CP. Artillery and Transportation provided perimeter security at night. We took turns monitoring sit-reps on the radio each hour as rifle companies made nightly situation reports on their status. This info was radioed to Brigade.

Everybody worked together as a team, making life the smoothest I experienced in the Army—no more chickenshit duties, details, inspections, bickering, and hassle. Everyone had jobs and responsibilities. Once completed, they helped others with their chores. The men of Staff were happy with me as a member; it meant one more body to assist in the abundant tasks.

Murphy and Sergeant Grassburg were still coordinating Personnel with the companies operating in the jungle, Crow finished putting up the colonel's hooch, and Jim O'Riley returned from erecting the Supply tent.

If you want to stay alive in combat you have to be smart, constantly thinking, "What if...?" Dumb and ignorant soldiers are the first statistics.

We split the radio watch six ways from sunset to sunrise. The men were still wound up and excited; no one wanted to sleep early. Forward CP would be here for two more days before moving to another location. Everyone could afford to stay up late with limited watch, catching a nap the next day if needed. Nobody walked around after sunset, but you could hear people still up by an occasional laugh, a flash of light as a tent flap slid open, and sounds from the latrine.

We put the lantern out at 2200 and crawled into our cots. Hans had the watch at the time. He became very quiet at sunset, almost acting hospitable and friendly, not his usual cocky and belligerent self.

I had just fallen asleep when I was startled awake by shots fired from outside, immediately followed by outgoing volleys.

The VC watched us in the afternoon and returned with a six-man ambush patrol. Their objective: shoot Americans. By the time they returned at night, they couldn't see any to shoot and ended up scattering several volleys around, aiming at black tent silhouettes.

Our gun positions were low, prone shelters, circled with sandbags and dispersed around the perimeter, impossible for the VC to see.

We vowed this would be the last time we would sleep at Forward CP without pants and above the ground in a canvas cot. I was glad I knew exactly where my pants, boots, pistol belt, and rifle were. It was pitch black inside; fortunately my equipment was stacked in sequence. Crow was next to me, matching me with a 10-second call to arms. We slid outside and crawled under HQ 4 when a second set of volleys splattered about. I scanned for anyone running about firing an unfamiliar sounding weapon.

Thankfully none of the anxious clerks from my tent did any firing; most was done by qualified troops on the south perimeter. Crow and I heard the sound of grass moving behind us. Hans slithered under the truck between us, completely decked out with full battle regalia: steel pot, flak vest, bayonet, first aid pack, canteen, weapon, grenades, extra ammo, etc.

Crow told me to continue watching the front, the direction of the firing, and Hans the rear; Hans crawled back, yet refused to stick his head out. A moment later, he crawled between us with a sheepish grin saying, "Where are they?"

Crow almost shot him, suggesting I watch the back.

I warned them to be careful; Staff officers were running between tents coordinating Artillery with Infantry. Also, they radioed the troops in perimeter to hold their fire and not reveal their positions.

I told Fong to stay on the floor of the tent with O'Riley. I didn't want him to be mistaken for the enemy and be shot by a trigger-happy truck driver or clerk.

The troops at the south portion of the perimeter were facing the edge of the jungle where the first shots were initiated. They waited until the firing stopped, aimed in that direction, released safeties, pried grenade pins back, and waited for the VC to fire again.

When the enemy fired short staccato bursts, troops saw the flashes, releasing a withering barrage of gunfire and grenades, immediately terminating the incoming fire.

The infantrymen searched, waited, and froze; absolutely nothing moved. After 10 minutes, each reloaded and cleaned his weapon with smiles and a few nervous chuckles.

The men returned to the tents, put their sleeping bags and mosquito nets on the ground, and fell asleep amazingly fast.

People began moving by 0530 when the eastern sky lit up. A mess hall tent was set up, but the cooks forgot to bring kerosene for the food burners. The colonel issued an executive order for kerosene by 0700; Recon Platoon drove to Brigade CP and borrowed enough to last until our supplies arrived later.

Personnel struggled up at sunrise. Jimmy O'Riley had the last radio watch; he gave us incentive, lying that the mess tent was open with hot chow. Wash racks and showers weren't set up because we would be moving tomorrow. The troops in the jungle wouldn't be returning to rest for another week.

The troops still had to be cautious with water consumption. Brigade CP had water purification equipment; distributing it to us was dangerous, requiring caution. This was "Charlie's" back yard; we had to play by his rules.

My digestive system was in the on-again off-again mode. When I ate the condensed C rations I'd be constipated. Chow in the field was served in mess kits washed in a trashcan with soapy water, barely heated by kerosene burners.

The can next to it was hot rinse and the final cold rinse. Suffice it to say, this was not sufficient to clean grease from over a hundred men. Consequently the men always had mild diarrhea at the Forward CP.

B Company, my old company from Cam Ranh Bay, found a cache of VC rice in over 150, 100-pound bags.

In the jungle the troops used land navigation to calculate their location with no roads, mountains, ridges, and buildings as reference. They relied on the compass and dead reckoning to orient with the map.

Bravo needed a fix from the air to mark the location of this cache.

Major Weeks was like a stallion straining at the bit. "Get me a chopper!" He was happy now. A Huey landed at the CP and flew him above Bravo in the jungle.

A Recon jeep mounted with an M-60 machine gun escorted Supply towing the water trailer to Brigade's water point for a fill and returned with kerosene.

The rifle companies complained their M-14 rifles were too long and got tangled in vines. Also, its ammo, double the basic load of 100 rounds, was heavy. Carrying 90 pounds of equipment is unwieldy; it's worse walking crouched, one step at a time in dense vegetation with a 95-degree temperature and 100-percent humidity. The supply officer, Captain Million, pursued older, lighter rifles in our arsenal.

The mosquitoes and flies were intense here; unfortunately there was another irritation—leeches. The small, black, one-inch worm climbed along the shirt, its rear sliding forward to the front, then the front forward until it lay flat. Back forward, then front forward and flat again.

The soldier could never tell when one was attached until he felt an itch. By then the leech would be attached, stuffed with blood, and looking like a fat, reddish black worm.

If a soldier unconsciously scratched the itch, he would find the finger full of his blood from the leach he broke. An attached leach was normally burned off with a cigarette

I must have looked funny walking around the CP with my shirt off, pistol belt and steel pot on, M-14 slung over my shoulder, and that monstrous camera swinging from my neck. The tent's large field radio battery was packed in heavy plastic bags, perfect to keep my camera dry during monsoons. This worked satisfactorily, but a camera of this enormous size in jungle combat soon proved ridiculous.

While assisting Staff, I didn't accomplish reporting. During lunch, First Lieutenant Kline told me of "civic action" by medics and engineers in local hamlets. I told him I preferred to be with the infantry, yet this was a beginning.

Medics told me I could ride shotgun; security was a commodity in constant demand.

The next day Battalion CP moved to the dirt runway of Phuoc Vinh airport where 2nd Brigade could be supplied more efficiently. Medics could treat several settlements here.

A local medical presence was impossible because the VC captured the doctors, resulting in a dire need for medical assistance. Capt. Pancho Milan, the battalion surgeon, and the available medics volunteered their services a week after the operation started.

Fong and I accompanied the medics on the first two visits. He explained who we were while the drivers passed out candy and gum to gain the civilians' confidence. There was little need for introductions after our first visit. There had been a lot of enemy propaganda about American cruelty; it didn't take long for these people to realize this as a fallacy. Adults and children with problems of every description continually mobbed the medics.

They became the most popular soldiers in the area. As they drove through the villages, children would throw bouquets of flowers while adults cheered and applauded. These "doctors" were taken to homes of people too sick to walk or to be carried by jeep. Captain Milan was called to assist a woman whom he said was having a breech birth. A chopper evacuated her to a military hospital in Saigon for a healthy birth. Later that day he was called to assist with another birth.

This assistance didn't end when Battalion CP left the area. While they treated the people, the medics instructed the civilians in how to care for each other's ailments. Trying to surmount the language barrier was the biggest problem. Nevertheless, the medics left behind rudimentary knowledge of simple medicine, care, and hygiene. If this was all that was accomplished during this operation, it could be considered a phenomenal success and a giant step forward for these people's welfare.

Intelligence asked if I wanted to ride shotgun for Recon. Reports had the VC monitoring our messages but doubted they could understand them. They were going to throw bait to see if it was snapped at. Recon would pass on a message to Alpha's 3rd Platoon on patrol. Later they would radio a conflicting one to see if the VC responded.

Two Recon jeeps were used, each with a 7.62-mm M-60 machine gun mounted on the rear deck. A "good ol' boy" from the South was the commander. This middle-aged guy was authentic from his almost unintelligible hillbilly accent, to the "blade" hanging from his side, and finally to the tobacco he chewed because he genuinely enjoyed the taste. The third guy on his jeep had an M-79 grenade launcher. My jeep had two of us with auto M-14s and the M-60. Each man each had three grenades hanging from his straightjacket-like flak vest. Weight wasn't a problem on a jeep. All this firepower and the confidence of being with capable people gave me a secure feeling I hoped would carry the edge. I was exploring Charlie's playground with a few of my pals but not worried.

Sarge oriented my map with the location of we were meeting the patrol, eight miles from town in a clearing somewhere in nowhere. Our dirt road led to a narrow clearing of elephant grass and giant anthills.

Refreshing afternoon showers cooled, washing away road dust and sweat. Puddles didn't form; water coated the entire claylike surface as an image-reflecting thin sheet.

The jungle was deathly quiet, without the typical jungle sounds of birds, monkeys, or dogs—even the jeeps were silent, an excellent indicator humans were watching.

Sarge motioned my jeep to come alongside. He whispered to keep our eyes on the mounds in the field. "Them anthills with stuff standing out of them, damn good place for Charlie. Keep out of the tracks of the other jeep." The clay was mucky; capable of sucking the jeeps down if we didn't make separate tracks. This clearing was a mudflat of yellow, jellylike clay covered by a slick of water with knee-high grass. He also suggested zigzagging, preventing becoming a target on a predictable course.

I felt like I was standing naked with eyes on me as we drove through this field. Yet I was confident that if the VC were watching, they wouldn't dare anything because of our superior firepower. I laugh thinking of myself driving over that flat in the back of the jeep, butt hanging from my mouth, bandoleer of ammo around my neck, a week-old beard, and a grenade with its pin loosened secured in my crotch.

This was a "walking on thin ice" feeling; we knew we were being watched. It was unnerving, wondering when and where they would start shooting.

We passed a thick clump of bushes near the end of the clearing. I scrutinized it closely because it was thick, making a good ambush site. Sarge noticed a narrow trail leading through a grove of mahogany trees surrounding the clearing. Plans called to meet the patrol in a field at the end of that trail in 15 minutes.

Sarge backed the jeeps down. If contact was made, we would blast forward, not dawdle out in reverse through a hail of gunfire. Everyone was sure we would find VC. This premonition wired me with a thousand volts. I still see almost every inch of that 100-yard two-lane dirt trail. Fortunately

I was wrong; we didn't meet any. They were watching, but apparently they didn't think it an opportune time to attack.

We reached the edge of the tree line and posted security while Sarge searched the field with his binoculars. A half-mile away 3rd Platoon was crossing the field, exactly when and where they were expected.

Sarge gave the platoon leader the message. The patrol filled their canteens, strapped on more bandoleers of ammo, and clipped additional grenades, replacing the ones tossed at VC in local tunnels this morning.

"Did you zap any?"

They didn't know, but got excited describing the action.

The jeeps cautiously drove back to the other clearing.

Sarge interrupted our concentration. "Look at them thar bushes. You men stay away, be security."

He meant the scrub of bushes I had noticed earlier. The machine gunner and driver stayed in the vehicle while Sarge climbed out and cautiously approached them.

"Well I'll be," he called out.

He pulled the branches down. Behind was a North Vietnamese 2½-ton truck crammed with supplies, bogged to the hubs, camouflaged, waiting to be excavated after we left. They had done a fantastic job; we never suspected it to be anything but a grove of bushes.

Headquarters' CP told us to leave it, that someone would get it later. We wanted to blow it up, but Sarge said to let it be, that they had to examine it for intelligence. I wonder if it happened and if anybody besides the VC managed to dig it out.

I returned with Recon in time for night chow, feeling a little taller than that morning.

We never learned if the VC were suckered into the radio ploy.

The next day I wrote two stories about my mission with Recon, then hung about Personnel rapping about those experiences. Sarge told me to leave the clerks alone because they had typing to finish.

I was reading *Stars and Stripes* when I heard movement in the grass by the rear of the tent. Crow and I investigated and discovered a slithering green "two-step-death" bamboo viper. I grabbed a broom, held the snake down behind the eyes while Crow grabbed an entrenching tool and decapitated it. Before tonight I thought he was all show and no go, but was pleasantly surprised how bona fide he acted in real danger. I think I must have surprised him with my prompt action also. With threats to our lives prevalent; occasions considered dangerous were mere incidentals of life.

We moved camp the next morning, taking only half an hour to ready the move to another nameless clearing.

I wrote a few more stories and took pictures around the CP. Unfortunately there weren't any pics adequate to warrant a flight to Bien Hoa to print.

Captain Million suggested I fly to the jungle with a supply chopper during delivery that afternoon. I asked Operations which company made contact. They said Major Weeks was with Bravo, which found another cache of rice. If there was action, the major would be in the middle of it; my best chances were with Bravo.

Five-gallon plastic jugs of water, cases of C rations, ammo, and grenades were loaded. A machine gunner was on each side of the chopper. Regardless I was armed with the auto M-14. I felt apprehensive landing in a jungle saturated with VC.

This cool, refreshing flight lasted only a scant 10 minutes; we landed in a small clearing Bravo had secured. The men acted so positive and strong, looking like authentic combat veterans since none had a chance to shave or change clothes since we started. I recognized the guys unloading the chopper from my platoon. They were happy to receive the water and rations while excited about their two caches of rice.

Their commanding officer, Captain J.J. Richards, West Point classmate of a high school buddy, was near the center of the field by a clump of bushes. I told him I'd be with him until the next supply in three days and wanted to see the captured rice. It was in the jungle and Brigade said they would move it later.

He told me to spend the night at the CP with him, the RTO, and medic. The chopper would be back in the morning for excess supplies; I could return on that flight if I cared. I thanked him, but after talking to Major Weeks I decided to stay until delivery three days hence.

The CO said 2nd Platoon would be point tomorrow and the one most likely to make contact.

I thanked him, scratched a spot in the ground, smoothed it out, stretched open my poncho, ate something, and discussed turns at radio watch. Although the shrubbery didn't offer much protection, we felt secure surrounded by troops guarding the perimeter. These were the same people I was with in the dunes of Cam Ranh Bay a little more than a month prior. Each man appeared to have grown in stature since I had seen him last. I guess everyone had. It was not growing up as much as it was gaining confidence and self-assurance. This was our coming of age; the men were becoming troops with a soul.

Kenny Campbell, the medic, and RTO were exhausted so I took first watch; Captain Richards fell asleep with them at dusk. I received sit-reps from each of the platoons and then called my report to Battalion Forward

CP. Hans was at the receiving end; I recognized his German accent, realizing he couldn't identify my voice.

"Sit-rep negative," I reported.

"Roger Duchess 2," the reply.

"Hitler was a fag, out."

"Wha, who's that?" he demanded.

"Out!"

At 0530, the sky got light. I fired up my first cigarette, opened some rations, rolled up my poncho, and began sweating again. My mouth tasted like cardboard; I hadn't been able to track down my duffel bag with toiletries and fresh clothes since this operation started.

The troops were dirty, needed shaves, their pants and shirts were ripped and stained, and they were smoking. Ammo belts hung around shoulders while shaving brushes, insect repellent, and water purification tablets were held by the rubber band securing the camouflage helmet cover with vegetation sticking out. Also machetes, knives, ropes, claymores, and smoke, concussion, and white phosphorous (WP) grenades were strung along pistol belts.

I was third man from point, entering the jungle at 0730. Point was always intense for the first man, having to keep the heading while being aware of trip wires, punji traps, mines, smells of the enemy, and ambushes. He had to push the thorn-encrusted vines and shrubbery aside, making a trail for the rest of his platoon. The heading had to be followed in a straight line. If the heading pointed through vines or quagmires of mud, point and the troops normally pressed directly through.

I developed an admiration for guys on point. I was probably under fire more frequently than most people in my battalion. It was optional which group I accompanied; if firing happened while I was near point, I could always hide behind a tree or anthill, which I did frequently. The point had no choice; stay, return fire, then push forward.

My M-14 with its big 7.62-mm NATO rounds felt heavy now. Frequently the front sight was snared by vines then yanked free. Patrolling began to be frustrating. I didn't want to roll my sleeves up because flies and mosquitoes feasted on my arms.

The humidity and moisture of the jungle kept us from being thirsty. Unfortunately it had an adverse effect on troops' hands, which turned white and shriveled as though submerged in hot, soapy water all day.

The jungle was absolutely silent, save for an occasional birdcall. Our soldiers could hear the man in front and behind breathing. Frequently this was the only way I could tell where the next man was. The jungle was so thick I could not see more than two feet in front—opaque like a fog bank.

The overhead entanglement of vines, branches, moss, and ferns completely blocked the sun.

The 150 men in this company assembled along the edge of a clearing for lunch after patrolling. As Major Weeks prepared chow, his RTO called; Charlie Company had found supplies, their CO was wondering if he could get there to examine this cache. Our battalion, the 1st of the 18th, had found more supplies than the other two battalions combined. This discovery would add to our total.

The major saw me and wanted to know what I was doing there.

"Looking for a story, sir."

There were plenty of stories all over. The Communists were stockpiling supplies for a push on Saigon, 40 miles away; local VC were getting help from North Vietnam.

I had snapped two rolls of photos since the beginning of the sweep, but didn't have anything worthwhile yet and jumped on the supply chopper the next afternoon amongst catcalls that I couldn't handle it in the boonies with real men. My return to the Forward CP was good timing; they were leaving for another location and, fortunately, all the equipment had been packed.

The guys in my tent wanted to know which company I stayed with. When I said Bravo; they put two and two together and realized I was the one that called Hitler a fag.

I sat in the back of HQ 1 while Peter and Sergeant Grassburg went over their checklist of equipment.

Crow roared up in the colonel's jeep.

"You hot shit," he bellowed. "Jimmy said you were with Bravo two nights ago; you're the one who told the kraut Hitler was gay. He's really pissed!"

"He can't do anything."

His screaming woke everyone.

Peter claimed he wanted to call in artillery.

I said Hans didn't dare take his safety off.

Sergeant Grassburg told us to be quiet and for Crow to keep the jeep away as he was making ruts. We were almost ready and didn't want the colonel's jeep to get stuck. Also he cautioned me not to upset Burg Baker; I would be his shotgun for the mail run this afternoon.

Our new camp was five miles away down a dirt road, through a small field, across a shallow stream, and next to the strip of jungle the three rifle companies were sweeping.

Sergeant Grassburg let me use the typewriter as soon as the tents were up. Establishing CP took less time since it was universally accepted to sleep on the ground.

I wrote two stories about the rice found and my patrol, forced down a mess kit of hot diarrhea-type mess food, and told Hans I would join him to Brigade CP for mail. I could ride shotgun and deliver my stories to the Information Office while there. Also I looked for a chopper ride to Bien Hoa to print my photos but couldn't find one.

Later, after I returned to CP, a supply chopper arrived. The supply officer, Captain Million, called me, saying it was going to Bravo with supplies. They had captured a hooch with over a hundred bags of rice and needed ammo and grenades.

The chopper landed in a football field-sized clearing. Bravo had enough men to secure only the landing zone (LZ); the rest were deployed in ambush sites and patrols throughout the jungles. Capt. J.J. Richards sat at a corner of this field by two humps of earth, a tree, and some brush. Major Weeks was there also along with both RTOs, a medic, and two rifle sergeants. The officers and NCOs formulated plans there for several days and for what to do with the rice.

Richards told me of rice on the other side of the clearing; 100 bags under a hooch. Three men guarded it down a trail, about 50 meters inside. He called before I left so that I wouldn't surprise them running down the trail.

I lit a cigarette, feeling like it might be my last.

A couple of random shots were fired inside the jungle. The VC were trying to draw our fire to know where our ambushes were. J.J. didn't flinch; he merely continued the night defenses.

He called the platoons in the jungles and told them to keep calm with the firing and send someone for the supplies.

That was the fastest-burning cigarette I had ever smoked as I prepared to leave.

Capt. J.J. reminded me to radio before I returned.

The trail to the rice cache was 50 yards away, through a field of five-foot-tall elephant grass. Initially, I gingerly walked across the field. Halfway to the tree line, a bad guy began shooting at me. The sounds of the shots rained down from the trees instead of ground level. I didn't see where the bullets landed, but could tell by the shock sounds the rifle muzzle faced directly at me.

The troops remained cool, not divulging their positions by firing back.

I could have moved faster if I hadn't had a monstrous camera swinging sideways from my neck. Twenty feet from the jungle, I found myself in midair, landing to my neck in water, sucked into a flooded VC foxhole concealed inside tall grass. These secluded foxholes were positioned in LZs facilitating ambushing arriving helicopters. I felt myself falling in slow motion and instinctively raised my rifle and camera above my head. When my feet landed, I immediately bounced up, keeping my equipment dry. The camera still had the plastic bag around it which I speculated kept it dry.

I scrambled out and ran the remaining 20 feet without being shot at again. Our guns remained quiet.

I called out to the troops guarding the rice, identifying myself along the narrow meandering trail. They shouted back to hurry.

After I rounded the third bend, I saw a sight that reminded me of cowboy and Indian movies. Their hooch was four posts supporting a peaked tin roof 15 feet above a hundred bags of rice. The men stacked bags of rice outside in defensive configurations, settlers in wagon trains under attack by Indians. That was how they felt because the VC had been shooting at them all day, evident by bullet holes in the bark of surrounding trees.

I couldn't believe how cool these guys were. I had been shot at and was shaking like a leaf. They were here by themselves all day with snipers repeatedly firing and now nonchalantly instructing me to keep my butt down. This was guerrilla warfare; I was finally involved with the real thing.

"You want to take pictures of us?"

I nodded, lit my last cig, and glanced at the stash behind. It was packed in 100-pound white bags with two hands shaking in front of U.S. and Vietnamese flags. On the top and bottom was printed in both English and Vietnamese, "Peace Through Friendship."

I mentioned the paradox of this rice in enemy hands. A trooper was upset, feeling we were let down by politicians and people of our government. This rice was destined for needy people in the villages and hamlets. Rather than being selective and screening recipients, bureaucrats designated to distribute it carelessly gave it to anyone who asked, simplifying their workload. Nobody monitored who received the rice; consequently the wrong people took it. I wrote to Bob Dole's 1997 presidential election committee, reflecting my sentiments about the Democrats in power impartially doling out welfare. Republicans were probably on the same committee because I never received recognition.

They complained about inefficiency, supposing the war was the government's idea to stimulate our economy, and pointed out captured VC supplies labeled "Made in the U.S.A."

I suggested confiscation from overrun Vietnamese outposts.

A G.I. grunted he would overrun some politicians in D.C. when he got out.

They wanted to know what would be done with the rice.

Brigade was supposed to take it.

"Before we left the other stuff where we found it. Vietnamese troops were to get it."

They suggested burying tear-gas grenades between the bags and "pop" them; poisoning the rice, which might have initiated a United Nations combat edict for civil rights violation.

There was tear gas in the supply chopper.

I took the camera out of its plastic bag and shook it. A little water eased out, but not enough to have damaged the film. The film advance worked properly as did the F-stop and light meter.

As I prepared to crawl out for photos, the men told me to keep my head low. If the VC fired, I was to freeze; I wouldn't get hit. Also, they assured me that "Charlie" had been shooting high all day.

I finished my third cigarette in 10 minutes, slid over the rice bags, and crawled low 10 feet into the bush. Bullet holes in the trees made by VC bullets were obvious, some a foot above the ground. It was not how high they were that bothered me; it was how low they had been coming in.

Those guys covering me looked like soldiers. They wore a two-week growth of beard, wet clothes with salt stains in the armpits and shirt collars unbuttoned to the waist, and a butt hanging. Their fortress had grenades and bandoleers of ammo resting on surrounding bags of rice with knives and machetes stuck into them.

"Yeah, these guys don't have that combat look," I chuckled.

I took several pictures; then had my subjects change positions for more. They thought I should return before the VC began firing again.

I crawled backward and called the CP, warning I would be returning. Another cigarette was sufficient time to warn the troops.

More water seeped out of my camera and the film advance began to stick. "I hope this roll of film is OK," I dreamed.

Captain Richards radioed it was safe. This time I ran across the field.

Major Weeks was in a frenzy: Charlie had found more rice, medical supplies, ammo, and papers and choppers weren't available. He spread a map out and squatted, pointing about it to Captain Richards; Charlie wouldn't take more than half an hour to walk to.

J.J. confirmed a 260-degree course would take him directly there; if he came to a stream, it would mean he missed them. The CO cautioned his troops Major Weeks would pass through, while indicating the VC were around and doubted they meant business.

The major called to his RTO, "Mount up Tom, we're going for a walk," and submerged into the jungle before Tom reattached his gear.

Tom gave me an "oh, what the hell," look as he struggled past with the same expression as that on a person's face before his first skydive.

I told the guys I'd hook up with them for the night and proceeded to nest my spot, finding a smooth place between the tree and a clump of clay.

I returned to the pagan rituals of prehistoric man, scratching a spot in the earth, making my nest for the night. The sooner I felt comfortable with this primitive environment and forget civilization, the better my chance to remain alive. I held a C ration can over a heat tablet, stirred a chopped onion and Tabasco sauce inside, gave a few stirs and bingo, the meal was delicious—back in civilization.

The day had been eventful and hectic; I was exhausted, volunteering for a later radio watch. I stretched my poncho across the ground after whacking off humps of earth, setting my helmet and pistol belt on the ground by it. Next I wrapped the poncho around my body, snuggling my rifle between my arms and legs like a woman. Since nights come fast in the jungle, I took particular care to allow time for a last cigarette before sunset.

I immediately fell asleep, jarred awake later by the inhumane sound of a soldier cracking up. His raspy bellow shattered the still night air. I was a kid investigating an empty house at night and somebody screamed directly behind me; although I would have reasons to be afraid later, his screams petrified me now.

They were horrifying, as though the VC were torturing him. I heard a shuffling; the medic ran past to him. He bellowed again, immediately muffled, then silent.

The medic escorted the soldier past me to Captain Richards. The man appeared normal. His sergeant said he acted removed and aloof earlier in the day, thinking it odd he was quiet now. He didn't make a special issue of it, thinking he was tired. I expected a mortar attack from the enemy who heard this outburst but fortunately nothing happened. "Doc" kept him doped up the remainder of the night.

I was anxious to see how my photos came out and left in the morning with the Medevac chopper and patient for their flight to Battalion CP. Dr. Milan looked at him while I had coffee and examined my camera. It was impossible to rewind the film. I managed to open the camera and take the film out, which was damp with the shutter frozen closed—my camera was ruined. A supply convoy was leaving for Bien Hoa so I hitched a ride to the PX to buy another.

The Air Force guys in the photo lab wouldn't let me in because I was too dirty. I threatened to toss a grenade. They reminded me I would never get my work done in that case. The men looked at my great film of the rice heist, two other exposed rolls, and camera while I waited outside the lab. Everything had been ruined; the two full rolls in the pack were also wet and couldn't be processed. My "Greatest Photo of the Vietnam War," the men in the rice hooch, had washed away.

A lieutenant presents captured VC medicine to the orphans and the Canadian monk pastor of the Ho Nai parish.

Martin helped me out at their PX, showing me the type of camera that would be practical. Waterproof cameras hadn't arrived yet, so I settled for a tiny Canon Demi-S 35mm that took a half-frame photo. This would fit perfectly into the heavy plastic bags the RTO's batteries came packed in. I placed an elastic band around the package and stuck it into the top shirt pocket. Perfect!

I hitched a ride to base camp at Ho Nai village and learned some captured VC medical supplies were given to their orphanage. 1st Lt. Jose Wilson, civic action officer, told me he would let me know the next time he visited this orphanage, asking if more enemy supplies would be arriving.

We were still securing equipment. I was surprised and thrilled enemy material had been recovered, evacuated quickly, and delivered to different Battalion Civic Action Offices. This alleviated Howard's complaint that VC supplies were left in the jungle for them to reclaim.

I showed Pfc. Wadsworth my new camera; he gave me an iced Coke. I couldn't chat because I needed to return to the jungle. The mess tent gave me onions and Tabasco sauce while Supply provided a packet of heat tablets. I put everything inside a couple of socks, tied the ends, and strung them from the top of my suspenders where they would ride comfortably.

The battalion executive officer, Maj. Albert Ridding, stopped by Personnel tent and told me a chopper was leaving from Brigade base camp to our Forward CP. A driver gave me the 10-minute drive.

"Old mamma-san" was pedaling her beers by the main gate to Brigade. She didn't recognize me at first because of my two-week growth.

She did after I spoke, asking where I had been.

Told her I killed "beaucoup" VC at Phuoc Vinh, later realizing she was probably VC watching movements at Brigade Headquarters. Also, I would meet her daughter there, shack up, and almost get killed by a VC patrol outside her mud hut. That's another story.

There wasn't any danger of disclosing secret operations by mentioning them because, remember, before we entered an area, we dropped leaflets, warning the enemy about impending operations.

I figured I had time to get laid, but realized it would cost me more than the standard 200 P's because I was so dirty. A small shower rinsed me off, helping me feel more presentable when I approached the chopper pilots for a ride to the Forward CP.

They gave me a brief stare.

I said that I was the PIO, public information office, of the 1st of the 18th "Vanguards."

They nodded. "In back."

The two door machine gunners ignored me.

Hans and Murphy were at the LZ for supplies. They told me the current CP was adjacent to a rubber plantation where showers, mess tents, and commodes were established for troops brought back for a break later that day. The men would have a few days to clean up and relax before going back to work.

I changed my socks, wolfed down hot chow, and napped in the tent.

The CP was getting brave again, back to sleeping on mosquito-netted canvas cots. Supply finished setting up the shower and latrine equipment. Also, 400 new sets of jungle fatigues, Cokes, beer, and ice had been delivered. The cooks scheduled fresh meat, vegetables, and fruit for the next day. Medical Platoon wouldn't be treating people in local hamlets and villages; they would be busy treating men's bites, sprains, skin rot, allergies, and infections.

Supplies were plentiful now; 1st Brigade would be arriving in Phuoc Vinh province from Fort Riley in two weeks. Much of their supplies were

VC base camp. A soldier destroys a captured bag of VC rice with straps attached so it could be carried like a backpack.

arriving by convoy and plane at Phuoc Vinh. We experienced a novelty—
a surplus of equipment. A helicopter became available at the CP, kept
on constant standby, allowing for immediate evacuation of sick and
wounded. Major Weeks was in the boonies all the time, but someone
would periodically need it for a direction fix or to evacuate enemy equipment.

I was anxious for troops to return to CP; by then good chow would
be available and water for showers. Battalion discovered 200 tons of enemy
rice, medical supplies, and weapons; there would be many newsworthy stories to write once I heard their experiences.

The greatest find so far was an ammo factory. C Company entered a
complex and found bowls of warm rice and baskets of fresh fish. They had
dumped tools and equipment into water-filled tunnels and trenches running under huts. Spec 4 Mickey Flare and Pfc. Albert Hanson grabbed
steel rods and probed beneath the water, then stripped, dove in, and discovered the sunken items. By late afternoon they had recovered hundreds
of feet of one-inch steel rods, shrapnel for Claymore mines, many explosives, over 20 mines, and 200 hand grenades.

I didn't have a chance to track down my duffel bag and toilet articles;
fortunately I got a toothbrush when I bought my new camera. The humidity and continuous sweating had a steam room effect, thoroughly cleaning
pores, while three or four rain showers each day, streams, and ponds rinsed
the body. We discovered that unclean teeth and an abundance of bugs were
the most critical health challenges. Recently I scorched a leech and was
stung by a scorpion. A few point men had pushed into bee's nests and
stung so seriously they had to be evacuated.

Our current CP was close to the troops, bordered by a rubber plantation on the left and a field the other side. Its elephant grass was three
feet tall with four-foot anthills and scattered trees. Supply had found some
"grease guns," Thompson submachine guns, and a few auto carbines, which
were left at our tent for NCOs or officers who wanted something lighter
to carry than the M-14.

The morning chow was delightful: ham, scrambled eggs, hash browns
with ketchup, toast and butter, and black coffee. Later, the guys at my tent
shared iced Cokes. Civilization returned.

It was obvious to the local VC where we were in their jungle; all they
had to do was follow C ration cans, hacked bushes and vines, and cigarette butts with filters. It appeared the American soldiers were converging
at a river crossing to be loaded into a convoy. A squad of VC tracked each
of the companies. When they merged at the deep, fast-moving river, a
decision had to be made when to attack: before, during, or after the cross-

Father Confroy serving mass in the boonies on three cases of C rations used as an altar.

ing. This depended on what the Americans did for security. If the VC wanted to attack, they realized they had to do so before dark because Americans never convoy at night.

I found my duffel bag and took my first shower, shampoo, and shave in two and a half weeks. Fresh pants, clean boots, ham and eggs, two iced Cokes, and the facilities of a commode. I felt human again.

After lunch Hans and I drove to Brigade CP where we joined the rest of the convoy. Bravo Company arrived at the river and secured it for the rest of Battalion. I couldn't wait to arrive there; Hans was becoming intolerable again.

The convoy arrived at the river at 1400, two miles from our CP. It was at a fast-moving stream 20 yards wide, running parallel to a service road for the neighboring rubber plantation. A rope was strung across the stream, helping the troops cross. This crossing turned out to be longer and more tedious than anticipated because of the depth and the speed of the current. Also many men didn't know how to swim and were terrified. This was ironic since many had been in firefights the past two weeks, yet they were deathly afraid of a stream.

Each carried over 60 pounds of equipment also contributing to their dilemma. Two from Bravo were Hawaiian surfers who volunteered to strip and coax struggling men along.

Captain Richards took charge of this crossing. He was everywhere, from the crossing site, to the convoy trucks where men who had crossed were napping, and to the different OPs along the riverbank and rubber trees.

Heroes come in many sizes, shapes, and forms. A most unpretentious pair were the battalion surgeon, Capt. Poncho Milan, and the chaplain, Father Thomas Confroy. Dr. Milan set an imposing figure at 6'4", 245 pounds with a round, jovial, babyface that never ceased to shine. He had the dubious distinction of being the second heaviest person in our battalion, comprised mostly of men like tall, lanky willows.

Father was a Benedictine monk, owning nothing; even his meager Army pay went to the Order. I had known the chaplain when the Big Red One was in the States and was editor of our weekly battalion newspaper, *Rimrock Register*. The last sermon this mild, gentle man with bifocals gave before we shipped out was about how we would be called upon to do something contrary to God's teaching. We would have to do what our country asked, contrary to a Christian's love for his fellow man. We would be faced with the ultimate reality, the final physical actuality of death. He felt what every priest must know: the feeling of compassion. And he asked God protect to us.

Eighteen hundred hours. Troops of Bravo toiled at the crossing and then stretched out by the edge of the rubber plantation, happy and relaxed. The men had accomplished an outstanding job the past few weeks and were ready for a rest, wash, fresh clothes, hot chow, cold beer, medical patch work, and mail.

Charlie, on the jungle side of the river, drew into a defensive perimeter for the night. A cluster of men appeared at river's edge, preparing to cross.

The rubber plantation lifted from the road adjacent to the river to a ridgeline 200 yards behind. This ridge extended parallel to the road for two miles ending near our Forward CP.

The VC couldn't believe we would convoy at night. They thought we were tricking them into making a move. They moved men forward just in case we made the move.

If troops weren't napping, they were laughing and talking about the operation. Everyone was euphoric; they had found more rice than the other battalions combined, along with a truck loaded with military equipment and supplies, caches of medical inventory, eight base camps, and had zapped or captured 21 VC while not having one man shot. These men were excellent soldiers.

Alpha Company Capt. Allen Armstrong, appeared out of an Army enlistment ad: tall, rugged, and blond, a handsome man, Airborne Ranger qualified who had earned his commission at the demanding Infantry Officers Candidate School at Fort Benning, Georgia. When he spoke, this curly blond officer's voice boomed with authority and confidence. He was popular with his men because he always put them first, thinking and caring for each. They were his men.

The transportation officer, Capt. Bill Million, was responsible for the convoy movement. He noticed troops accumulating by the riverbank at 1800, an hour before dark. Million told Jimmy O'Riley to radio Captain Richards, inquiring about his crossing status.

"My men are across; I think it's Alpha."

Million went to the crossing where he saw Armstrong and questioned him.

"My men never complained. I pushed them hard and they produced. They did an outstanding job. I promised hot chow and cold beer tonight."

Captain Million observed Alpha had not half finished crossing yet. Regardless, Armstrong assured him, they were moving well and he would assist.

Captain Million called Battalion that Alpha was crossing and they could be loaded before dark.

Major Weeks commented with something unprintable about this and reminded him about security.

After Alpha exchanged security duties with Bravo, Captain Armstrong assured Battalion there wasn't any danger.

I was with Jimmy O'Riley at his jeep when Captain Million began this communication. My stomach turned; it appeared impossible Alpha would be crossed and loaded before dark.

Jimmy had some C rations and a mess kit in the jeep. I chopped an onion and included it with two cans of C's and Tabasco sauce in the kit. Jim made a stove out of rocks and cooked this concoction with heat tablets.

Hans came by and wanted some; I refused, telling him to go away and that I would be riding with O'Riley. He wanted to know if we would be leaving soon because it was getting dark.

At dark it became evident to the VC we were still crossing troops.

Their largest weapon was a mortar.

The trees behind the ridge didn't have many branches. A mortar could be lobbed there while rows between rubber trees provided visibility to their target. Rounds could be walked around until they hit their target. VC soldiers waited in place for their signal.

I walked down the row of 21 various types of trucks parked bumper to bumper. American Indian Archie Sharp, the driver of HQ 23, was upset; the troops loading onto his immaculate "deuce and a half" were muddy and wet. He despised anyone getting his spotless truck dirty. The .50-caliber machine gun mounted above his cab became covered by dust kicked up by the troops.

Sharp was upset because his gun wasn't clean now. The infantrymen ribbed him about a truck driver knowing how to fire a big 50.

I sat along the edge of the road, resting my back against a tree while speaking with Jimmy. I could feel the nervous apprehension of his boss, Captain Million, nervously pacing the length of his convoy. The sun had set and Alpha Company hadn't loaded yet.

2100 hours. "Saddle up, move out, hot chow and cold beer waiting a few miles away," bellowed Captain Armstrong.

OPs and LPs were pulled in while the men still joked about the next time they were going to get laid. Some were stealing a smoke in cupped hands, marginally shielding the glow.

I climbed into the jeep with O'Riley and Captain Million, number two in the convoy. My flak vest was on, but I kept it open for ventilation. Captain Million reviewed the route on his map. I mentioned it was fortunate we didn't have a moon that night.

The VC noticed we were ready to move now and moved closer while waiting for their signal.

The lead driver asked Captain Million which way to go.

He directed down the road about two miles on the right.

"Duchess 2, looks like everybody's ready, over."

2130 hours. "This is Duchess 2, crank 'em up."

Both company commanders reported they were ready. Million told the lead jeep to move. I stretched my legs out, relaxing in the back of the jeep with my feet resting on the opposite bench and pistol belt unbuckled, held slackly by the harness resting over my shoulders.

Captain Million radioed Battalion we were moving. I watched the three-quarter-ton behind us follow then spun forward, hearing three gradual shots fired in front and above, one second apart. I hoped it was a misfire until, to be colloquial but descriptive, all hell broke loose. Guns fired at us inside the groves of rubber trees. Their flashes danced about the rubber trees like strings of firecrackers. I swung behind and saw Dante's inferno. Each of the 300 men in the convoy immediately returned the fire as fast as his weapon could. I twisted front again and saw the guy sitting in back of the jeep slump dead.

He was shot and went down. That was it—all the action to this sequence. There is nothing more dramatic than a slump dead. He was sitting up alive one moment, hit, and flopped to the floor dead. Death is swift and effortless in combat.

I turned behind again and saw an extraordinary sight: flashes from our muzzle bursts and tracers resembling a red screen of fire pushed through the trees. I was stunned by this trauma, numbed to the deafening din created by our guns firing simultaneously. I saw demonstrations of firepower during training, but never as dramatic as now. I couldn't see incoming rounds because of the brilliance from our rifle flashes in the black night.

The VC that killed the guy in front must have swung back to us, missed, then continued to spray behind and drilled the driver of that truck when he came into range. He slipped under the dash the moment he was hit; his truck veered off the road, bumped into a tree, and halted the convoy. A second later, the two VC who did the shooting burst out of the jungle and ran toward us on the road. I have no idea why they left their seclusion.

During basic training to qualify to fire with M-14s automatic, we were taught to hold the stock tightly against the shoulder and lean forward because the muzzle wants to climb. Firing a 12-gauge shotgun gives an idea of how an M-14 kicks.

I aimed at one of these VC running 10 feet behind me and fired my M-14 auto, burying a burst of six 7.62-mm NATO rounds into his chest. The first one hit in the center, causing him to lean forward as he fell. It appeared the subsequent five rounds propped him up, preventing his continued fall. Momentum kept him moving ahead while his legs performed by the still-functioning nervous system. My vise grip on the rifle prohibited the barrel from climbing, resulting in the subsequent second to sixth bullets hitting him in what appeared to be the same spot.

He fell when I stopped shooting. I can still visualize almost every detail and see that VC in my sights with each bullet going directly into the same hole. He had shot at me earlier, missed, and then I shot him. If you get someone in your sights and miss, it might be your last mistake. This was the real thing. The black night was illuminated in red from the gunfire of men trying to kill us.

After the initial fusillade, our troops gained the upper hand because of superior firepower. We learned that during an ambush we had to return fire immediately, even though the assailant wasn't in the sights. The rapid response is significant to destroy the enemy's concentration and aim, resulting in missed shots.

The enemy's return fire immediately slackened to sporadic random shots, providing an opportunity for the troops in the stalled convoy to jump off their trucks. Ditches lining both sides of the road offered protection.

I heard a muffled "whoomp-whoomp" explosive sound.

"Mortars! Keep your heads down!"

The warning came too late for a platoon of Alpha; a round exploded in their midst as they were about abandon the truck. Three were killed and the remainder of the 45 wounded.

The troops were firing so indiscriminately they were in danger of running out of ammo. Some of the NCOs and officers began running amongst them, cautioning about this. 1st Lt. Leon Holton lost his life at that time leading his men.

Ron Milan, the former lieutenant of Castro, took charge of the situation. He hustled between the men in his platoon, kept their heads down because of the mortars, cautioned about wasting ammo, pointed targets out, and was shot in the head doing his duty.

C Company remaining the other side of the river couldn't conceive what happened initially, seeing only flashes and tracers. The furious mortar bursts were so bright the men standing and firing from the trucks were illuminated before jumping into ditches, creating an intense drama for the troops watching the show. It was difficult in this madness to refrain from firing, yet necessary to prevent the enemy from knowing your disposition.

Captain Million tried to ascertain the status of the situation, but Captain Armstrong had the battalion frequency tied up, giving instructions to his company on the wrong frequency—battalion instead of company!

Four rounds smashed into the engine of Pfc. Sharp's truck. Steam shot out of the radiator, the manifold roared, the block knocked, and the roar turned in to a whimper—nothing. The Indian was furious—they had destroyed his truck! He stood on the front seat with a foot on the dash for balance, placed the M-14 selector on full, and fired at every muzzle flash he saw. After he had used all five magazines, he dropped the empty rifle to the seat. The hot barrel burned the neck of a man, treated later by a medic and awarded the Purple Heart.

Sharp climbed the body of the truck and began firing his devastating .50-caliber gun until exhausting that ammo also.

Our jeep and the one in front sped out of the ambush along the narrow dirt road, positive there were more ahead. I didn't know the guys in the lead jeep. Half a mile away, the gunfire seemed as loud and close as before. This was a nightmare; you run as hard as you can but remain in one spot without moving.

The jeep in front stopped at an intersection not on the map and the passenger looked back at Captain Million giving a "what do I do now?" signal. I told Jimmy and the driver of the front jeep to get out; they provided security while Million oriented our location on the map. I had Jimmy watch the back where the sky was lit by gunfire and the other driver look to the front while I scanned the sides.

We still couldn't contact Battalion because Captain Armstrong had the frequency tied up, screaming hysterically. Captain Million used the free brigade frequency to report the ambush. Also he told them about an intersection not on the map. They directed us to continue along the road; they would contact Battalion Forward CP to let them know our status and to expect us shortly.

I crawled over to the other jeep and rearranged the body because it had almost bounced out earlier. Now I noticed a sound I hadn't heard before, the muffled "whoomping" sound of incoming mortar rounds exploding on the stalled convoy.

That booming voice of authority and confidence that once belonged to Captain Armstrong, had cracked, then shattered. He extensively occupied the frequency shrieking, "They're here, they're firing, they're shooting at us."

During a break in his transmission, Captain Million immediately transmitted details to Battalion while conveying to the companies the current status. Later he told Battalion that most of the incoming rounds had ceased although the mortar still fired. He directed the companies to restrain their shooting, that they should get back in the trucks, and make sure when they left they did so with all their men and equipment. Also he mentioned this intersection not on their maps. I was amazed how Million kept his wits, never imagining he could be this cool under fire.

Prior to this traumatic experience, he reminded me of the type who would hawk refrigerators at a discount store. I never claimed to be a qualified judge of character.

We roared from the intersection, arriving at the CP in five minutes. It was in a state of alert, prepared for battle; gun positions were placed at strategic locations and a guard station halted us. Men were running different ways, each seemingly knew where he was going and what duty he had. The tension of uncertainty was prevalent. Tragedy was occurring. Was the attack headed this way? What should be done prepping? Would we sit and wait for them to come for us? Were we sufficiently prepared?

Even though we were only two miles from the ambush, we could still hear the sounds of combat almost as audibly as if we were in the middle. That incessant "whoomp whoomp" was more pronounced and noticeable than I expected for an ambush a few miles away. The motor rounds appeared to be following us. "They might be zeroing in on the CP," I tormented myself.

I took my flak vest off and sat on my helmet in a stupor.

Gradually the enemy's shooting at the ambush site became almost negligible; most had been killed or wounded.

The mortar finally stopped firing—they had run out of ammo. The remaining troops loaded the wounded into the trucks. Sharp's disabled truck was four from the end. It was left with the one that received the direct mortar hit. These trucks blocked the road so the remaining two were abandoned.

All the truck engines had been left running during the ambush. When the dead and wounded were loaded, the convoy left with a lurch and troops in the ditches scrambled to keep from being left behind.

Unfortunately, the squad posted as rear LP was abandoned. These six men commented on the sudden silence. They crawled back toward the trucks and realized, to their dismay after passing four abandoned vehicles, they had been left behind. They wisely decided against joining C Company on the opposite side of the river. There was an excellent possibility they would have been shot by the anxious troops, so they formed a perimeter next to a truck and waited for dawn.

There was still shooting when the first group of trucks returned to CP. The nightmarish task began of segregating the wounded soldiers into groups, contingent upon the severity of wounds. Father Confroy helped Dr. Milan and the medics unload and sort. I watched in a trance.

This sparsely populated grove of trees blocked the starlight, creating mysterious, dark images of moving troops. These creatures were arriving by truck, unloading, and helping others. One of shadows helping called to me, "Ray, are you OK?!"

It was Hans. I was surprised. Surprised he cared and surprised he wasn't shot.

I was exhausted from the trauma and tossed my armor vest and helmet into the trench running adjacent to the dirt road, propped my back against a rubber tree, and left the chore of sorting the wounded to the men of Headquarters Company

The medics made the first analysis of the wounded. The most seriously wounded were carried to the medic tent where Father helped Dr. Milan prep them for surgery. He exposed their wounds, cleansed them, and held the only light in the perimeter, a flashlight, for the doctor operating. It was more difficult for the medics outside to make their prognosis and treatments in the dark, doing the basic first echelon work on the simple cases while the more serious were patched and plugged temporarily until Dr. and Father had an opportunity to treat them.

More trucks arrived after the firing and mortars finally stopped.

First Lt. Peter Kovacic had been an advisor with the Vietnamese army for eight months before becoming attached to Battalion. His platoon was already low on ammunition before the ambush and completely out by the time they arrived at the CP. He found Headquarters Company's ammo cache and began to distribute it to his platoon. Staff Sergeant Stand declared it belonged to Headquarters Company and couldn't be used by anyone else.

"Sergeant, my men have just been in an ambush and fired all their ammo. If the VC attacks here, all this ammo is not going to do anybody any good if we can't use it."

Headquarters' ammo became theirs.

The aviation section at Brigade Forward CP was alerted, scrambling one chopper. The firing was initially intense with the sky lit, enabling the chopper crew to see the ambush next to the river without navigational aids.

I heard the telltale sound of the UH-IB chopper disturbing the now deathly silent night air, cursing the heck of a time for him to come. The shooting was over and here comes our cavalry.

The Huey has M-60 machine guns on each side capable of firing 500 7.62-mm NATO rounds per minute with every sixth round a tracer, allowing its trajectory to be visible as a red streak in the night.

Two medics opened the flap on the med tent to bring in another soldier. Father told them he had just finished with someone who they could move out. More plasma was needed; a medic brought some in.

A strong breeze caught the flap, making it flutter, emitting muzzle like flashes of light.

One of the door gunners saw flashes ahead.

They swung around for a look and thought they saw more.

Reality aggressively returned when I recognized the "chauka-chauka" sound of a helicopter overhead and indisputable "crack-crack-crack" of M-60 machine guns firing directly at me above. My intuition told me earlier I should not take my gear off. I should have paid more attention because I needed my flak vest and helmet now. I frantically crawled about groping in the dark, attempting to locate my equipment. I felt the helmet, flopped it on backward, while continuing to search for the vest. Tracers skipped through the trees while invisible, seemingly innocuous, five bullets flew between them. The rest of the men hugged the tree trunks, crawled under vehicles, or dove into trenches.

Dr. and Father stood their ground in the med tent. They did not flinch or shut off the flashlight, continuing work on men while bullets indiscriminately pierced their tent.

I have seen magnificent statements of war in history books—"We have not yet begun to fight"—and heard it in movies—"I love the smell of napalm...." None ever made the impact of Headquarters Capt. Richard Barrell deliberately tramping through the middle of the camp strafed by machine gun fire. "If he makes another pass," he growled, "BRING HIM DOWN!"

This was a gripping statement to me; we would shoot at and try to kill fellow Americans. By shooting them down, we would prevent further deaths of our men.

Operations contacted Brigade when the chopper fired, managing to halt it before the next pass. Everybody waited with safeties off and definitely would have shot him out of the sky. I finally had my vest and helmet on, ready for the pass, and prepared to shoot him down.

Officers met in the Personnel tent preparing for defense of the CP, while discussing an imminent attack; the enemy appeared to hold the advantage.

Sergeant Stand approached me. "Pezzoli, we need security out there." Meaning in the field, outside of the CP.

"Grab two people from Commo and set up an LP 400 meters, alert us of an attack."

The squad left at the ambush site heard the sound of the chopper firing in the distance, thinking it an army of VC attacking the CP. They couldn't imagine any left alive after noticing them carrying and dragging their comrades out of the plantation. The trucks recovered some in front of them.

It was obvious the men posted along the perimeter were jumpy as I passed through. We walked to each, introduced ourselves, made sure they had the right password, and told them if we saw VC we would kill as many as possible before running back to the perimeter yelling the password all the way.

"No sweat," they assured us. Their nonchalance scared me.

We left our lines to go "out there," certain we would never live to see tomorrow. Three hundred yards in the depths of this opaque field, I stumbled across a creek a yard wide, one foot shallow, with elephant grass lying across the top like a carpet.

We established our LP at 2100; the men were tired and had me take first watch.

I could hardly keep my eyes open and tried to keep awake by frightening myself, remembering what I had been through earlier.

I managed to stay awake for an hour, then noticed what the stranded squad had been watching: forms of the enemy on the other side of our meadow dragging away their dead and wounded. Unreal! I awoke the other two. We became as giddy as high school boys looking down a girl's bathing suit, watching the enemy completely oblivious of our presence devote the remainder of the night to dragging away casualties.

There was no longer a danger of attack.

I had the last watch at 0500 and saw the sky brighten: time for my first cigarette. We headed back to our lines commenting on the perspective of the field in the light and how lucky we were to return alive. A gun position called us over—the mess hall was serving hot chow.

I was surprised to see Fr. Confroy still up, vigorously walking among the wounded offering words of encouragement and comfort. He had been up the entire night involved with the ordeal of working with the injured. Regardless of his exhaustion, he appeared smart and alert. Father was a pillar of strength.

The action from the ambush was over. The wounded and dead were loaded into trucks and choppers for evacuation. Six men killed and 40 wounded was the score for our side of the card; we didn't know about the VC. The only indication we had about their status was many were firing initially from treetops, behind trees, and along the edge of the road the entire length of our 21-vehicle convoy. Gradually their firing slowed and eventually stopped.

We also saw what the squad left behind had seen. Also, the enemy's slaughter was validated by three of the four trucks left behind with .50-caliber machine guns and ammo untouched.

All 40 of the wounded during that ambush fully recovered at medical centers in the States. God was by their side that night in the crude aid station at the Forward CP because two of His angels were by their side.

We were punched in the nose by the VC and learned a lesson passed on to other troops in Vietnam: the VC watches you all the time. If you are stupid enough to let your guard down, you're going to be punched in the nose. We also learned big .50s were not needed to fight a guerrilla war. If one of these weapons was captured, it could bring down planes and choppers. All were immediately removed from the trucks in Vietnam. A convoy at night meant a court-martial, and Armstrong lost his command in the morning.

We had the unique distinction, claimed by several military papers, of being involved in the largest ambush of American troops to date. This notoriety remained another month until something called the Ia Drang Valley occurred.

The troops spent the next two days washing, soaking, eating, drinking, and mostly sleeping at the CP.

There was a week left to this operation, with a few areas to be searched. Division had daydreams of locating more VC supplies. The stuff we managed to find was of marginal importance, though the absence of the VC was ominous. They had taken a terrible toll in that ambush.

Our entire brigade captured over 500 tons of rice plus supplies of sundry nature.

A new CP was set up again in the town of Phuoc Vinh by the city square. I didn't want to write anything about the ambush out of respect for the deceased guys. If a friend gets a bloody nose because he was stupid, you don't broadcast it, while their souls can be found in the Wall.

I looked for something positive to write about or photograph. Sergeant Grassburg suggested accompanying the Medical Platoon still treating the local people. Spec 5 Jerry Peters said he'd enjoy having me accompany him.

I took a few photos, made some notes, nothing much.

A father came by with his baby, who had a fever. The infant became nervous when Peters examined him and began to cry. Peters had the father pull the baby's pants down while preparing a syringe of penicillin; I could see a good photo opportunity. So did Pfc. James Smith, the driver, who maneuvered himself into position between Peters and the father for the photo. The baby cried louder when Peters inserted the needle. The father smiled and Smithy stood between them knowledgeably looking down with his hands on his hips. This picture made many major U.S. papers.

I was finally able to compose at least one Great War Photo.

The operation was winding down; the VC faded away and no more supplies were found. October 24, the CP moved for the last time before returning to base camp at Ho Nai. The troops were scheduled to go on a day pass to Saigon.

I helped Staff break camp for the last time. Spirits were high; everybody was joking, talking, and singing. Hans picked up the mail delivery at the airport accompanied by some major newspapers. Splashed across the front page were stories and photos of the October 1965 war protest. Everybody stopped what they were doing and looked in disbelief at what they read. One of the guys pleaded, "What's wrong with them? Don't they know what we've been doing here?"

Not really. The media had never been interested in humanitarian efforts like ours with the villagers. Many people did see my baby photo because it showed something, but certainly wasn't as sensational as the media would have liked. It would have distributed more if it were an article or photo of violence.

I hopped a chopper ride to Bien Hoa and stumbled into the photo lab. Thanks to the guidance of the Air Force, I didn't blow the development of my film.

The photo lab asked if I was near that Big Red One ambush. I told them a little about it. The whole routine of those of us living in the boonies

A medic gives an infant a shot while his driver supervises.

was unimaginable to these guys who lived in air-conditioned quarters, had Vietnamese maids and servants, worked in clean, dry clothes, and drank fresh, cool water out of a glass.

The Vietnamese that worked with them were the more fortunate of their people. They had good-paying jobs and clean work while living under the protection of American soldiers.

I hitched a ride to my base camp after finishing the photos. The base camp desk personnel wanted to know more about the ambush. I showed them my photos and wrote about the medics, all the VC rice and equipment we captured, and the people in the villages. The troops were to return home in two days.

Lt. Angle, my boss in 2nd Brigade PIO, called me the next day. Brass thought the picture of the baby getting the shot was fantastic, especially in light of our recent ambush, and wanted a dozen more copies ASAP. I hitched to Bien Hoa to print them. These professional photographers had mixed emotions about the shot, a "ho-hum."

Freddie Jones greeted me enthusiastically at Brigade Information Office, Lt. Angle's mistaken interpretation of an infantry NCO. He said MAC-V Information Office in Saigon wanted that photo now and he was going to take me. I was excited because this would be my first opportunity for free time in the city.

We delivered the pictures to Haas Faas and Peter Arnett. These mouthpieces of American news, conduits through AP and UPI, normally sat through military briefings in the morning, spun their twist, and submitted stories by noon that were gobbled up. After that they dined at exclusive restaurants about Tu Do Street on substantial expense accounts. I was surprised they cared for copies of my sensitive photo.

After we left, this bumbling, buffoonish NCO told me he had to pick something up at the major PX there. That "something" happened to be its largest portable stereo tape recorder, delivered to "Someone in Cholon who had been helping his department." That someone happened to be a very sexy Fu who, he claimed, was his girlfriend. These women would tell a person like him, who was desperate and in most cases married and unattractive, that she was his girlfriend.

"Oh, sweetie, this is nice but it's too small for our apartment."

"Our apartment" was probably cofinanced by several other guys.

The Bumbler's friend said she was busy with work all the time, consequently he was supposed to call her before he could visit his apartment "to make sure she was there."

Fu wanted me to meet another friend, Lin, who was sick in the next room. She had a fever now, would be looking for a "boyfriend" when she got better, and was anxious to meet me.

Lin was lying on a mat in a cubbyhole next door. I squatted by her but couldn't communicate because she didn't know English. She had a round face and a little heavier then most. Her forehead was warm and complexion pale; probably had some type of flu. I elected not to pursue our association much further because I wasn't sure what she might have been sick from.

Sarge returned with a stereo console he exchanged the portable for.

"These Oriental women," he lamented during the ride back to camp, "are really temperamental. Are you going to see Lin anymore?"

We had passes to Saigon the next several days. I said I would see her if she felt any better then.

"She wants you for a boyfriend."

"Sure thing."

The troops returned to base camp, spruced up themselves and their equipment, and convoyed to Saigon for booze, broads, and bravado. The passes had to be completed in three days; that was when "Operation Copperhead" began. I maintained my equipment and acquired a more practical tool for my trade, a semi/fully automatic carbine. Other troops secured excess World War II grease guns and Thompson submachine guns lying about Supply. These weapons and their ammo, .45 caliber, were lighter than the M-14, but unfortunately not as accurate and deadly. We didn't need accuracy in close combat as much as the convenience of a small, light weapon capable of automatic fire.

I took my camera with the last group on pass, wearing shorts and a T-shirt: a trip to the beach in Cape Cod.

Everybody knew I was their reporter. I asked for photos and they perked up like roosters because they were proud of themselves. With their combat gear on, they looked like something out of a recruiting poster. They were all one, all equal, part of the same team. Now their civilian clothes revealed their social backgrounds.

One guy had a black polo shirt with a Coors Beer emblem on the chest. He sat erect with his shoulders back, chest out, stomach in, and a stern look on his face.

Posed next to him was a plain Okie: nondescript face, tan pants, open collar shirt, all most likely PX purchased, and hair held back by something sticky.

On the other side sat a black guy looking like he just arrived from Africa, not purified by Hollywood with Caucasian features. His intense stare amplified the features of his proud race.

The rest of the guys were characterless.

We were released near the government palace in downtown Saigon. I clicked several pictures then headed to Lin's house. She was expecting me because "Bumbler" had been there with Fu the day before and mentioned I might come. She looked a lot better then; she might have been run down before and needed rest. A lot of people in Vietnam did not receive proper nutrition.

I didn't know what to do with her on our "date." I could have taken her on a bus into the country for the day. That would have been stupid because I didn't have a gun and could have been shot at by the bad guys. She knew of a small place where we could have lunch.

I couldn't understand the menu and didn't have the slightest idea what the dishes consisted of, so I gestured I wanted beef with vegetables, rice, and sake. My lunch looked like a typical Oriental meal.

She asked if I wanted her to be my girlfriend. She could live in Bien Hoa, only 20 minutes from my base camp. I think she was sincere, liked me, and wanted to see more of me. She and her friends had a hard time pronouncing my name, Ray, so they called me "Bien Hoa." I could put her up if I didn't spend most of my time in the boonies. There was the danger if I saw too much of her, I would, in all probability, end up having a kid I didn't want.

I said good-bye to her later at the convoy pick-up point; this was the last time I would see Lin. I made a few trips into the city later; free time was a luxury not allowing sufficient time to meet her again. Later I heard she had her own apartment; she must have found a guy.

Most of the troops were drunk when they loaded the convoy—par for the course for everyone. What started out as a group of clean-scrubbed neatly attired young men at reveille turned into a drunken, noisy mob with snakes, parrots, a monkey, and two bar maidens attempting to be smuggled back to camp.

I noticed a heartwarming sight on our return: many Vietnamese families parked along superhighway #1 from Saigon to Bien Hoa participating in the final stages of packing up picnics. A picnic in the country was not common for the Vietnamese, or had the same significance to them as it does for us. It meant that if you went too far past the influence of the government, some hood might rob and kill you, saying it was on behalf of the Party. This danger lessened after we began exerting our presence.

By the time we reached base, most of the drunken rabble was asleep. We played, had fun, were little boys again; but we had our job to do, leaving for work at sunrise.

This time we would keep our guard up, stay on our toes, be constantly alert, remember our previous mistakes, and not let a sucker punch in the nose depress us. Our noses had been only bloodied while the enemy had been killed!

Chapter 8

Our Work Is Cut Out for Us

"Operation Copperhead" was an appropriate name for the action we unexpectedly found. Battalion would be leaving by helicopters November 5 for a week of search and destroy in a fan-shaped jungle 35 miles from Saigon toward Cambodia between Di-An and Phu Loi. The size of this area wasn't as impressive as the enemy activity encountered. The North Vietnamese were infiltrating along the newly constructed Ho Chi Minh Trail and building a holding area within striking distance of Saigon, the capital. The media called this the "Iron Triangle"; it sounded catchy.

I was in Vietnam during the period of the North Vietnamese buildup. Consequently, and thankfully, we didn't meet any large units, only mostly minute infiltrating groups.

Each of our companies was assigned a Vietnamese dog handler whose help was marginal. We were stalking the world's smartest prey, the human being. He could think; animals only act on instinct. In the same respect, we, the stalkers, were professional hunters that could think also and out-wit the prey. At times our contact with the VC was precisely where they expected us to be, providing them an opportunity to ambush us. Each time we made contact with a base camp they fired first, hearing a twig snap or a limb swish as we crept forward during our search.

Many times the Viet Cong hid underground in tunnels or in trenches that surrounded their base camp where the dog couldn't get the scent. In many cases we detected the VC before the dog did because we knew the foul smell emanating from camps was definitely human, which the dog did not know. We didn't realize it initially, but the VC could tell we were around because we emanated a particular smell also. Captured VC said they laughed about Americans saying we smelled sweet. Their cadre said we were soft and needed perfume to tolerate the jungle.

The media found a topic which always was a guaranteed copy: the enemy body count and friendly WIA and KIA (wounded and killed in action). Important accomplishments like halting enemy infiltration and terror, securing land under government control, civic action programs, and stimulating the economy were secondary. The objective of the mission for the media became "how high the body count." This is absolutely ridiculous: imagine the 101st Airborne at Bastogne running from their perimeter and counting the bodies of Germans they had just repelled.

This operation would be in an area cleared for the newly arrived remainder of the Big Red One. Major Weeks suggested I go with Charlie Company; they would most likely make contact. The other two companies would be reserve, searching a neighboring area.

We were entering a new phase of the war with transportation to the operations by helicopters. Truck convoys became outmoded and impractical while choppers were small and fast, difficult to hit. Each was nimble getting in and out of difficult terrain yet proficient in laying down a devastating base of firepower.

Our 20-minute flight was the last opportunity to nap for the next four days. Many stretched their feet forward, pushed their helmets over their eyes, and dozed while being buffeted by air currents.

The jungle always looked innocuous from the air, lush, green, and pure, making it impossible to visualize what lay in store below.

I noticed a dot in the jungle a mile ahead, the clearing for our landing in the enemy's back yard.

Each LZ is a potential ambush site where you are most defenseless. Skimming over the treetops at 85 mph then dropping into a gap in the trees with hostile eyes watching was slithering into a black void with unknown destruction waiting below. Yet, if the enemy did fire during landing, a withering response from six infantrymen's weapons and two machine-gunners in each chopper would slap him hard.

The men in Charlie Company wanted to know why I was there.

"You guys are the ones that are going to find VC; Bravo and Alpha are reserve."

Second Platoon was point for the day; I took my usual place near the front. I wanted to be close enough to film the firefight, but careful not to interfere with the maneuvering and integrity of the squad under fire.

Patrolling the jungle was not a walk in the park. It was creeping bent over with 85 pounds of equipment snared by vines and branches. The jungle was so thick at times a person couldn't see the men three feet in front of and behind him. The temperature and humidity were intolerable. The point man was responsible for the land navigation, using a compass to maintain the heading and a machete to chop a path maintaining the course. He had to be aware of telltale VC signs in the jungle: smell, booby traps, mines, punji traps, trip wires, and voices, to mention a few.

The company established a defensive perimeter an hour before sunset with three men to a position, each taking turns at watch. I spent the night with the company commander's staff of RTO and medic, making a nest inside some bushes and vines.

My clothes normally dried by sunset. I put dry socks on and wrapped my poncho around me like a mummy to keep warm. This cocoon also offered limited protection against mosquitoes and flies.

I became a welcome addition the company staffs, assisting each with the night workload of monitoring the radio.

Each report received at CP was a barely audible whisper from the men on the fringe of the perimeter. Each call to CP was reassurance, contact with the outside world from the world of night.

Many North Vietnamese assembled there. This was convenient because they had the protection of the Cambodian border to store supplies; Americans and South Vietnamese were prohibited from entering. Cambodia, at this location, was less than 50 miles from Saigon, the country's business and cultural hub. Prior to infiltrating the South, the North Vietnamese had guerrilla warfare training in their jungles, using base camp tunnel complexes like those of the Viet Cong in the South. When it became evident America was entering the war, the Communists studied U.S. combat tactics. A practical method was watching readily available Hollywood war movies.

Reports they received the first week in November indicated Americans were in their jungles. Helicopters were seen and their LZs had evidence of groups of men moving in a particular direction: grass and bushes trodden over, bushes hacked, human feces and toilet paper, and empty C ration cans. Also found were cigarettes and military matchbooks.

There were no base camps large enough to shelter a significant North Vietnamese unit, so their troops were broken down into groups no larger than 20. It was better for them, they deduced, to lose 20 men than have 100 surrounded in the jungle with helicopters, bombers, and artillery raining havoc. Scouts were deployed to find and track Americans. If their destination was determined and if it was feasible, an ambush would be sprung along the route. Yet if Communist troops were at a base camp, they would try to hold off and fight the Americans.

The North Vietnamese thought they held the advantage with their camouflaged camps: surrounding trenches and tunnels extending beyond with hidden trap doors to pop out of. An infantryman could be heard and seen from inside the perimeter well before he was close enough to see it. By the time he got that close, he would be dead—they thought.

It was easy that day to follow a group of Americans in the jungle. They had an armored personnel carrier (APC) following parallel along a narrow oxcart road.

This province had been a prolific producer of rice with service roads framing the rice farms along the tree lines. Viet Cong terror had forced these farmers to leave for populated areas where the government offered protection.

The North Vietnamese platoon following C Company was new in the South; they had an opportunity for their first big victory.

The VC decided, from the Americans' direction, on a projected course after a river-crossing site. Their camp would be directly in the G.I.s' route. It would be easier to fight them there than at the river crossing where they would have to contend with the APC.

I was third from the point man and heard a rapid series of shots fired my direction from a high-powered rifle I hadn't heard fired before. Previously most of their weapons were carbines captured from Vietnamese troops. Their slides made the identifiable metal, clacking sound when fired.

I dove on the ground, melting into the contour of the earth. My carbine was on auto, safety off, and pointed in the direction of the firing. My chin was flush with the stock while my eyes searched left and right for any movement or flashes. The man in front dove to the right. I couldn't see more than a few feet in the vegetation and immediately lost him. I heard him fire a few bursts at someone, feeling reassured he was still next to me. I was afraid the Reds were going to shoot at him, miss, and hit me. Fortunately, no one fired back; he must have killed the man.

Somebody else shot in my direction, this time from the left front.

I wasn't sure where the guy behind me was because I had lost sight of him also.

I jumped when a whisper behind me asked, "What's going on here?"

The platoon leader had crawled up to me.

It sounded like a base camp with troops in the trenches.

He whispered for some men to come forward, then crawled back to reposition them.

The leader of the point squad, Sgt. Bobby Tall, was a lanky career man from rural southern Illinois. He consolidated the point so everybody was within whispering and visual distance and adjusted them on line facing the camp. The second enemy rifle was still firing on my left; I visualized the shape of this perimeter by the sound of the shots at me. It appeared to be circled by trenches with men firing; I heard their shots but couldn't see any movement or flashes.

Several North Vietnamese were secluded inside a pit in front of the camp, their design of an early warning system.

The training these soldiers received in the North never explained that when an American is shot at he immediately dives on the ground. When he is shot at from a trench, he stands no longer but is on the ground and bullets fired are projected above him.

Another fact they were never aware of was that most Americans have been exposed to guns since they were old enough to walk. One of the first things a father buys his son after his first steps is a cap gun, holster, and pistol belt. As soon as they are old enough to comprehend, American kids are watching cop shows, cowboys, and war flicks either in the movies or on TV. An American kid digests the fun, innocence, and glory of killing at an early age. Shooting people is normal—second nature.

Some of the VC crawled through tunnels in front to trap doors they supposed would open in the midst of G.I.s.

One of them opened the outside tunnel flap, which had been camouflaged with small branches, leaves, and grass. His heart was thumping from the firing, the long frantic crawl, and the dead, stifling tunnel air.

He waited by the shallow end of the tunnel near its exit to catch his breath and listen for sounds of G.I.s before breaking out.

Sgt. Tall heard someone yelling something in Vietnamese from the base camp and fired a burst at the sound. Immediately after, he felt like he had been hit in the head with a sledgehammer.

The North Vietnamese had heard Tall's shots, burst out of the tunnel, and saw his camouflaged helmet in front of him. He had forgotten to release the safety on his weapon after crawling through the tunnel. Hastily releasing the safety destroyed his aim and concentration, sending only one of his three bullet bursts into the top of Tall's helmet.

Sgt. Tall didn't comprehend what happened, but instinctively spun on his stomach, spotting the person that just shot at him. He squeezed off a round that hit his assailant in the face, immediately killing him. The bullet had slightly grazed Sarge's head, ruined his helmet, and caused a ringing in his ears that made hearing difficult for an hour.

"Be aware of the tunnel entrances," he cautioned his squad, "covered with twigs and leaves."

One of his men noticed the ground was spongy under his hand and pulled back the leaves, exposing another tunnel. He ripped the twigs, moss, and leaves off. A North Vietnamese standing directly below the cover jumped to the side as the grenade floated in.

He grabbed and tossed it back.

Fortunately for the G.I., he remembered what he had been taught during grenade training: "Watch them till they land, then cover." He eyed the tunnel, saw the grenade fly out, caught it, and threw it back. There was an immediate explosion sending a piece of fabric and flesh outside.

After this incident, troops made sure grenades were "cooked-off" before thrown in VC camps. The pin was pulled, lever released, and two seconds counted before thrown, leaving only two seconds to explode, allowing the enemy insufficient time to react, pick it up, and toss it back.

I wasn't aware of what happened to Sgt. Tall and his squad. All I heard were shots and an explosion from their direction.

"Look out!" a person in front of me called a fraction of a second before bursting through the shrubbery. I had quick decisions to make. I knew there were men near the left flank and nobody in front—had to be the enemy! If I shot at him and missed, I might hit an American on my left. Yet, I couldn't let him get away, so I tackled him.

College football taught me a proper tackle; I made, perhaps, the best in my life. I sprang to the left, catching him with my head on the left of his waist and my right shoulder in his crotch. Knees locked, his momentum carried him forward. I pulled his legs back with my arms and twisted 180 degrees; lifting him in the air, then fell on top of him.

During jungle training in Florida, we completed a week of Ranger Jungle Training, learning how to kill a person with our bare hands. If you place your hands around the throat and apply even pressure with the thumbs on the air tubes, you can kill the person in five seconds. I hadn't reached the point yet where I enjoyed killing people so I tried to kill him in a sanitary way by choking him.

After squeezing a few seconds, he began to look pale, his eyes rolling back. "He's about to die!" I thought. In a flash, his hand punched forward, my right arm partially blocking his thrust. I felt a sharp pain in my side as his knife entered a half-inch, a jolt of electricity. I thought I was killing him but he almost killed me because I took too much time. You can't be nice to a person you're killing! Just kill him the fastest, most efficient way possible.

That's exactly what I did and should have done earlier, the much more dramatic Ranger method:

I opened my hands and clapped both ears simultaneously, exploding his eardrums while destroying the inner ear. Next I carefully placed my thumbs on the outside of each eye and pushed in, plucking them into my hand without leaving much mess.

Now that my enemy was neutralized, I took his knife, which had dropped on the ground next to me, drew it across his throat one way, then back the other. He gurgled a little before he stopped breathing, showing no great dramatics in death. I was surprised how clean his body was, thinking he would have been dirty and smelly like others we found. He was freshly shaven with clean hair and nails. The clothes looked new, like he was recently outfitted; his tan shirt, pants, and floppy bush hat were relatively sweat free.

Killing him was an elation and rush unlike anything I had ever experienced. It was like hitting a grand slam, shooting the game-winning basket, or a hole in one. This was a sensation I would be experiencing more, liking, and looking forward to.

I didn't know if he was the one who shot at me earlier, but decided to continue hugging the ground before I became a statistic also.

Before I flattened, I gave my victim a quick once over to ensure he actually died.

The firing stopped and the CO had the men pull back to regroup before dark. The medic looked at the slit on my side, put something into it and over it, and gave me a shot preventing infection. This was only a puncture; I didn't want it reported.

Only one of the troops was shot in this engagement, wounded in the side and not serious. He was going to be evacuated by the APC but it became hung up on a soft shoulder. They were trying to get closer to us during the engagement; instead, the vehicle became stalled and impotent. A helicopter was dispatched to take him to Brigade's hospital. The troops convoyed home in two days. I took the chopper also to develop photos, write stories, and get laid.

The box score for that camp was three confirmed VC bodies, the good guys zero.

"Click," the combat switch just turned off.

Chapter 9

The Light at the End of the Tunnel Grows Dark

"Operation Cold Duck," November 5–9, that's all the time it took. It seemed more like a lifetime because of everything that happened. Reflecting on it, I realize this was the transition from killing out of fear to killing for pleasure. If a group we weren't with made contact everyone was envious, wishing to be there. They received a rush whenever a VC was zapped.

From then on, I wanted to be with the troops whenever they were in the jungle, which was most of the time. The elements were brutal on our equipment, requiring extensive maintenance.

A homemade 36-round carbine magazine, made by and recovered from the VC, was lying on a crate in Headquarters tent. Most here carried M-14s and didn't need it; I claimed it for my carbine. The contraption looked in fair condition, which was surprising considering it was homemade and not maintained properly. I soaked it in oil, cleaned it thoroughly, and worked 36 rounds through the chamber.

The golden rule of rifle ownership proclaims test-firing a new weapon before using it. There was a gully to the right of camp where weapons were periodically tested. Naturally, before this occurs, the entire camp is notified so the shooting is not mistaken as hostile. I didn't consider alerting the camp to fire my weapon and test the magazine; it appeared to be functioning satisfactorily. Each time I pulled the slide back, a bullet ejected sharply while the next slid into the chamber smoothly.

The new operation would be in that same area as our last, at Di-An-Phu Loi. Sensing devices deposited in jungles indicated human movement. The Big Red One Headquarters would be established nearby; the Brass wanted to rest peaceably so another sweep was requested.

Operations said Bravo would make contact. This was supposed to be a filler operation to keep the troops busy until the next multibattalion operation was coordinated. We would have preferred for that week off to sleep, eat, and screw.

I showered at 0330, had chow, strapped on equipment, and joined my old company at the camp LZ. My platoon had some new members; I didn't know if they were replacements for people who were shot, discharged, or cracked up. Harry, my old pal from the dunes of Cam Ranh, had made corporal.

"Hey, Ray," he asked, "are we the ones that are going to find them this time?"

I told him I recommended Bravo so the guys could make rank. Everyone assured me all they wanted was a discharge.

The sky lightened at 0530. At 0540 I lit my first cigarette. The sun appeared at 0550, I began to sweat at 0551, and the choppers arrived at 0600 swirling clouds of dust. The combat cycle of Vietnam began again.

When the helicopters arrived, they hovered two feet in ground effect. The LZ at the base camp was packed, orange clay blown into a dust cloud by chopper prop blast, coating the weapons with a fine film of orange dust. Fortunately the LZ in most of the jungle clearings was grass, making it unnecessary to clean the weapons after landing. This was only a small price to pay for the practicality of convoying by chopper.

The support elements needed to convoy to establish the Forward CP. After it was established, helicopters took C rations, water, ammo, and personnel to troops in neighboring jungles. Deliveries were normally accomplished an hour before sunset into many tiny clearings. Frequently the clearings were so tight that chopper's blades clipped leaves from the surrounding vegetation.

Resupply was normally every three days. On the following morning, the chopper returned to get unused supplies. There was a mad dash loading red duffel bags with collapsed plastic water tubs, letters to be mailed, and leftover boxes of C rations. Pilots were always apprehensive during this minute on the ground; they were an easy target for snipers in treetops. Fortunately, we never lost a chopper.

Support personnel never wanted to spend time in the intimidating jungles. In contrast, the infantrymen felt more at home in the jungle than in the sky, on roads, in their base camp, or in the cities. Some of my closest calls were outside jungles.

I had switched to Alpha in the late afternoon of the fourth day and was four behind the point man as several bursts of automatic fire scattered from the dense jungle growth, missing him. Many of us, including myself, owe our lives to the poor training and marksmanship of these creeps.

The squad crawled on line with the point man and returned fire. I found a two-foot anthill and ducked behind it, removing myself from their integrity. The squad sergeant coordinated the shooting from his men so they wouldn't deplete their ammo while revealing their location. I didn't shoot because I couldn't see a target. Also, I didn't want the VC to know I was hiding there. While the platoon was being reshuffled behind me, I was completely unaware of their status. Minutes later I saw several troops behind and others to the left.

The squad sergeant thought he might be able to make it into the VC trenches if he slid to the right flank, then forward and, hopefully, over the trench if he made the right guess. He crouched and ran three feet until a vine firmly snared his canteen. The fraction of a second he hesitated to untangle it cost him his life, shot in the back the moment he spun to untangle it. The two men with him saw gun flashes in the opaque jungle leaves and laid down a heavy base of fire. The firing from the front ceased.

They called back for a medic to retrieve the sergeant. Two more automatic weapons began firing my way again as the medic ran up from the rear. He hesitated next to me for directions. I warned they were probably firing at him, that he should stay low, and that wounded man was on the right flank 15 yards away. He plunged through snaring vines and springy brush, into the intense gunfire. I expected him to become another casualty and was delighted when he returned moments later, escorting the wounded man. This man appeared heavy for an infantryman; I surmised he was a recent arrival.

I heard a crashing sound to my right. The medic was running next to the wounded man loping over vines and branches. He stumbled on a root and fell on his face. I yelled to the troops behind to stop shooting in our direction. The medic and I struggled to get him to his feet, but he had lost his strength.

"Grab his arms," I directed to the medic. "We'll carry him."

The VC were the only ones firing now; the medic and I could finally hear each other talk. We put our arms around the man and strained to haul him to the trail behind, collapsing when we reached it. Doc and I stretched him out on the trail to carry him.

He took his pistol belt off before running, facilitating his movement; unfortunately the poncho was left behind with it.

I took mine, spread it on the ground, and rolled him inside, fashioning a makeshift stretcher. Two soldiers on the trail grabbed the other corners and helped carry him to a clearing for Medevac. He was dead by the time we labored there five minutes later.

The VC were still entrenched by sunset; Alpha's Company, Captain Barrell, had the troops withdraw to form a perimeter in the clearing. His staff established their CP in a clump of bushes near the center of the clearing. I scratched a nest next to them while the troops coordinated defenses.

The medic was here with the body also. The CO didn't call in a chopper for him because it was too late; the sergeant's corpse could be evacuated in the morning by Supply.

I was still shaking at dusk, not realizing it was from the continuous showers. Normally they stopped at 1700, giving the clothes several hours to dry before the balmy night.

At 1915 the sky, normally brilliantly lit by stars, was completely blotted out by rain clouds. The CO made adjustments with the RTO while the medic and I planned the night's radio watch. We slid the body out of my poncho and stretched it prone next to me in a stately manner, head forward and fingers clasped across the chest.

I chose the second watch to allow a nap of badly needed sleep. I folded over the sides of my poncho and slid inside, not realizing how cold it was until I tried to sleep. The normally refreshing rain turned cold with sunset, flooding me in the poncho. Normally, body heat captured by the poncho dried damp clothes. However, the temperature was to cold to prevent drying tonight.

A foul aroma permeated my little domicile. I thought it came from the body next to me and quizzically inhaled it to identify the source. It didn't have the stench and I assumed it was because the night was cold and wet, prohibiting decomposition.

The frigid and sopping night was the first time in Vietnam there were no flies and mosquitoes, the only positive thing about that night.

I began to shake, sometimes very violently, experiencing another Vietnam first—completely exhausted and unable to sleep.

I glanced at the body of the buddy next to me. He was serene: the face steel gray with drops of rain scattered on it, his eyes closed, while his face appeared relaxed as though asleep. The soldier was at peace, a corpse to be placed in a body bag and flown to Saigon the next day. One of our men was going home. The only place I would see his name was etched in granite at the Wall in 2002. The media never considered him newsworthy.

This was a guy that got zapped. Most of the men in my unit in 1965 were in their early 20s, older than the teenagers drafted later. We knew fellow soldiers by name but didn't make friends; if somebody got it, what a shame. The safekeeping of our lives was more important than remorse over someone's death; soldiers didn't want sorrow over a death to numb their combat senses and tried to keep combat impersonal. Words such as "dead, shot, and killed," were never used in context with G.I.s.

"Gosh, I envy you," I thought. "It's all over now. I'd like to join you wherever you are, but be able to return tomorrow." Earlier he was alive, warm, breathing, walking, with memories, a family, and aspirations; now he was just a body.

The cold and damp penetrated my bones.

I thought I could warm up by withdrawing my head inside and sealing both ends to capture my body heat. This couldn't work because my body didn't emit heat. The frigid night air chilled the body-warmed water was sloshing inside.

I realized it was compulsory to sleep; still, violent shaking kept me awake. I tried to use mind over matter and think myself to sleep, but the stench inside was too nauseous.

I hadn't realized the G.I. bled to death inside my poncho. We carried him to the clearing where he died in the poncho and let the body lie until we pulled it out later. We hadn't noticed the man's blood filling the poncho. When I wrapped it around me, I was unaware I would become saturated with most of a soldier's blood.

I was afraid I would die of hypothermia. My only solace was that everybody experienced the same trauma in this inclement weather. Fortunately for them, they didn't have to tolerate the reek.

Pfc. Bobby Day, the RTO, finished the radio work with Captain Barrell by 2100 hours and I resumed radio watch. I heard most of their conversations with Brigade and Division while trying to sleep. We were scheduled for removal the next day, whenever choppers became available. The CO and RTO never showed indications they were cold. Bobby said he was so tired he couldn't keep his eyes open. This seemed odd because I was wide awake from violent shaking.

I sat up and began monitoring the radio, feeling warmer now than when I was lying down, probably because of exerted energy. My frantic trembling finally stopped yet I was still cold and wet. I hoped to become bored with radio watch like normal, relaxing enough to sleep.

That guy's blood had apparently mixed with the rain and saturated my clothes and hair. I put my helmet on to keep my head warm and dry when I emerged from the poncho. The odor was prominent outside also. This whole episode was a traumatic experience. I couldn't think rationally enough to realize this stink emanated from inside my poncho and on my person. The body next to me didn't smell because it had been consecrated pure by the rain.

Normal body temperature is 98.6; my body didn't feel that warm but it must have been warm enough to start cooking the blood inside my poncho, causing it to spoil and turn repulsive.

I recognized Crow's voice when I called the sit-rep to Battalion Forward CP at 2200 and 2300 hrs. I wanted to identify myself and say something about my situation but didn't; it would have violated radio integrity. He was at the Forward CP, probably only five miles away, sitting in a canvas chair in Headquarters tent, wearing a T-shirt, smoking a cigarette, and nursing a beer.

I felt drowsy after the 2300 report and thought I should take advantage of this relaxed feeling to sleep. The medic rested soundly next to me, turning only once after he fell asleep. The corpse looked more alive than he did. I couldn't fathom how he could sleep so soundly in this weather and was reluctant to disturb him for watch because of his tranquility.

I touched his shoulder. He awoke immediately; I sealed myself inside the poncho, hoping to capture enough scarce body heat to sleep. The combined smells of spoiled blood, rubberized poncho, and probably my B.O. began to overwhelm me. The continuous rain couldn't wash away any of the smells, as I hoped. The experience was like a bad dream where my body does something completely contrary to reason, like falling up a cliff instead of down.

My body trembled so intensely I was afraid something inside would break. The body is supposed to heat up when it shakes and I wondered why it hadn't. I finally tried sleeping with my head outside. It appeared to help because the stink wasn't so prominent. The blood must have been flushed from my hair.

The RTO woke me at 0500 hours. He could hardly keep his eyes open and needed more rest before our day began at first light in half an hour, and just did the sit-rep.

I sat up and glanced around the jet-black void. The body hadn't moved; it still looked more rejuvenated than the medic and RTO. Rain wasn't falling, yet drops remained on the face. I started shaking again. I needed hot cigarette smoke.

First light in Vietnam was 15 minutes away but I couldn't wait. I tucked my head inside the smelly poncho and lit one. It tasted better than sex and heated me up, scattering my bone-deep chill. By the time I finished, the sky was painted red in the east. This nightmare appeared to evaporate, now seeming a minor triviality: reality was this combat patrol in Vietnam. We started getting up, lighting up, parking gear, and opening C rations.

A final rain shower sufficiently wet my chow, washed me more, and with the rising temperature thawed me.

The CO received a call from Operations informing him he would receive his lift to CP sometime in the afternoon, that he should go back to the VC camp for enemy supplies, and that a "slick" would arrive in an hour for the body.

At 0600 we heard several short bursts of automatic M-14 fire from the trail to the VC camp. Troops of the squad straddling the trail were replacements. VC from the camp walked into them. The troops hesitated before shooting, it being the first time they saw the enemy face to face.

The first three VC were helping a wounded comrade; they spotted the G.I.s and hesitated also. A moment later the replacements regained their composure and blasted at the enemy without aiming first.

Initially there were bursts of fire both ways. Gunsmoke filled the air, a grenade exploded, then confusion. When the smoke cleared, none of the Americans had been hit, the VC were gone, and a line of blood led away.

The sky cleared of rain clouds by 0700, the sun began its notorious ascent, and a supply chopper arrived for the body. I decided to escape with it instead of waiting for later in the afternoon. I helped the medic load the body that, after it warmed up, looked and smelled more like a corpse. We didn't have anything to cover the body with and unceremoniously laid it on the floor between the two machine gunners. They appeared oblivious to everything: not saying a word to me, looking in my direction, or glancing at the body. I don't imagine either the body or I were pleasant.

We landed at Brigade Headquarters, Long Binh, across from the Widow's Village where wives of fallen Viet soldiers were housed. I bought a carton of cigarettes at the PX then walked to my base camp. A jeep picked me up and drove me the rest of the way home.

I lugged myself into my "office," the Personnel tent, dropped my gear on the floor, and glared at two clerks using typewriters.

Armed Forces Radio was blaring. Periodically, after we moved from the sand dunes, I heard current music with a beat instead of the normal radio garbage of John Philip Sousa marches, Tommy Dorsey big band music, and "wing. My mind cheerfully fled from my current disposition of melancholy to the vibes on the radio. I took a shaving brush from the elastic band securing my camouflaged helmet cover and applied oil to my carbine, which had been in water all night. Music was booming and my foot began tapping by the time the song was over.

The DJ broke my trance yelling, "Good morning Viet—nammm! How's everybody out there in this tropical paradise?"

"What's that guy hollering about?" I demanded.

"Is the Big Red One enjoying their R&R? Understand you men enjoyed an overnight near Di-An. How was it out there, Big Red One? Fifty-two degrees last night; was that cool? I'll play music to warm you up."

I threatened to blow up the radio.

The guys suggested I'd have to clean up the mess, and that instead I should wash and have chow.

Most of the blood had washed off my body, clothes, and poncho after sunrise, but I still vented a sour aroma. A fresh shower, shave, deodorant, lotion, toothpaste, clean clothes, hot chow, and music from that fantastic addition to our military arsenal, the DJ, Adrian Cronauer, helped ease my pain. I was consecrated from the worst day of my life.

"Good morning, Vietnam!" As loud and clear as Robin Williams ever wailed in the movie. This was beginning of a new day.

The Forward CP convoy returned after 1200 hours and the infantry arrived in choppers at 1700. Later I wrote stories of human-interest trivia. Out of respect for the buddy who died in my poncho, I never mentioned this incident until now. I was afraid the media would make a circus out of the sacred death of this beautiful man.

There were increased anti-Vietnam demonstrations, mostly by college students who had the money and social background to go to college, avoiding the draft. This guy, and many others I wrote about, were merely everyday Americans doing what would turn out to be the most important thing in their lives. I fell into that category also.

At midafternoon, I stretched out on my canvas cot, watching the world through my mosquito net and drifting into never-never land.

The CP convoy returned and the guys—Hans, Crow, O'Riley, Murphy, Fung, and Peter—flooded the tent with their equipment and commotion. The radio went on again and gear clanged to the floor of wooden pallets. The cooler was filled with beer and ice and everybody talked at once. They were also happy to return for clean clothes, hot food, fresh water, mosquito nets, and pussy. Each was planning an excuse to explore the latest whorehouses. I was always the first one they looked to for an excuse to leave the compound.

"Ray, you awake? Need someone to take you to Bien Hoa for pictures?"

I told them to shut up, or they would never go with me again.

"Ew-w-w, must have combat fatigue."

"Is the beer cold yet?"

I fell asleep for a few hours, had chow before the mess hall closed, then fell asleep again to be interrupted only once for radio watch.

Jimmy O'Riley drove me to the photo lab the next day after receiving a "Dear John" letter from his girl in New York. He was a shy, sensitive guy who just got the shaft. I knew a house with new, young, relatively inexperienced prostitutes and treated him to one, hoping it might help.

I considered having the medics test my blood because I still felt tired, lacking my normal gusto. Some of the troops caught a mild form of VD, mostly from the whores in sleazy places. They were often seen in the back part of the medic tent, bent over, pants down, hands on their knees with their butts sticking out for penicillin shots. The medics checked my blood for VD; fortunately the test was negative.

The next day, Sunday, was the first time we used our new chapel, built from scraps of wood and tin by Mike. This chapel helped put me on the road to a renewed belief and trust in religion and God. It was shared by all the religions, as churches should be. We felt a deep love and affection for God, which many of us never experienced before. Also we could feel God's reciprocal love for us. I served every mass Father Confroy celebrated around me.

November 13, more long-range patrolling and search and destroy in the Di-an-Phu Loi areas near the Big Red One's main base camp. We were to leave the next day for three weeks, have to take sufficient supplies, and plan on having Thanksgiving out there somewhere.

"Operation Viper" was 25 miles north of our base camp. We were looking for a VC regiment that "ralliers" (VC who surrendered) said was located there. Before we attacked, we still had to drop leaflets warning that Americans would be looking for Viet Cong.

I told Major Weeks this was ridiculous and asked if it was Colonel Salisbury's idea.

"Brigade was afraid Jane Fonda would complain if we don't warn the enemy that we're going to pay him a visit," he grunted.

We disembarked from the choppers and headed through a field of tall elephant grass to the jungle beyond. The Air Force "softened them up." Three F-100s made strafing runs ahead. The next strike was made by two F-5s, which dove perpendicularly at their targets, pulled up at the last minute and sat their craft on their tails, shooting up like a rocket.

All the strafing, bombing, and napalm made us feel secure until we arrived at our objective, a regiment-sized camp hidden under mahogany trees and jungle canopy. Not one single bomb touched it. This base camp was half a mile long and at least quarter of a mile wide. All the low shrubbery, branches, and vines had been cleared, leaving an area the size of a small town existing under the canopy of overhead jungle growth.

The land rose gradually from front to rear; the back portion of the camp was 400 yards above the front, yielding an excellent field of fire. The last hundred yards of the camp rose sharply and was studded with bunkers, trenches, and punji traps. We were involved in a full brigade operation with the other two battalions, totaling 1,000 men. We waited inside the tree line while the entire brigade assembled on line before proceeding inside.

I attached myself to Alpha, planning to enter with them in the first wave. Only a third of the brigade would make the initial assault; the remainder would be reserve until needed. Four hundred men moved out in a slow, deliberate patrol pace, eyes sweeping the jungle canopy above, fortifications ahead, and one-foot grass below our feet.

"Mines," the man next to me casually said. His alert eyes detected the three prongs of a "Bouncing Betty" under his foot as he placed it down. They are the diameter of medium paper clip and stick out an inch from the mine, which blasts three feet above the ground when detonated and explodes. It was incredible he could discern these prongs, less than an inch above the ground, in tall grass, while noticing everything around him.

Concentration was the answer. People seldom experience full concentration, especially for half or all day: an airline pilot a few hours, a college student during exams, an athlete during a game, but not all day and part of the night. If anyone lets his mind slip into semiconsciousness, he quickly ends up dead. I found I was more frequently exhausted mentally than physically.

I acknowledged the mine and turned to the trooper behind me, whispering, "mine," pointing to the spot. He took a piece of C ration toilet paper and laid it on top so others would notice it. Everybody saw what was happening and didn't have to be warned.

When we reached the base of the hump, several squads remained behind the mahogany trees to provide back-up firepower if we needed as we ran the remaining 75 yards to the camp's crest. As I ran past each of the gun positions, I thanked God they had been vacated. If occupied, I would probably be dead.

There were a few bursts of fire from the troops on the left flank, but my group didn't find anyone. I had a funny feeling in my guts when I reached the top, like a kid nosing around an unattended girls' locker room, peeking into their lockers, checking out their bras and panties, fantasizing about what filled them.

The top of the ridge was still. VC had been here and probably were watching from a secluded spot. Several men ran to the left; I followed them, discovering a kitchen with pots of warm food. While nosing around here, I saw something reinforcing the trauma of this of war: the fresh skin of a monkey was on the table in their kitchen. They had been forced to skin and eat monkey to survive.

This was commensurate with what I had learned about the Viet Cong so far; that most who voluntarily entered didn't have any idea what they were getting into.

The trench around a VC camp where I was being fired at only minutes earlier. Note the tunnel leading outside the camp. They fired above your feet.

Brigade reserve followed us to the crest line, joining the exploration of the camp. I should have thanked Jane Fonda; those warning leaflets we dropped saved my life, frightening the VC away. I felt like a condemned man sitting on the electric chair during a power failure as I looked down the hill and imagined myself charging up the hill past these installations.

There were 60 tunnels, 40 bunkers, over 125 booby traps, punji traps, barbed wire, and trenches with firing ports. All the tunnels were connected, many leading beyond the perimeter. We were aware we should have been statistics.

I had my meal next to Alpha's CP. Captain Barrell's men returned with more enemy supplies: rice, pots and pans, knives and ammo, a few mines and grenades, and Communist propaganda. I kept a few posters of the North Vietnamese leader, Ho Chi Minh, extolling the virtues of the working class in a lengthy poem. I asked our Vietnamese interpreter, Fong, if Ho wrote it. He laughed and said Ho couldn't write. I mailed these posters to my friends as Christmas greetings.

The brigade divided into company-sized patrols, departing to different destinations a half hour apart.

Nobody, to my knowledge, ever returned to destroy these camps, tunnels, trenches, and fortifications. We had a timetable to fulfill for each area searched; destroy was something we never seemed to have time to do. The only thing we managed to do was to push the enemy farther into the jungle where he was more difficult to locate. The large regiment whose base camp we discovered broke into smaller units and scattered throughout a 15-mile radius. Brigade discovered fractions of it, but never a unit large enough to conduct a conclusive battle.

There were so many different patrols in the jungle that each battalion had to have its operations officer flying in a chopper, orienting through colored grenades. The VC were monitoring our radio messages and began popping grenades at the same time to confuse the spotter or to draw him into an ambush.

A VC camp operations table underground. The overhead covering of bamboo struts, plastic sheet cover, and camouflage vegetation are visable.

Major Weeks was spotting for a company. He radioed, "Pop a red." Seconds later, the red smoke of two grenades lifted out of the green canopy below, a few hundred yards apart. A Huey gunship was security for the major in his observation chopper. Weeks told the gunship to standby and asked if they "monitored the last situation."

"Roger, monitored."

The company commander also realized VC were intercepting the messages, so when Major Weeks radioed, "Pop one" again, the CO answered,

"Duchess 3, have an orange." A few seconds later a second orange came out of the jungle—where the VC were hiding. The gunship flew directly into the smoke, fired both 7.62-mm Gatling guns, each spraying 750 rounds per minute, and released 24 rockets from both pods.

I later asked the major if he was able to register a kill for them.

"Pezzoli, you know to register a kill you have to be close enough to the body to physically verify it. No. 1, I wasn't up close enough and no. 2, there weren't enough left to verify."

We made frequent contact with small groups of that VC unit. Some of our companies became broken into smaller platoon-sized patrols with 45 men. This was more manageable in guerrilla conflict; nevertheless, it was still too large for the jungle.

Four days after the operation began three VC ambushed us along a small trail. They fired several short bursts with automatic weapons and then hesitated. I was two from the point then. The foliage along the sides of the path was sparse. I could clearly see my men in front and behind along the trail. Nobody was hit; the VC missed clear shots again.

We immediately hit the ground at the first shots and returned fire a fraction of a second later. I glanced in the direction of the firing before I fell and noticed the leaves flickering in a bush the bullets were fired from. Six of us immediately shot back on automatic. When the VC weapons stopped firing, I eased to my knees, did a two-second cook-off with a grenade and threw it like a baseball directly at the bush I saw move. I never took my eyes off the grenade until it entered that bush, and then hit the ground simultaneously with the grenade explosion. Everyone else went prone as soon as they saw my grenade in the air. This action was orchestrated so smoothly one might have thought it rehearsed.

Troops near me sprayed a few more bursts, but didn't receive any response. We decided against going into the jungle and looking behind the bushes for bodies because they might be booby-trapped.

We moved out again. Half an hour later we came to an intersection of trails that wasn't on the map. The platoon leader called the company CO who said to establish a squad ambush and continue patrolling ahead because contact had been made there with a larger enemy force.

I couldn't decide if I should continue with the patrol or stay at the ambush site. Reports were about larger forces ahead, while there seemed to be action here also. I spoke with the squad while they established their positions along this fork of trails. They had mixed feelings about making contact here.

When the remainder of the patrol moved out, the last man let me know they were leaving. I finished my conversation, still considering staying. I was tired of walking, but the prospect of making contact with a large VC force ahead enticed me to run down the trail and catch the patrol before they walked too far. I had run past two bends and almost caught up with them when I heard a burst from a Thompson back at the ambush site. I wheeled around and ran there. As I ran, I touched the safety of my carbine, ensuring it was off and also fingering the selector insuring the weapon was on full automatic.

A three-foot square anthill divided the trail intersection like the traffic light on an island. I dropped behind it, positioned my rifle on the top, and searched for VC.

"He's in front!" one of the men shouted who had just shot a VC that ran into the fork. The jolt from the two .45-caliber Thompson rounds had knocked him off the trail into the brush where the shooter saw bushes moving, indicating he was still alive.

I focused my eyes from my cover in the middle of the Y of trails. The wounded VC was flopping about in the shrubbery immediately in front, six feet away on the left of the Y. I saw a flash of his blue shirt through parting leaves in a bush directly in front. I didn't have my sights on him, but squeezed the trigger anyway, knowing I could spray at him on automatic, hitting him eventually.

The prized 36-round VC magazine I had thoroughly nurtured before but never test fired was in my rifle now. My first round jammed. The cool confidence I flaunted while hiding behind this cover with an automatic weapon, aiming at a wounded and dying enemy, transformed into a rush of panic. I removed this banana-shaped magazine, pulled the slide back, ejected the jammed round, replaced the magazine, and chambered the next one.

When the bush moved again in the same spot, I aimed directly at it and shot again. Again the alarming "bang, cluck." The carbine jammed a second time. I removed the magazine again, cleared it, and was about to insert the standard-issue 20-round magazine when I heard M-14 auto fire behind that bush. While inserting the new magazine and chambering a round, the bush flung open and a G.I. stepped out and walked deliberately and forcefully to me.

"Man, you almost shot me that time."

No words were appropriate now, due to my stupidity, I had almost killed a soldier and lost my soul.

His eyes were aflame, his furious stare penetrating directly through me. I'm sure he would have enjoyed killing me. He had just killed a VC five seconds before and experienced me as the same threat to his life.

"Yeah, I'm sorry, my rifle jammed," a feeble response.

I violated two principles resulting in my almost killing an American soldier: I didn't test fire a new piece of equipment on my weapon and didn't have my sight on the target the second time I fired. Our excellent training prevented more than the two deaths of our troops attributed to friendly fire. My story of this goof-up was published in several military papers, a crucial lesson on fire discipline run amok where fire discipline is paramount importance.

Troops dragged the body into the intersection to see it better. He was, as we found many VC, young and surprisingly neat and clean, wearing a pistol belt with a packet of cooked rice fastened in the back and a crude grenade on his side, but no papers, identification, or maps. There was no reason to have his body evacuated for Intelligence; we left it in the trail so his comrades would know we were around.

The platoon remained there for half an hour, then the entire unit, including the ambush squad, continued patrolling the trail. The platoon leader wanted to move out because we weren't in satisfactory defensives after announcing our presence.

This was the last time I saw the guy I almost shot, who never mentioned it to anyone. Two other men at the ambush site saw this, but remained silent also.

Our objective was reaching a clearing before sunset for supplies. I cleared the ammo from the VC magazine and left it by the body. If a VC found it, I hoped he would have a malfunction also and get killed trying to use it.

We made the clearing by 1700, established a perimeter, received supplies, and prepared for the night. I enjoyed the "wop-wop-wop" sound the Huey's blades made as they approached our LZ, my contact with the real world outside.

Later that night, an ambush squad saw five VC walking across a clearing and held fire, making certain they weren't Vietnamese soldiers. They could see weapons; also they knew Americans, Vietnamese, and Popular Force troops never patrolled at night deep in enemy territory.

Each of the men selected a target; when the enemy was 20 yards away, they opened fire on full.

The five figures dropped, either from being shot or for cover. One G.I. had a M-79 grenade launcher and saturated the area with grenades. I was next to the platoon leader and his staff then. He radioed the men to remain in position and not look for bodies or survivors. They had seclusion and the VC didn't.

I reported the ambush to Battalion who advised the other platoons were making contact also; they felt the VC were up to something and we

One of two VC killed in the night ambush, their bodies bloated by internal gases and covered with ravenous insects. The arm of this corpse was still in the crawl position when he died.

did not pull out of defense that night. I remained on the radio another hour monitoring "sit-reps" and whatever else was happening.

The medic took over at 2100. My radio watch began again at 0400. I slept for five hours, which was a good night's rest.

I awoke the lieutenant for a 0500 call. The CO told him to move us out at sunrise. Brigade thought the VC had consolidated during the night and might be assembled in a local patch of jungle.

The troops were pulled in and prepared to move after the chopper removed surplus supplies. The squad that ambushed the VC that night didn't have time to search for victims.

We never found the large consolidated VC force suspected although patrols made frequent contact with smaller units.

Two days later we passed a village near the site where our squad ambushed the VC patrol three nights previous. The village chief indicated he wanted to talk to someone of authority. SSgt. Calvin Jefferson, the life of the squad with a continuous mischievous gleam in his eyes, told the chief he was the boss. This gregarious fellow was so convincing he could have passed himself off as a black, jive-arsing General Westmoreland.

We thought this body might be mined. The local village chief cautiously pulled it over to be examined.

He passed the word back to the platoon leader that he was investigating something in the village. Fearing a potential ambush, the lieutenant gave him another squad and drew up defenses with the remaining two squads. I followed.

Jefferson, the chief, several villagers, and the rest of the squad proceeded to a clearing by the village.

We found two bodies bloated with internal gases and smelling worse than the blood left in my poncho by the guy that bled to death. They had been lying in the open for three nights and two days at temperatures ranging between 80–130 degrees, partially decomposed by the elements and consumed by indigenous insects, flies, and animals.

One of the bodies was wearing a blue shirt and pants, shower thongs, an empty pistol belt, and a felt hat with a broad brim. He was lying on his stomach, one hand on the ground, elbow in the air, the position he died in while crawling from our ambush.

Jefferson told the chief not to touch the body because it might be mined. One of the men carefully tied a rope around his arm and gradually pulled the corpse over after everybody found cover. The man wasn't mined.

We saw one of the things that stopped him; a chunk had been blown out of his hip. His pockets were flat and looked empty, the reason men used not to stick their hands inside checking papers. Sergeant Jefferson called everybody a candy arse and went through the pockets like they were a virgin's panties.

"Nothing," Sergeant Jefferson grumbled, wiping his hands on the damp leaves.

The other body was lying on its back without a shirt or shoes on. The shirt had been yanked over his head, apparently so he could look at one of his wounds, the hole on the left side of his chest under the armpit. The right arm was blown off at the elbow while the left had cloth wrapped around it from the hand to the elbow. Bugs covered the exposed part of the body like pepper on a prime rib. We thought even he was too deteriorated for Sergeant Jefferson to touch after he said that it wasn't necessary to check this guy's pockets.

"Let's not waste our time; he doesn't have pockets. Gotta go back with the platoon for chow before we move out."

I took some pictures of these bodies, vowing to God this would be the last time I photographed bodies lest I end up in the same condition. I was superstitious like everyone else.

The men spoke about their difficulty comprehending the culture of the Communists who left their wounded friends on the battlefield to die. One of the men speculated the VC were chopped up so badly they weren't

His friend had part of his side, right arm, left foot, and fruitlessly wrapped left arm blown off by a 40-mm M-79 grenade.

able to help. We found out later they always left their wounded if the injured men were too weak to walk.

Thanksgiving was two days away; we would spend 24 hours at the Forward CP for turkey, clean clothes, showers, mail, and religious services. My patrol arrived at the battalion CP the next day as did the others. All the men looked tired; they had done a lot of work and didn't receive much rest. Everybody's spirits were high with the prospects of the earlier mentioned treats. Contact had been made, the enemy killed and disrupted, and not one of our men injured.

I returned with barely time to shower, shave, and change clothes, catching a ride to Bien Hoa with Hans on a mail run, for I was anxious to print photos.

I had been frustrated with the photos of my tiny Canon half-frame lately. Many photos came out dark because of my insufficient experience in photography; I didn't understand using a film with a higher ASA would squeeze more light out of the murky jungle interior.

I might have been able achieve that "Great Vietnamese War Photo" if I had used the proper film. I almost lost my life in the quest of this goal, but did manage to achieve another: showing the guys someone cared for them, respected them, and was proud of their achievements. During my time as reporter in Vietnam, from September 1965 to June 1966, it was still possible for the news media to say something decent. My human-interest photos and stories were being published with regularity.

I finished my photo work and went to the PX where I bought a carton of Winstons, had an ice cream, wrote captions for my photos, sent a letter home, and was picked up by Hans as I fell asleep at the table.

We found and joined a convoy of three vehicles returning to the Forward CP.

The CP was relatively safe, so we slept on canvas cots. I cleaned my equipment, had chow at the mess tent, made plans for a late radio watch, and fell asleep.

This Thanksgiving would be meaningful. For the first time during most of our young lives, we realized there was much to be thankful for. We were still alive, had survived life-threatening experiences, and had endured living conditions close to those of animals.

The troops would vegetate at the CP for 24 hours with nothing to do but sleep, eat a Thanksgiving dinner of turkey with all the fixings, and catch up on mail. Enjoying the luxury of hygiene with showers, shaves, and fresh clothes was critical.

This setting was a million light years from my hometown of Wareham, adjacent to Plymouth, Massachusetts. During Thanksgiving we found a dusting of snow on the frozen ground, icicles on roofs in the morning, and heard cheers from my high school's traditional football game.

This year was different. We were on a humid, sweltering, insect-infested flatland 30 miles north of Saigon surrounded by Viet Cong trying to kill everybody.

The turkey and fixings were piled on metal mess kits washed earlier in trash cans filled with soapy semi-hot, semi-clean water.

Fong was part of our family. We explained the history of Thanksgiving. Also, we described turkey, mashed potatoes, yams, gravy, and cranberry sauce. One of the guys half-wittily asked him if his country had a holiday like this. He hesitated for a second and he stammered, "My country is only 10 years old. I hope before long we will have something to be thankful about."

I read in military newspapers that the Korean "Tiger Division," which had arrived less than a month before, had completely eliminated VC opposition 15 miles north of our Forward CP. They were Asians and fought the war like Asians and as a war should be fought—for keeps. Their hands weren't tied like ours; whatever they did wasn't under the scrutiny of the world.

The VC teased the Koreans when they first arrived and quickly realized that if you antagonize a bull, you'll get horns in an uncomfortable place. It took less than a week for Charlie to get the message. After that, the Koreans saw no VC.

We weren't ready to give up, even though we felt frustrated.

The choppers picked us up the next morning, continuing our sweep for another week. We never completely rested during breaks because the VC threat was constant. I was not the only one unable to unwind; four men had cracked up so far. I feared I might join them soon.

Most of the streams were shallow and narrow, making crossing easy; the challenging part was scaling down the sides before they were crossed. This meant rappelling down an almost perpendicular bank, 15 to 20 feet tall, crossing, then climbing the opposite side. The banks were studded with shrubs and vines, offering excellent handles and rungs, assisting in descent and ascent. These crossings would have been difficult wearing simple gym clothes; our task was compounded by the unruly assortment and weight of equipment. Vines and shrubbery snared our 60 to 80 pounds of equipment by its irregular, protruding edges. Crossing a simple six-foot-wide stream took a platoon over half an hour after security had been established on both sides. Helpers were stationed along both of the banks assisting. Others helped passing heavy equipment.

Contact was made with a VC camp in two days. I could tell the guns fired on the point were from a trench or foxhole because its tell-tale "crack"

Right foreground: I am climbing a typical perpendicular stream bank.

sound was low, close to the ground. His rapid response of several bursts from a Grease Gun caught the enemy off guard and forced him to duck. The point dove on the ground and called two behind to crawl on line and return a base of fire. I was number four and crawled a few feet forward, not enough to remain in visual contact but within the whispering distance. If I remained absolutely still, I could blend in completely with the surroundings.

After our guns opened fire, more fired inside from what I perceived to be their perimeter. The troops behind me held their fire because they didn't know our exact location.

A VC directly in front fired a carbine on auto. Naturally I knew it was automatic because it fired in bursts and was a carbine because the slide made a "clanking" sound moving forward and back. I flattened myself to 10 inches and pointed my rifle at the sound five feet away. Bullets hit tree limbs and leaves a foot above, making a "tick-ticking" sound knocking pieces off. He was in a trench, mistakenly firing up; the trajectory carried rounds over my head.

He was so close I could distinctly hear him remove his magazine when it ran out of ammo. The carbine was firing "crack, crack, crack," pause, "crack, crack, crack," pause, then "crack, cluck," and silence. I distinctly heard, "sch-h-h-h," the metal sound of his magazine withdrawn from the weapon.

"Now," I thought, "is a good time to give him a mouth full of lead."

Fortunately, I reasoned that I had no cover, only concealment; I didn't know exactly where he was, although he sounded directly in front. Also, he did not know my location. If I shot at him and missed, he would know exactly where I was—directly in front. The only thing between him and me was elephant grass, vines, and leaves, while he had a trench for protection.

I didn't fire, instead I dug my face into the ground further and heard, "sch-h-h-h," the fresh magazine inserted and "click," the metal tab securing it. I was certain that if I fired at him he would duck and be missed. And I was also certain that as soon as I stopped shooting to replace my magazine with a full one, he would have found his target and killed me. You can call me a live coward, but I am still alive and went on to kill at least eight more VC.

That incessant "crack, crack" and "tick, tick" sound of leaves continued. I forced my face deeper into the ground and roots so hard it cut, waiting for one to find its mark. Again, this was a bad dream, unreal because I couldn't do anything except lie waiting to get shot.

I watched the red ants climbing about their world of blades of grass. "I'm envious of you. I wish I was with you. Do you want to trade places?"

If I threw a grenade, he might not know where it came from. Still, I was afraid to throw one because trees, bushes or vines could knock it down closer to me than to him.

A jet flew over; at the same time I heard a man behind pop a smoke grenade, marking our location for an air strike. One F-4D Phantom, then another made strafing runs, firing 20-mm cannon from their Gatling guns, 750 rounds a minute exploding on contact. They fired so fast we heard "vroom-m-m" rather than the auto weapon sound of "rat-tat-tat."

The cannon rounds hit directly in front, exploding like a string of firecrackers. After the second plane made its run I heard something falling above me. "Grenade!" I panicked and snatched it to toss back, but dropped the metal shaft immediately; it burned my hand. I picked up one of the jet's 20-mm casings.

I was impressed by the accuracy of the Air Force. The cannon on the first two runs and the bombs on the third were placed directly in front and a few feet from us. They appeared to go directly into the VC perimeter.

After the jets' passes, two Vietnamese Skyraiders labored, initiating their runs, taking eternally after the jets' lightning speeds. They released their ordinance and strained, clawing for altitude. A moment later two bombs exploded behind our lines. "Cancel the air strike!" radioed the platoon leader.

The VC stopped firing during the strike; I didn't know if any had been hit. Three men ran to the VC perimeter when it lifted. I rose to my knees and whispered to the man behind we were going in.

I ran five feet to the right where the men had been, then forward watching for vines, trip wires, punji traps, and VC. I hadn't run more then half a dozen steps before crossing the trench into the shrubbery-hidden base camp.

Several shots to my left; the point fired into a tunnel. I saw a punji trap next to me by the perimeter trench. These four-foot square, four-foot deep pits were filled with sharp bamboo shafts supposedly covered with poison. I never saw one of these traps concealed and never heard of anyone falling into one. Strangely though, there were two instances where they saved men's lives. In each case they came under fire from base camp bunkers, kicked over the pointed stakes, jumped in, returned fire, and threw grenades routing the enemy.

The trench was five feet deep and had two bunkers with firing ports in front. There was so much going on when I entered the perimeter; I didn't see the VC who shot at me earlier. The tunnel the point man was firing into was near where I thought he was. He could have been firing at my assailant attempting to escape through the tunnel.

The trench made an irregular circle around the camp with individual and two-man foxholes or gun positions at different intervals. All the bushes, vines, and low tree branches were cleared. The overhead jungle canopy was dense, obliterating the sky, making the camp obscure.

I glanced over my shoulder and saw men behind jump the trench and run to the right. The commotion was extreme now; my thumping heart hurt while I panted like an out-of-shape athlete.

I reached a well in the center of the camp and hid behind it in a defensive position, waiting for more troops to arrive. The camp had a system of tunnels branching out from the perimeter trench. Next to the well was an underground kitchen 15 feet deep and eight feet square with bamboo rods supporting a plastic sheet with leaves on it. A compartment was next to it acting as a damper for the smoke, dispersing it through a long tunnel.

After the camp was secured, volunteers went into the tunnels exploring them. They discovered living quarters consisting of tables and beds doubling as dispensaries and classrooms. A room had penicillin, syringes, vitamins, malaria tablets, and other medicines.

One tunnel was 200 yards long, the length of two football fields. Most of these tunnels started from the center of the camp and extended to the trenches encircling the perimeter. Others passed beneath them to the jungle beyond as escape routes. These were similar to the one the VC who ran into me must have used.

At other camps, VC popped out of tunnels to shoot the troops attacking. In each case they missed in their haste and were, instead, killed themselves.

These tunnels were ventilated by five-inch holes angled up to the surface. Their openings were ingeniously constructed with a sharp 90-degree turn in one direction immediately followed by another turn in the opposite direction. This guarded effectively against grenade blasts and bullets. The clay was so dense braces weren't needed to support tunnels and cavities. Entrances to the tunnels were shafts 15 feet deep with toe and foot slots carved into the walls, consequently the men who searched these tunnels had to be light and nimble

The tunnels were three feet high and two feet wide, making them cramped for many Americans. Incredibly, we never had problems finding volunteers.

The man would remove his helmet, pack, and pistol belt, take a flashlight and a .45 pistol, and lower himself into the black void, an adventure for many. During my almost 12 months we never lost a man there while managing to find, capture, and kill almost a hundred VC.

Later, one of the men was surprised when a VC from an adjacent tunnel grabbed his pistol. The man dropped his flashlight, released the pistol, grabbed the VC's lips with both hands, and pulled his mouth apart before he could fire. This VC surrendered easily.

The enemy left six backpacks here. The rule of thumb was first come, first served. I was the first there and searched for souvenirs. These were supposed to be turned into S-2 Intelligence, which we did as soon as we finished exploring them. This was exciting, like opening Christmas presents.

I found something in the second pack making this effort worthwhile, a VC hammock. It was light, made of cloth from parachute material, and sowed to carved wooden shafts at each end. We had captured hammocks like this before, but never the size of this. My six-foot two-inch frame fit comfortably. The rest of the men arrived, excitedly exploring like kids.

Only two hours of sun were left; a perimeter became established. I was excited to try out my new bed, but had to wait until I finished assisting discovering and destroying equipment. This was another of the chain of holding camps, or relay stations, for infiltrating North Vietnamese.

Grenades killed two VC while another was zapped by an M-14. Nobody knew what happened to the other three VC we thought were there. Blood lined the entrance of a tunnel. The most important accomplishment of these operations was discovering and mapping these camps. Later, after more troops brought the 1st Infantry Division to full strength, they would know exactly where VC camps were located. The Communists crowed about their extensive tunnel complexes there after we gave them South Vietnam. We managed to keep them squirming in mud.

I thought I would sleep soundly in the hammock, but I was nervous and jumpy after the firing. On days like this one with several hours of light and sufficient time, we heated C rations for enjoyable treats in the boonies.

Continuous perspiration was tolerable because we realized it would be washed off several times a day by monsoons, streams, or both. Unfortunately, nothing discouraged the flies, mosquitoes, leeches, ants, and bugs always prevalent.

To make my existence tolerable, I fantasized about choppers "whoomp-whoomping" over treetops, picking me up and flying to base camp a cool 1,000 feet above steamy jungles.

The word was we would be leaving by convoy in two days.

I had interesting stories to write, but not many photos because of insufficient light. Life in the jungle was tiring and frustrating. No more Resupply choppers were slated; I would have to leave with the convoy.

The next two days were uneventful; I was hoping for action that would require choppers for a lift. The same monotony, the same leaves, the same vines, the same heat, the same wet clothes, the same shriveled hands, the same leaves, the same vines....

We were scheduled to return home at Ho Nai that day. I didn't feel like eating C rations that morning, wanting refrigerated apples instead. We might have to patrol for the day if trucks weren't available.

I was sitting with the platoon leader, RTO, and medic when the CO called, confirming we would be leaving in the morning and to secure a convoy pick-up point.

The platoon left the jungle at 0830 and followed a dirt road leading to a clearing five miles away. We could count on arriving at base camp by noon for hot chow, showers, mail, and cold drinks.

I felt hot by 0900, although the temperature was no warmer than normal, and dizzy if I turned my head; all I saw were Infantrymen walking on sand, like mirages in the desert. I slipped on a small rock, falling on the shoulder of the road. The guy next to me asked if I was OK. I was.

Water in my canteen had been "purified" by the engineers from another of their unknown sources and tasted that way. "Maybe," I thought, "the water in the well at the VC camp would have tasted better." I forced a few swallows and struggled forward.

I was lightheaded and saw blotches floating over the road, as I felt with the flu. My skin was prickly; I saw spots and hallucinated a little. At times, when you're short of breath or before you go under from anesthesia, the mind runs rampant with imagination, a severely erratic thought process. This is exactly how I felt.

I fantasized I had been killed and this was the afterlife. I was destined to spend eternity walking in 130-degree weather with 85 pounds of equipment hanging from my body with these inanimate, nameless, dead G.I.s.

We arrived at the pickup point, I lay under a bush but couldn't feel a breeze. This was a perfect time to sleep, but I couldn't.

The convoy came an hour later. I crawled in the back with the men and was amazed how most slept while the truck bounced along the dirt road, sending billows of encrusting yellow dust. Their heads nodded back and forth, each bouncing off the other like pool balls; I still couldn't sleep.

We reached camp at noon.

Hot chow and a shower didn't help so I visited the medics who said all I needed was rest. I realized I might be cracking up so I told Personnel Sergeant Grassburg that I needed an out of country rest and recuperation(R & R) to any place available.

Manila had a new R &R Center that would be opening the next day. I could go if I had all my stories and photos finished.

That light at the end of the tunnel, the glimpse that promised hope, was out. I had to get away.

Chapter 10

The Never-Never Land
Full of Sugar and Spice
and Everything Nice and a
Grove of Yum Yum Trees

I knocked out a few stories after my shower and turned them in to Lieutenant Kline to review. Preparing for my R&R in Manila on the next day gave me a lift.

The flight to Manila took over two hours. There were 30 guys wearing khakis with a tie and carrying a suitcase of civvies. I didn't know any; everyone sat quietly, each embroidered in his individual thoughts. A few napped, some looked out the window, while most stoically gazed forward.

R&Rs were bused to the Manila USO and processed by a lady looking like the typical USO worker in World War II movies. I was surprised how efficient and sincere she was, not plastic and artificial.

A middle-aged man dressed in expensive casual clothes approached me and introduced himself. "Hi, I see you're Italian, I am too. My name is Lee Talesco, VP of San Miguel Beer. Have you heard of it?"

"No, I'm from Massachusetts."

He owned one of the largest breweries in the Pacific and thought we were doing a super job. He wanted to show his appreciation by inviting me for lunch each day. I took his business card, saying when I found a hotel I would call for his driver.

I put his card in my pocket and walked outside taking pictures along the coast. I felt naked without my rifle, grenades and pistol belt. This was the first time in six months nobody was trying to kill me. Also, everyone spoke English, American culture was prevalent. I was exhausted from the last operation and felt I was dreaming.

The troops in my group each went their own way. I found Hotel Philipineous reasonably priced and reserved a room, yet I was too excited for a nap. I called Lee, made plans for lunch the next day, put on shorts, sneaks and T-shirt, and began investigating the city. The Old Spanish City was historically significant, the indigenous food seemed Asian, and San Miguel beer tasted good.

Manila had "dance places." Barmaids approached, smiled, and suggested a watered-down drink for a commission. I understood you could take a barmaid home if you offered her enough.

I had to get some sleep and would search the next day.

I was sticky and showered again, turned the air conditioner down, crawled between fresh, clean sheets, into a flat, smooth, soft, bug-free bed, and virtually passed out.

Lee's secretary called at 1000, confirming our lunch. His conversation during lunch at the country club was the monologue of two pilots discussing the preflight checklist. I realized the importance of his position and expressed my appreciation for the time he shared.

He mentioned his gratitude, again, for America coming to Southeast Asia assisting with a Communist problem attempting to take foothold in his country. His 13-year-old son was anxious to meet an American G.I. Also, he wanted me to meet his wife and daughter whenever I had a chance.

I thanked him again for his concern but was lost explaining I didn't want anything from him or anybody else. I merely wanted to be by myself for the first time in over six months with no commitments. I related fleeting bits about what I had been involved with, but was reluctant to give details because I had six more months of combat to go. Superstition.

He was perceptive, saw he was cornering me, and backed off. He added that I might care, at my convenience, to see the volcanic depression of Taal, 50 miles away. Also the World War II cemetery for those killed in the Pacific was magnificent and I might care to see Corregidor too. Call my intentions the day before and his driver would accommodate.

Later in the afternoon, the driver left me at hotel row. I casually strolled the walk next to the ocean, watching life. I realized another reason why it was pleasant walking about the city; the air was warm and the humidity was high, but there were no mosquitoes, flies, and bugs.

I took a nap in the hotel room on my freshly made bed and woke up at 1800 hours, thirsty, hungry, and horny. The first two drives were satisfied quickly in the hotel restaurant while the third would require time, patience, and decisions.

The evening came to Manila: hotel row with its dance places, restaurants, and side-street bars lit up and life began. I planned to scope out a

The final resting place for many American heroes, the World War II Pacific Cemetery in the Philippines.

few bars before visiting the one from the previous night. The Can-Can Club with a few men and many attractive women caught my eye.

I bought a brew, quaffing it at their nondescript bar. American-style rock music blared on the speaker system while a few G.I.s danced. My eyes scouted the booths.

"Hi, my name is Shirley."

She was tall for a Filipino and slim with Oriental features. Her jet-black buffed-up hair amplified her delicate features. She spoke English hesitatingly with a sexy accent. I danced with her once and was immediately turned on. I enjoyed her so much I even bought her a house drink of expensive colored water. She had intriguing looks, a unique-sounding dialogue, and didn't pressure me to buy her more drinks. I was in love!

It was fantastic having someone nice to clutch and become close to. She said she wanted to spend the remainder of my leave with me, but had to work nights. That was all right, I could visit later in the evening, buy a few "drinks," and dance to closing with her. She said she would enjoy tours with Lee's driver. What a fantastic break: we would be together and have free transportation at our disposal.

I tried to forget about Vietnam; not my past, but what might happen after I returned. I was a fish on the line; the angler gave me slack, yet I was still hooked. This line was attached to the reel, which would eventually be whirled in. I couldn't let my emotions run amok because my line was connected to the reel in Vietnam.

We visited the World War II Memorial Cemetery, drifting through rows of crosses marking the graves of dead soldiers. These stately rows of crosses meandered over hill and dale, punctuated by a tree here, a bush there, flowerbeds, and a few subtly situated hedges. I experienced peace and tranquility relating to the fallen soldiers and their misfortune, understanding their pain.

We sat on a bench, reflecting over the tombs of heroes, creating an unreal, mystical pathos. We sat silent for three hours; she knew I had to go back and was apprehensive about seeing me again. This was a pleasant dream; unfortunately all dreams end.

Two days later we visited Taal, a depression in the earth's crust 50 miles across the top and a quarter of a mile deep. We had lunch. I bought lunch for the driver because I didn't anticipate staying at this magnificent vista as long as we did.

Shirley and I strolled the rim, admiring its extraordinary view, not talking but communicating.

The driver left us at my hotel. We showered, played a good radio station, crawled between the sheets, and wrapped ourselves up with each other.

Lee said his family would be home the next day and wanted them to meet me. The wife, son, and daughter looked like Middle America, where Lee was a vibrant Southern Californian. Their differences were hot and cold. I enjoyed their wholesome family life, reminding me of home. Lee wrote later that his young son was disappointed I didn't tell him about the VC we killed. I replied we didn't get any and didn't like to discuss it.

I met Shirley at work.

We spent the next day at the beach by my hotel. The week was fading fast. I had enjoyed many experiences; paradoxically, I felt I just arrived.

We visited Corregidor the next day and saw where the Japanese had held American prisoners below the ramparts of the Spanish fort. The prisoners were cramped in narrow, dark, dank, rock passageways and rooms. I imagined myself held by the VC inside tunnels, wondering if I would be as strong, appreciating these troops' endurance, and offering my highest respect.

Shirley and I spent the last day in the hotel room. I told the chambermaids not to come in, only leave fresh towels outside the door. Shirley reminded me to call Lee and his family to thank them.

In one more day, no more tall, sweet-smelling lady. No air conditioning, fresh sheets, dishes and ice cubes. No more clean body, freshly shaven face, or dry shoes. I would have to coat myself with insect repellent again.

The Old Spanish Fortress in Manila where the Japanese kept Americans prisoner during World War II.

Back to the warm stagnant water flavored with purification tablets, which I had to fight bugs to drink. Back to ... I didn't want to think about it.

Shirley took the last night off and cooked dinner at her simple flat containing only the basic essentials of furniture; she didn't require much. I wanted to buy her a gift before I departed, but couldn't decide what until she turned the radio on. It was a small, cheap portable blaring static, my answer.

That night she gave me a Barong Tagalog, an embroidered formal Philippine shirt with pearl cuff links. It must have cost more than she made in a month. The next morning we left her apartment early and walked to the PX, arriving as it opened to buy the biggest "ghetto-blaster" in the place. I found a big, black beauty with woofer, tweeter, and midrange speakers on each end.

This was the best radio she had ever owned. I also bought a brightly colored fabric belt and fashioned a sling to support it over her tiny frame when she carried it.

We stretched out at the beach together, fitting perfectly together like matching puzzle pieces. I advised her how to adjust the balance of stereo, tone, and fine-tuning.

We stood up, wiped the sand off, pressed together one more time, and flagged down a taxi to the airport.

The remainder of my group arrived in every mode of travel: taxi, bus, rent-a-car, and one guy on a bicycle with a girl on the handlebars. Most had women. Photos were taken while hugs, kisses, promises, and presents were exchanged.

"Will you write to me Ray?"

"Of course, Shirley. I will never forget you."

Everybody was quiet on the return flight while we were reeled back into our reality—Vietnam.

Reality became evident during the convoy back to base camp: three miles outside of Saigon proper, the driver and his shotgun put magazines back into their M-14s, chambering a round.

"Lock and load," the guy next to me sarcastically muttered, "welcome home."

The guys at camp commented about my tan. They said I was missing action on the current operation and the battalion had a new CO who was really cool, Lt. Col. Bill Staples.

A convoy was leaving for the Forward CP tomorrow at 0700 hours.

I wrote a letter to Shirley, saying I enjoyed her and would be busy. This was the last letter I wrote to her. I received two from her but never wanted to reply because I had a war to fight and my life to save.

Getting laid was no problem here; guys in my tent said there were nice ones by 1st Division Headquarters at Di-An and a man could still get them for $2.

Chapter 11

Christmas with a Meaning

The convoy arrived at the Forward CP at 1000 hrs. I asked for supply officer Captain Million's tent to inquire about departure of the next Supply chopper. Crow, the driver for the battalion commanding officer, was here also.

"Crow, what are you doing here; there's bad guys trying to zap your butt."

He said our new CO was crazy and wanted him in the jungle with him; even Sgt. Maj. James Rocks went.

Resupply was slated for early afternoon for Charlie Company

All three companies had been finding an equal amount and the three 2nd Brigade battalions had killed quite a few. They had found a dozen base camps, 3,000 pounds of rice, Russian carbines, and a Chinese-made heavy 7.62-mm Russian machine gun. Bravo found a supply depot with a flour mill, rice storage facilities, and livestock. They even found hot chow on the tables at one of the places.

Captain Million thought I stood a better chance finding action by going to Charlie. He told me to grab chow and give a hand later with ice and heavy plastic bags to pack soft drinks with ice for the guys.

I was thrilled helping with this treat. The Viet Cong and North Vietnamese troops were, in most cases, forgotten and completely ignored by their governments, their bodies left unceremoniously rotting in the tropical sun.

We loaded the soda into four plastic bags. Also we packed four 30-gallon plastic tubs of water, one case of grenades, 50 bandoleers of 7.62-mm ammo, and a case of .45-caliber ammo for the Thompsons and Grease Guns.

As soon as a monsoon evaporated, we departed. The LZ was secured by a platoon patrol that arrived before the rest of their company. Guys who recognized me as the reporter who had stories of them in military papers enthusiastically greeted me. I told them Santa had a treat in the green, rubberized plastic bags.

"Soft drinks packed in ice!"

The platoon leader showed me his CP near the edge of the clearing. I strung my hammock, strategically situating my equipment after dusting it off, and walked around the partial perimeter talking with troops preparing defenses. They asked about my leave in the Philippines because they were contemplating going there themselves.

I was astonished how comfortable it felt back in the boonies with the men. I nonchalantly walked about them, asking their condition, how they were maintaining in the jungle, and what they had been doing against the VC.

They were always positive, laughing and joking about what they would do to Charlie if and when they got their hands on him.

The remaining two platoons arrived at this nameless spot we would call "home" for the night. I noticed activity by my hammock, marking the arrival of Charlie Company's CO and his staff. I didn't want to interfere with them establishing camp, so I continued talking with the troops while sipping a Coke.

After the CO finished setting camp, I returned to my hammock. There was sufficient ice in the bags for the staff and me to put into our canteen cups and enjoy ice cubes with water. Elation! Our men temporarily forgot the heat, bugs, danger, and what was becoming increasingly irritating to us—that adverse coverage of the war by media.

This was the first time battalion's top-ranking NCO, Sergeant Major Rocks, spread his poncho in the boonies. He usually was only as far forward as the Forward CP, not in the boonies for an evening perimeter.

While I was discussing the more interesting aspects of my leave with the medic and RTO, I noticed a new soldier making his "hooch" for the night. He was in his early 40, blond, handsome, sharp featured, wearing a three-day beard and dark glasses, smoking a long, thin foreign cigarette rolled inside dark tobacco, and carrying a sexy-looking Swedish K submachine gun.

Charlie's CO, Capt. Richard Tamagini, introduced me to this man: our new battalion commander, Lt. Col. Bill Staples.

We conveyed formalities.

After the colonel learned I always accompanied the troops, I became "Scoop" to him.

Our battalion just received a much-needed infusion of fresh blood that had a remarkable effect on our attitude and performance. He was the type of man whose decisions and judgments were trusted and respected.

The remainder of the week was spent with small-scale platoon-sized patrols. Most of the enemy contacted were small groups of North Vietnamese. Three had been killed in different ambushes with equipment captured from porters carrying it to a combat area. The entire operation was especially successful because no one was shot. The enemy didn't have an opportunity to assemble large forces. He was out there and knew we were also; consequently every unit commander was alert for any mistake the Viet Cong might make. Unfortunately, the COs realized, this was also vice versa.

We didn't find much else. The troops returned the day before Christmas. This mission throughout the enemy's infiltration route from Cambodia into the Iron Triangle had been highly successful. A considerable amount of equipment was captured, yet our stealth had been so meticulous that we weren't fired on once.

Our excellent preparedness was paying off. I attribute it not to our military training as much as our American lifestyle, reveling in violence. When men were boys, they played cops and robbers, cowboys and Indians, in each case glorifying in the killing of others. The advent of TV plunged this violence into a child's eyes each night so killing, and how to do it, became a common and accepted facet of life.

Many of the toys children play with are merely tools of the killing trade so they can better fantasize killing. I was glad I played those games of hide and seek, kill and destroy, when I was a kid. The first time I came under fire, I felt I had been there before.

It was ironic that many protesting the war were the same ones who would later strap a pair of cap guns on their infant son, encourage him to shoot at someone, and exclaim how cute he looked. Considering our advanced preparedness to war, it became evident that the only ones who could defeat us in this conflict would be ourselves.

The convoy crossed the train tracks to our base camp opposite the North Vietnamese refugee Catholic village, Ho Nai. The local Communists had been harassing them, killing farm animals, poisoning the water wells, and pilfering crops. When Battalion moved outside them, the commanding officer and chaplain told their Canadian monk his people would be persecuted no more. American troops would guarantee their safety.

The convoy snaked across the railroad crossing and meandered into the compound of tents. I immediately noticed my "home" was made "standing tall" by the others who never visited the jungles. My dull green Army tent appeared to glow in the afternoon sun.

The pallets had been scrubbed clean, the tent's sides uniformly rolled up with branches inserted along the top edge, simulating mistletoe.

The guys had found a scraggly bush, fuller than most, and erected it in our tent. They fashioned a garland of toilet paper and clumps of medic's cotton around the branches. Empty cans of soft drinks and beer had been punctured and strategically placed in the tree's smattering of branches. Jimmy O'Riley fashioned a star out of green bamboo and managed to secure it to the treetop while strips of aluminum foil sufficed for tinsel.

My tent looked extraordinarily appealing now; I couldn't wait for the convoy to stop and jumped out as the jeep slowed, scrambling home, while trying not to lose my 60 pounds of equipment.

The men procured a 40-watt bulb, socket, and extension cord, which they secured to the treetop behind the star. This would provide satisfactory illumination, considering our two ineffective propane burners.

After I peeled off the muddy boots and walked barefooted on the clean pallets to my cot, I was astonished at the base of the Christmas tree. White cotton medical sheets were placed around the bottom, resembling snow. Piled around were a portion of the hundreds of pounds of Christmas cards, letters, presents, and food from people in the States we didn't know. This display of generosity was astonishing during a time of increasing resistance to the troops.

People were completely oblivious to the gender, race, class, and religion of its recipient, sending mail to "Any GI in Vietnam." There was one universal message: "Good luck, we're thinking of you, thanks for helping out those people, and let God be with and protect you." This was gratifying, citizens remembering G.I.s over Christmas.

Christmas carols played on Armed Forces Radio as I removed my equipment. When *Jingle Bells* began playing, I noticed my foot tapping.

I finished scrubbing my boots and body in our shower. This contraption consisted of a faucet welded into a 50-gallon, atmosphere-heated water drum resting on stilts with no concealing sides.

I hustled through this pleasure to make mess hall before chow closed. The cooks were involved in preparation and oblivious to my presence.

Christmas dinner the next day was special; 40 of the village orphans were our guests.

I returned to my tent with the mess kit to eat while I looked through my mail. I also wanted to stake my claim on the bounty of letters and gifts stacked under our tree from gracious Americans.

"Hope you have an enjoyable Christmas, Ray." I could feel my mother's pain as I read the message in her card. She was happy I had not been injured; yet concerned about the time left.

We instinctively wish a "Merry Christmas" without considering the significance of the words: "happy, joyous, healthy, merry, peace," frequently taken for granted and used as mere salutation. I was living adjacent to a village of people who now had a reason to be happy; we were protecting their freedom of religion.

Mike, our battalion carpenter, and Murphy and Wadsworth the clerks, rotated to the States as I arrived. I shouted good-bye as they disappeared down the dusty camp road with a look of quandary on their faces, wondering if they would ever have jobs as significant as the ones they were leaving and if Mike and Wadsworth would turn gay, if they weren't already.

I met their replacements, Rick and Lansen, when I plopped my equipment in the tent and immediately liked them. First they asked if they could drink beer in the tent and second how easy it was to get laid.

Jimmy O'Riley, Hans, Crow, and I contributed for a case of beer. We would have a welcome aboard party tonight.

I had stories to write, but decided to develop film this afternoon if possible. The Air Force closed on holidays; I would have to wait several days to print.

I arranged for Rick to ride shotgun to the air base and drove the safer route. That is, the nice ride through Tan Heip so he wouldn't be frightened by the desolate and still dangerous back way. Also, this route had nicer girls.

Immediately outside the village, I stopped at a bar with an enclosed patio on the side. We could comfortably sit outside nursing a beer while being entertained by the maidens using tempting persuasion to get us interested.

We could relax isolated without being seen by Brass. When you find the one you like, and after testing and tasting her, the price bargaining process begins.

Rick was shocked when I explained they initially ask only $4.

"Yeah, yeah," he said, "let's grab 'em before they change their minds."

I told him to cool it and let me do the talking.

"No way! Beaucoup money—200 P!" The bartering game began. After I yelled a few Vietnamese words, they knew I was a vet and agreed with 200 P, $2 for something you'd be proud of in your hometown.

Rick didn't last long and wanted to go back for seconds. We didn't have time; I had work at the lab, stuff to buy at the PX, and needed to return before sunset. Also, there would be opportunities later. I didn't want him to become a glutton; I wanted him to savor it.

Rick had a difficult time restraining his enthusiasm when we returned. Sergeant Grassburg returned with the Forward CP convoy also and began indoctrinating his two new clerks. Rick kept trying to explain to Lansen how beautiful the body was on the girl he paid only $2 for without Grassburg catching on. The Sarge never had this situation with Murphy, Wadsworth, and Mike; consequently the ultraconservative Baptist wasn't sure what all this excitement was about.

Hans came into the Personnel tent with three sacks of mail addressed, "TO ANY GI IN VIETNAM." A "don't forget the guy in Vietnam campaign" by people in the States. He divided the mail into groups passed out to companies. There were over 50 well-wishing Christmas greetings for our tent alone. Postmarks into piles reciprocal to each state divided our cards; I received the ones from New England.

Battalion received over 20 boxes of Christmas treats, some from our parents, but most from considerate Americans. The troops enjoyed the letters, cards, greetings, and sweets immensely. Unfortunately we never had time to write, explaining our gratitude. When the tour of duty is only half over and you realize your life is only as long as the second you are alive, it's difficult to think of anything except survival

Contributing to my most meaningful Christmas was a Christmas card we believed was the longest greeting received in Vietnam. S-4 Supply Officer Bill Million's wife organized her Saginaw, Michigan, Civics Class to send a 25-foot scroll with 175 messages and warm words of support from ninth-grade students.

The scroll was passed between the enthusiastic men. We felt these ninth graders were more mature intellectually about Vietnam than older American students protesting in U.S. colleges. The cliché, "Wisdom from the mouths of babes," was appropriate.

The Vietnamese were celebrating their Tet tradition, similar to the Chinese New Year where celebrations were rampant. This country was at war and in no mood to celebrate anything, yet we were surprised to be placed on alert, anticipating an offensive. Many were wishing for it so we could get the VC in the open, en masse, killing more. American troops had to wait two more years for that. Some of the men thought the alert was the Army's intention to keep them around the camp instead of drinking in the village because nothing happened.

Second Brigade remained in base camps for four days, our longest break between operations.

It was the first day Christmas carols were played on the radio, which lasted for three days.

I went to our wash rack, brushed my teeth and splashed off. Silver moonlight poured through a crystalline sky reflecting off the pale tan clay surrounding our base camp, reminiscent of fields of snow.

"Ray." I was brought back to reality. "*Mary Poppins* is playing at Charlie Company in 15 minutes on a sheet between two poles."

Julie Andrews carried me back to my innocent life in Wareham, where I had been an altar boy serving the Christmas midnight mass. Each night at home I slept in a dry bed and my family ate fresh food from plates. A TV played in the living room and we safely walked the streets.

Jimmy O'Riley and I returned to our tent after the movie. Rick and Lansen were laughing about the girls Rick had grabbed that afternoon. I removed myself and walked past the rows of tents to our perimeter. I needed time to meditate, feeling it important for me to be here.

Surprisingly the "whoomp" of a rocket flare didn't startle my thoughts on this silent night. An outpost beyond the perimeter heard movement and investigated with an illuminating flare. It "pooped" its luminous white brilliance, cascading glitter from a teetering parachute drifting toward the sounds. The Star of David directing the Magi to the manger in Bethlehem.

Another flare was fired; the sky quickly returned to its dazzling black. I visualized what I believed as a child: Santa Claus on a sleigh, sailing through the sky behind eight prancing reindeer. I used to stare into the sky in my back yard to see him on his journey to homes of children, though never seeing him because, as my mother reminded me, Santa doesn't come until midnight and I couldn't stay up that late.

A machine gun fired at sounds in the jungle. Red streaks of tracers darted through the darkness, resembling lights of reindeer dancing through the sky.

I still had sleep deficit from the combat operation, so I returned to my tent and crawled into the luxury of a canvas cot surrounded by mosquito nets, falling asleep to *Silent Night* on the radio.

Reveille on Christmas Day was 0600. Since I was attached to Personnel and didn't have to make formation, I stayed in bed another hour. It was a fruitless venture though; the other guys were up for their duties, making their usual commotion.

After morning chow I wrote captions for my photos and stories. A large Christmas dinner was planned later. I could take my material to the 1st Infantry Division Public Information Office in the morning, see Bob Hope's USO show with Anita Bryant, Carol Baker, and Joey Heatherton, and return in time for the meal. This was a paradoxical Christmas: carols playing on the radio, gifts opened and exchanged, cards and letters read aloud, fruitcake in everyone's hand, and the joyous feelings of gratitude, goodwill to all, adoration of God, and peace on Earth—offset by the double alert for a suspected enemy attack during Christmas truce.

When I returned, Sgt. Maj. James Rocks said we had invited 40 children from the Ho Nai orphanage for Christmas dinner, split into groups of 10, one for each of the companies.

Their Canadian monk guided his flock across the tracks at 1300. Several noticed them and ran over to escort them, dividing into groups.

Rick asked me to help escort our group to Headquarters' mess tent.

As the kids timidly followed, it occurred to me they probably had never seen black people before and the only white person in their lives had been their silver-haired monk.

Their bashfulness ceased, however, as soon as they reached the mess. The men completely overwhelmed these kids with affection and gifts in a most heartfelt outpouring of love. In these kids, the men undoubtedly saw their children, their siblings, and even themselves.

Differences in culture disappeared, replaced by a magnificent bliss. The kids loved it. We reminded the men, completely smitten by our guests, that they would be busy in combat soon and would never see the kids again.

The feast was sumptuous: turkey, mashed potatoes and gravy, corn, yams, squash, peas, rolls, butter, salad, cranberry sauce, and pumpkin pie. The men hovered over the kids through each course, attempting to explain these previously unknown dishes. After several mouthfuls, the kids knew they were eating delicious food and needed no further coaching.

The men worried later when a heavy nine-year-old boy digested three helpings and indicated he wanted a fourth. Fung informed the boy he shouldn't feel obligated to continue eating. The boy smiled, nodded, and pushed his plate forward for another.

Later in the afternoon, after more gifts and hugs, the kids became drowsy and had to be returned for a nap. Several hundred men insisted on helping with the task.

The scene was enchanting: sleepy-eyed youngsters carried on shoulders, dozed in arms, and cradled.

The arms of two men held a boy, with a couple of girls chauffeured in the colonel's jeep.

We reached the orphanage; the men realized they would never see these kids again.

The irony was, as these children shook our hands and hugged us, thanking us for the banquet, we felt indebted for their visit and help in forgetting the war. We hoped they would never forget us.

Some of us, we knew, were celebrating our last Christmas. We recognized God had intended this for those never to commemorate this holiday again.

We had been humbled, humbled by the gifts from strangers back home and humbled by the innocence and gratitude of orphans. But, more than anything, humbled by the knowledge that God had handed us the most meaningful Christmas of our lives.

Nine years later the Communists took control of South Vietnam and God died.

Unfortunately the American public had to wait until December 1998 to learn this story when the *Catholic Digest* had the opportunity to print it.

Chapter 12

The Roller Coaster
Ride Begins

One underlying fact kept me going: I knew that I had reached the top of my hill. The end would arrive as long as I remained strong and managed to keep on track.

The expected Tet offensive never materialized. My battalion prepared for another sweep of the Di An-Phu Loi area in the Iron Triangle on December 30.

I experienced that obnoxious old feeling.

As it is on the roller coaster ride, once I reached the top of the first hill, I could view the entire ride ahead and knew what to expect before I arrived. By now I was beginning to see the end of the ride; all I had to do was hang on that long.

The chapel Mike built was dedicated December 26 and I served the first mass for Father Confroy. During an awards ceremony December 29, Maj. Gen. Jonathan O. Seaman, commanding general, 1st Infantry Division, presented a Bronze Star, 30 Purple Hearts, and two Army Commendation Medals. The next day the choppers dropped us off at another of those nameless clearings surrounded by jungle.

My platoon-sized patrol made contact the second day while I was four from point. We came on line, with the remainder of the platoon reassembling to our rear. I could tell by the sound of gunshots that the rifles were pointed up, fired from the trench, and the bullets were spraying the bush above making that innocent "tick, tick" sound hitting the leaves.

I felt the soft camouflaged cover of a tunnel under my hand while we crawled to the left flank. I motioned to it, ripping it off so "Charlie" would know his tunnel had been exposed, hopefully discouraging any idea using it against us. Exposing it would also help the guys behind to be aware of danger.

I could hear the VC excitedly yelling to each other in front.

The man to my right sprang forward. I followed. Four steps later the five of us were in the compound. Three of the men began firing at somebody on the left. The man I was following ran to the right side. I selected running down the middle.

While panting forward in a crouched stance, I saw the outline of a rectangular shape in the grass and stopped by it. The camouflaged cover of a tunnel! "Cook off a grenade," I remembered. "Release the lever, a two count, explodes in two seconds."

I crouched on the side of this entrance flap with my carbine held by its neck and index finger snug against the trigger. "If I opened that flap from the front," I visualized, "I'd be in danger of getting a mouth full of lead." I warily opened the hatch from the side with the grenade hand while easing the muzzle inside as it opened.

When this flap was perpendicular and falling back, I released the grenade lever and began the two-count cook-off.

I glanced across the hole and to my astonishment Major Weeks was cooking off a grenade also. His eyes were wide as beer bottle bottoms while his red handlebar mustache appeared aflame.

I must have looked as terrified as he.

It may sound ridiculous now, retaining military protocol in combat and nonchalantly informed him, "After you, sir."

"Oh, thank you, Pezzoli."

"Crack! Crack!" The two grenades exploded in the tunnel a second after we released them. We didn't bother to stick our heads into the dusty hole to see if we had blown up any VC because there was more to search.

While the perimeter of the camp was being secured, I found eight backpacks belonging to North Vietnamese and searched through for worthwhile mementos before turning the packs into Intelligence.

Men searching the tunnels found blood at the bottom of the shaft Major Weeks and I threw our grenades into. They had two confirmed VC bodies at other locations and "possibles" at three more. None of our guys were hit.

I walked along the five-foot deep trench that circumscribed the perimeter and came to the location opposite where I had been lying and attacking the camp, imagining how it must have felt for the VC defender, firing at me.

I would have felt better in his place because I could see absolutely no protection for me except for a few leaves obstructing the view. I wasn't far from him either, only about five feet. The only reason I was alive is attributed to poor North Vietnamese training.

If he had stuck his head above the trench, aimed, then sprayed his bullets six inches above the ground, I would not be writing now.

The troops were becoming like alarm clocks. Set the dial for sleep, they're unconscious immediately. Set it for radio watch wake up or guard duty and "clang, buzz," immediately conscious.

I wanted to return in a week for stories and photos, so I took a supply chopper to Bien Hoa. I wasn't very dirty yet so the Air Force let me into their lab without suggesting a wash first. I became more proficient processing photos; consequently I finished by noon with sufficient time for the PX before hitching to base camp with a departing jeep.

A shower, hot chow, and iced soft drinks would be rewarding.

Two short stories and captions for four pictures only took two hours. I wanted to get them to Division Headquarters that day so I could hitch to Forward CP in the morning.

Hans had to pick up mail at Headquarters later in the afternoon. Both Rick and Lansen claimed they had finished their work and had to pick up Personnel papers also. The reason they wanted to go was to scope out whorehouses opening there.

We checked out and sampled the product at a number of new places before Headquarters. A place immediately outside the perimeter had nice, very clean young ones, far superior to others we had seen earlier. We made note, planning to stop later.

They looked brand new. A female friend in the States later asked about these women, their thoughts, feelings, emotions, and goals.

"We received instant pleasure, enjoying them immensely because tomorrow we might be dead," I told her.

We rationalized we were helping them financially, providing a standard and quality of life they otherwise would have difficulty obtaining.

On our return, Lansen and I went in first. We grabbed the two we had negotiated with earlier who invited us into adjacent rooms separated by low tin walls. The ladies told us MPs were busting people and suggested we keep the jeep away; the other two drove off.

The girl I was with was the most attractive Vietnamese woman I had seen. She was tiny with the delicate features of a porcelain figurine. A delicacy to be savored, not guzzled like the heathens we were. I lay on the straw mat with her tiny body wrapped in my arms after my sex act, which lasted the typical five minutes, relishing this delicacy. Rick and Hans returned with the jeep and banged on the tin walls, demanding we hurry so they could get their turns before the MPs came. Lansen and I didn't flinch, lying there totally absorbed with our women.

"Bang, clunk, rumble." The walls of my room began to shake. Rick and the girl he wanted slid over the wall to get inside. I gallantly shielded my lady as she delicately held her silk pants in front to cover her private parts.

There was additional commotion in the partition next to mine. Hans and his woman just did the same to Lansen's, demanding their time also. Lansen and I put our clothes on and drove away for five minutes while the other two did their thing.

"This war is really hell, isn't it," laughed Lansen, driving down the dusty road to a bar and a beer.

I spent the night at the base camp. The following morning I went to Brigade Headquarters and hitched a ride with a convoy of Civic Action vehicles departing for our Forward CP. This program was an unheralded area of goodwill which the news media unfortunately failed to mention; human-interest activities in Vietnam weren't newsworthy.

My battalion constructed a two-classroom schoolhouse and furniture for over 100 students in a local village. We sponsored an orphanage also and assisted them in devising a balanced diet.

The artillery unit had constructed numerous latrines. Engineers were rebuilding roads and clearing hundreds of acres of land to create a "home-town" for refugees from Communist terror.

I rode with the Medical Battalion conducting medical patrols in many of the isolated, unsecured areas along our route where "Charlie's" threat was always prevalent. Many times, during prior patrols, medics were unescorted by infantrymen; the only personnel in these visits were the medic, driver, and a Vietnamese interpreter. By the end of our year, Brigade had administered over 15,000 treatments.

By the time most rotated to the States or were discharged, over 100 tons of relief commodities had been passed out to refugees and orphans. Our convoy stopped near our sweep, assisting a man the surgeons trained with first-echelon medical practices. Also, they brought more medical supplies. Of course our media never told you about this, but the souls in the Vietnam Wall do.

I arrived at CP about noon and noticed excitement at the Supply tent—Remington 12-gauge pump shotguns. Each squad would have one; the weapon could fire seven rounds of 00 buck in seven seconds. The soldier carried 20 rounds in crossed bandoleers, resembling a Mexican bandito. Great holes could be blown in the jungle, et al, by holding the trigger back and sliding the pump rapidly.

Also the M-79 grenade launchers received new canister rounds capable of saturating an area with deadly sprays of pellets.

Hunting the VC with a 12-gauge pump, bandoleer of ammo, and God.

A chopper arrived to deliver the new weapons. I took the flight; the first stop, my old company, Bravo. The men acted like kids at Christmas as they received their new weapons. The search and destroy continued immediately after the new toys were passed out.

I tagged along with the point. Some seasoned VC cadre had noticed the chopper delivery and set up an ambush. They had not received AK-47s from the North yet. When they saw Bravo's point, they fired bolt-action 7.62-mm Chinese carbines. The point returned fire, M-14 on full, spraying a magazine of 20 rounds into them. They stopped firing and ducked.

The jungle wasn't thick as normal; we could tell exactly where the VC were. Initially, my ears told my eyes their location. My eyes saw flashes and smoke, telling my hand where to point my rifle.

A tree stood in front of me behind a two-foot mound, affording me a perfect view and protection. I told the two men in front I had my rifle on the VC. "You're covered, run forward." This trust of me was incredible. They believed with confidence that if they risked their lives, they were sure I could protect them.

I fired the 20-round magazine on full, pinning the VC on the left while the two men maneuvered forward. When they were clear of vines and branches, each tossed a cooked-off grenade.

The platoon sergeant ran behind my tree and asked if I got any. Maybe; they weren't firing any more. If they were wounded, I was sure the guys finished them off with grenades.

We heard several M-14 shots, then a spurt of auto M-14 fire on the right. I stayed behind the tree while the sergeant crept ahead, analyzing the situation.

The firing stopped.

Bushes crashed to my left; I was surprised to see my shy friend from Cam Ranh Bay, Harry Kerry, burst out. Emerging from this dense thicket was Harry, "Connie," that boyish, innocent, wholesome-looking all-American type lad with such devotion for his girl he placed her portrait on a sandbag at his foxhole.

First I noticed his stripes—he was now sergeant—and then I saw the bolt-action rifle he had taken from the VC he had just killed. Finally and most shocking, I saw the hard face of a man who had just killed someone. That upright, all-American boy was gone.

"Harry, you OK?"

His eyes shot directly through my heart; not saying a word, he just glared at me with the look I will never forget. "If looks could kill." Rephrased it was, "Looks of someone who just killed." He was a killer now, completely unrecognizable as the Harry I used to know. His soul had been captured.

After the firing stopped the troops began the normal sequence of events: reload the weapon, clean the breach, take a leak, and light a cigarette.

We anticipated more VC to arrive, answering our shooting. Four defensive ambush sites were established for naught. Bravo continued patrolling another three days but didn't make contact. On the third afternoon, Major Weeks said he was accompanying the chopper to Alpha Company which had seen indications of a large force.

I joined him.

Chapter 13

The Look from the Other Side of the Fence

"What's going on, Roland?" Alpha's CO, Captain Barrell, asked Major Weeks in his usual relaxed, refreshing manner, resembling James Coburn: sandy blond, lanky, and easygoing, speaking with a sharp, pointed, crisp dialogue.

Division Intelligence reported activity by a stream crossing ahead. Alpha would spend the night there with several LPs.

The men with shotguns were anxious to try them; unfortunately they hadn't made contact yet. I told them about my firefight with Bravo and massive firepower from the guy with his pump, blowing holes into the jungle and everything else. In the afternoon the point came to our objective stream inside steep banks, with fortifications near its crest. Two squads came on line to cover him inching down the perpendicular slope, climbing hand over hand down the shrub studded walls, struggling two steps up and back slide one.

The crest of the ridge was nude of vegetation except for stumps with three-foot anthills throughout its length. It was pockmarked with trenches and tunnels; one leading to a five-foot by 10-foot rectangle carved four feet into the clay. A hole was dug into the comer with a pot hanging over still smoldering teak. The VC had elected not to stay and fight.

Captain Barrell established night perimeter here because of its defensives and the stream of fast-running clear water. I found a perfect spot on the crest where a VC slept between a tree stump and two boulders. I could hang my hammock between a tree and narrow rock. Also, the location had steps forged into its wall leading to the stream where I could bathe in cool water. My hooch would be in the exact place a VC had dwelled earlier.

The CO told me 3rd Platoon was leaving for the LP.

I just finished establishing my defenses and was heating up C rations stuffed with onion and Tabasco over the enemy's smoldering campfire. This patrol would follow the trail along the crest to its intersection with another stream, a half mile away. This sounded easy, but I had acclimated here and didn't care for the concept of lying out there tonight. Also, I didn't think they would find any action either, feeling our chances were better at the VC camp where we might intercept residents returning.

I apologized but would not be able to take photos at night. If they found anything, I would get photos and stories in the morning.

Fifteen minutes later I finished my beef stew, washed it down with fresh, cool stream water, untied the laces in my boots, and stretched my feet forward as I snuggled against a moss-covered tree, preparing to catnap.

Two 20-mm Gatling cannon mounted on a jet make the unique "VROOO-MM" as they fire 750 rounds per minute, clattering like a string of firecrackers during contacting the ground. A 500-pound conventional bomb "CRACKS" with such velocity upon detonation that its shock wave is felt past the blast, while a 300-pound napalm bomb makes an innocuous "splashing" sound before the kerosene jelly erupts into a bright boiling orange fireball.

We heard these sounds from the same direction the patrol had gone 15 minutes earlier; our planes were bombing them!

The F-4D Phantom strikes like a bolt of lightning—you don't see or hear it.

The platoon patrol had yet to assume the character of men in combat as it departed: men were finishing C rations, involved in conversations, and most bunched together with their weapons casually held.

Platoon Sergeant Augette "Pappy" Canon cautioned them to button it up, we were still in "Charlie's" back yard, and not leave a trail of C ration cans.

Birds were busily chirping while a monkey screeched his approval. A recent shower cooled and consecrated the steamy jungle. This wide trail displayed signs of intensive travel. The point man stopped to examine rice along the side.

The simultaneous "VROOO-MM" of cannon and their chattering explosions startled the men to freeze in their tracks. The diving Phantom sat on its tail, blasting out of sight on its afterburner. The inconceivable fact our plane blasted them never occurred until noticing another begin an identical run.

"That's 3rd Platoon," Capt. Barrell screamed. "They're bombing our platoon!"

"Call the CP, cancel that air strike," he directed RTO Day.

"Mount up, we've got to help them."

This seemed foolhardy to me. The planes were still attacking; I doubted we could do anything when we arrived.

The men threw their equipment together and, oblivious to danger from enemy troops, dashed up the trail toward the patrol and screeching jets.

They released their ordinance and another pass was made before the strike terminated.

A squad attempted to escape by ducking off the trail into the jungle. The platoon leader, 2nd Lt. A.J. Peterson, hollered to his men, encouraging them to join in a nearby stream with deep sides where he "popped" two smoke grenades. Both jets had just launched their strafing run as the Air Force forward observer, flying overhead with his light observation aircraft, noticed smoke from these two grenades.

The squad that escaped off the trail ran into an impasse of entangled vines and sharp-pointed green bamboo pricks. Twenty-mm cannon rounds exploded about them, fortunately hitting no one.

The rest of the patrol had made it to the ostensible protection of the stream meandering beneath a maze of vines and dense bushes. Strike #2 seemed wide. Another smoke grenade was released, hopefully indicating "friendlies" below. RTO couldn't contact Brigade Headquarters to abort the strike because the perpendicular stream banks blocked his signal.

The Air Force FO saw the smoke grenade, this time a yellow, and mistook it as a VC trick simulating Americans. He swung the jets around for a strike at the yellow mark rising from the jungle canopy below.

The separated squad tangled in the undergrowth began hacking out of the maze with machetes.

Each plane began its pass. The first released two napalm bombs, which the troops cringing near the top of the stream bank could see flipping overhead like two fat cigars tumbling in slow motion. They hit the treetops; clear kerosene jelly spewed out before erupting into a boiling fireball, completely engulfing the jungle. The men ducked below the bank to avoid its intense heat.

The other bomb splattered into dense undergrowth, halted, ruptured, sprayed, and ignited. The men snared by vines were speckled by blazing jelly clinging to their bodies like fiery glue, while their fifth was completely incinerated by the primary fireball.

Sgt. Canon climbed up the slick, shrub-lined stream bank, searching for his missing squad. The men on top thought the blazing inferno had engulfed them. Canon told platoon leader Peterson that he was going over the top into the blazing jungle looking for them.

Survival was of primary importance; nobody tried to rationalize why our planes were attacking.

Passing a bomb crater made by the air strike. Note how all the vegetation was literally blown away.

The lush, green, damp jungle had quickly absorbed the napalm, leaving only the glob halted by the wall of dense vegetation intensely raging. While Sgt. Canon ported himself over smoldering embers, Lt. Peterson called directions.

A blinding flash of super-hot white almost completely surrounded Canon, who was shielded by teak trees. He was so close to one of the two exploding 500-lb. bombs that he couldn't hear the explosion. The teak absorbed the energy meant for him.

Unfortunately for Lt. Peterson, a piece of shrapnel sliced his forehead open like a knife through soft butter.

This blast blew away every growth of jungle vegetation—a giant vacuum, sucking up everything except the giant teaks. Canon ran into the smoldering bomb crater, positioning himself, arms overhead, right hand clasping the left wrist—the signal to halt.

Captain Barrell asked RTO Day if he had made contact yet.

Billy stopped and radioed Brigade again to stop the strike. He shouted forward to Barrell, saying there was interference. Moments later contact was made and the strike terminated.

The normally damp, sweet smell of jungle now smelled like a burning newspaper extinguished with water.

As we ran down the trail to the victim platoon, everyone was numbed, like watching an awful TV program and unable to switch the channel.

Barrell reached the fringe of the bombing and found the jungle completely void of vegetation.

The column slowed to a crawl to circumvent shrubbery blasted across the trail. I heard a "cracking" and stopped to see its source. The largest teak in the world made that noise; I skeptically looked at it. The "cracking" progressed to a tearing "roar." The tree, weakened by a bomb blast, fell directly toward me!

This was another bad dream; a massive teak tree was falling directly at me. I sprinted down the trail to escape from being pulverized, feeling the breeze as it thundered past me, pounding the ground. Fortunately no one was injured.

A few feet ahead, a limb screeched across the top of my helmet and some scratchy thing fell inside my collar. My intuition cautioned anxiety as I reached inside my shirt removing the prickly twig-feeling thing.

"Zap!" I was stung. A scorpion fell inside my shirt and was aggravated by my hand. I flattened my fatigue shirt against the bottom of my neck, sliding it back and forth, squashing that thorny thing. I undid my pistol belt, shook my collar, and a dead squashed scorpion dropped out.

The trail ahead had been scorched by napalm with three men of the burned men lying on the side. They had fist-sized holes burned through their equipment and fatigues with splotches of skin burned away. Nobody was crying in pain, yet they were dazed.

They pointed to the man entangled in the maze; everything was obliterated by napalm. The trapped man was burned black and crispy, most of his uniform and equipment dust. The only things left were remnants of a pistol belt, backpack, and harness. The napalm burned only this 20-square-foot area; the density of the jungle prohibited it from sliding, as it would in the open. Everything was obliterated.

While a medic began treating the burned soldiers, the body of the smoking dead man mesmerized me. Five minutes earlier he was an alive and recognizable human; now he was burned crisp like a piece of toast.

I hurriedly removed myself from his sickening sweet smell and hurried forward, accompanying Captain Barrell. Bombs incinerated chunks of jungle with black smoke still spiraling from craters.

A shout was made to Captain Barrell from a smoking bomb crater in this pockmarked area, exemplary of the moon; Sergeant Canon struggled out.

"They kept on comin' sir, kept on comin'. I signaled them but they kept on comin'," pleaded the man with saucer-sized eyes who watched certain death from 20-mm cannon fired at him.

Pappy stood in the crater, hoping the FO would notice Americans being bombed. He had been mistaken as the enemy and experienced the first pass of the second strike aimed directly at him. He stood his ground with both hands clasped over his head, signaling to abort. This courageous sergeant didn't flinch while both jets approached with their Gatling cannons spitting, dropping twin 500 pounders.

"You did your best, soldier," Captain Barrell said putting his arm around the frantic sergeant, attempting to soothe him.

"Medic, look at Pappy; give him something."

Calls came from the bank of the nearby stream. Two men propped up platoon leader Lt. Peterson at the crest of its bank, his forehead bleeding profusely.

A medic wrapped the wound. Peterson's helmet absorbed a deadly fragment of shrapnel while a sliver ricocheted off his forehead.

You might say God was looking after the platoon because only one was killed. I know He was watching me; it was merely by the roll of the dice I decided against joining them.

The Medevac chopper could not land in the jungle. The wounded were lifted through trees, winched to a hovering chopper above, strapped to a gurney like a papoose. This was the first time this method of evacuation had been utilized, initiating an evacuation method saving the lives of many soldiers in the future.

The men who survived the napalm had million-dollar wounds, allowing them to recover in the U.S. The platoon leader's forehead was split open; later the large scar disappeared. The Air Force FO needed a medical discharge, becoming despondent after fully comprehending his target had been G.I.s in the jungle—signaling to halt.

Who ever said war was fun? Part of this legend is on the Wall; this is the first time America's public will be aware of his death due to "friendlies."

Alpha Company spent the night in that hell of an area after the body and the wounded had been removed.

The following morning we patrolled to a clearing where choppers took the remainder of Alpha to the Forward CP for showers, hot chow, mail, fresh clothes, and 24 hours of rest. Father Confroy offered spiritual comfort to all.

I boarded a Supply lift to Charlie Company the next morning. The troops wanted to know details about the strike—I didn't feel like discussing it.

Me (foreground) serving mass with Father Confroy at a Forward CP.

We made contact the third day. Two carbines shot at the first two men, semi-automatic. The G.I.s returned a heavy base of fire holding the attention of the enemy, while the rest of their squad slipped around the right flank. I followed.

A rattling of outgoing rounds erupted when we burst into the camp; fortunately no one was hit. Six men ahead of me leaped over the perimeter trench, firing from either side of the camp while I skittered down the center.

A dozen backpacks belonging to North Vietnamese were standing in the rear. I crouched behind a tree by them securing this end until more men arrived. A few more short M-14 bursts finished off the remaining enemy.

First come, first serve—the souvenir rule.

I searched a pack and noticed a troop had joined in the treasure hunt.

"Anything good?" he asked.

"Nah, nothing yet, just some clothes."

I struck it rich with the next pack. A piece of red cloth was inside neatly folded. It was exactly what I suspected after opening it in the privacy of a bush: a homemade Russian flag. Also inside was a delicately painted tea set that appeared antique. This must have belonged to a high-ranking North Viet.

The guy next to me found a paper cylinder, eight inches by two, packed with hash. This helped to confirm our suspicions many VC were stoned, necessary to live their torturous existence.

In another pack I found two pairs of black silk pajamas I could give the guys at the Photo Lab; I always strove to show them my appreciation. Unfortunately, these were the only supplies we recovered besides two bodies next to a trail of blood leading beyond the camp through a tunnel.

The next day a chopper flew me to Big Red One headquarters where I hitched a ride to the photo lab before returning to my base camp.

The two specialist fours were thrilled with VC PJs. They slipped into them and ran about the shop, startling people in this top-secret facility, never considering how ridiculous they looked with pant legs eight inches short.

Martin received the tea set: "This is too nice—you keep it."

I told him I didn't need it, flourishing the Russian flag.

After I finished my photos, I stopped at the PX for a hamburger, cold soda, and carton of Winstons.

Staff at my base camp wanted details about the air strike's effect on the men; I had a difficult time expressing myself.

They told me that Military Air Command/Vietnam (MAC-V) designated that area for an air strike because of recent activity. Someone had slipped up and not coordinated with the Army first. It was an unfortunate coincidence that troops were passing by at the precise moment of the air strike.

I showered, shaved, changed my clothes, cleaned my equipment, woofed hot chow, quaffed a few cold beers, wrote stories (nothing about the air strike), captions for my pictures, radio watch that evening, and finally received a good night's rest in a sleeping bag, on my cot, inside a mosquito net using my flak jacket as pillow.

I spent half the day looking for a lift to the troops. In mid afternoon, I discovered a convoy to the Forward Command Post where I spent the night in Headquarters tent.

Jimmy O'Riley told me a chopper was scheduled for supply to Bravo in the morning. He also said we would be getting automatic M-16 rifles when the troops returned to Ho Nai. He had seen crates at 1st Division Supply. We would finally be ridding ourselves of World War II weapons for something more 21st century.

Bravo had discovered enemy equipment the day before I arrived. It was evacuated along with two men with infected cuts on their hands.

Bravo questioned me about the air strike. I changed the topic to something more positive, about the equipment recovered from North Viets and thrilling them about the new M-16s.

Two days later we established the CP in a field. I tied my hammock between two bushes and prepared to heat C rations before nightfall.

There was commotion behind, sounds seldom heard unless there was a problem. I grabbed my rifle and pistol belt and ran back to the tree line to investigate. Two men had killed a boa constrictor by hacking its head off with an entrenching tool.

"Let's eat it!"

I looked for dry branches while the men finished cutting the head off with a machete. They tied the tail around a skinny tree, cut a circle around the skin at the base of the tie, and gradually pulled the skin back. I was astonished how easily it came off without ripping.

"Ya got to skin 'im when 'e's still warm."

I found a tree split by lightning, ideal firewood because leaves kept a splintered section dry from daily rains.

Toilet paper was used to ignite it; in 15 minutes we had a crackling fire. The snake was strung along a spit, rotated above the flame, and liberally doused with Tabasco. It wasn't long before troops stopped by, investigating the delicious aroma. Bravo's CO, Captain Richards, checked out the commotion. He joked, saying he was concerned it smelled so good it might attract hungry VC.

The bouquet soon attracted many of the men from the perimeter. Everyone hacked off a chunk, decimating the eight-foot snake in short time.

Two days later, January 24, Bravo was lifted back to base camp.

Chapter 14

Getting the Tools of War

During two and a half years in the Army I became accustomed to used equipment from World War II and Korea. We had heard about the M-16 in the States but never dreamed our units would receive any, especially out of crates.

The jungle troops were issued M-16s if their slot called for a rifle. The weapon was distributed the day after we returned with troops excited like teenagers receiving sports cars for graduation. Each man went to the Supply tent, picked his rifle out of a crate, posted the serial number, and returned to camp for indoctrination. It felt natural, almost literally melting into our hands like a piece of chocolate.

The M-16, later called "the black rifle" by the VC, fired a .223-mm magnum round five times longer than its diameter. The instructor warned the round was so light, it could be easily deflected by a twig from its target. Conversely, it had five more rounds going toward the target in the first second the trigger was pulled auto than other rifles. Also, when the round hit, as we would graphically see later, it tumbled end over end, ripping a one-inch-wide swath.

The rifle was half the weight of the M-14 and, almost as equally important, was one-third the length. The ammo was lighter; consequently we carried more with less effort.

The biggest problem was firing bursts too long; the excessive heat might cause the barrel to warp. The M-16's incredibly fast rate of fire, six rounds per trigger squeeze, demanded constant maintenance for the close tolerance of the breech. It was suggested in development that the chamber be chromed, but President Kennedy's Whiz Kids discouraged it to keep production costs at a minimum. Consequently, every time the rifle fired, the breech had to be immediately swabbed with an oiled shaving brush, facilitating the fine tolerance between breach and bolt.

The VC soon called it "the black rifle," that wonderful M-16.

The Vietnamese Army Basic Training Camp near us allowed Battalion to set battle site zero on the rifles.

Test firing this new weapon was like driving a new Ferrari. Cautiously back out of the parking lot at the dealership. Drive slowly to get acquainted; outside the city come the back roads. Anticipation is titillating. There are no cars and the road is blessed with banked corners. The driver slams the accelerator to the floor and is united with the gods.

Touch the trigger, once, then again and 12 lethal rounds are released in two seconds. It doesn't kick or climb, merely exhibits a controllable shudder. The end of the barrel wiggles, further scattering bullets. The main disadvantage the troops discovered was that they couldn't see the target after a few bursts. Smoke from the rapid rounds obscured the target, making it impossible to see if it had been hit.

To eliminate the problem, a burst was fired and the muzzle pulled out of the line of sight. This caused suction, dragging the smoke away, so we could see the target.

The firepower from our new rifles completely destroyed the Vietnamese rifle range. They watched and smiled, enviously saying, "H-m-m, velly good gun, numba ten-thou!" Our engineers rebuilt their range.

Woods, the 1st Bn, 16th Inf PIO, took his first and last combat photo while squeezed between a machine gun team assault and the bad guys.

The brigade information officer, Lt. Angle, inquired about the status of my work in the jungles accompanying the troops.

I told him I was almost in the air strike. He cautioned he didn't want to lose me also.

Specialist Woods reported for the 2nd Battalion, 16th Infantry. He was a much more lucid writer than I, but he never accompanied troops in the boonies and consequently never had action photos in military papers. Each issue constantly had combat photos of my battalion. His envious CO commanded him to accompany the men for "good action photos."

Wilson had never ventured into the boonies and had absolutely no combat savvy. Somehow, while accompanying a patrol, he found himself sandwiched between a machine gun crew assaulting VC entrenched on the other side of a field. Suffice it to say, he got excellent combat pictures but they were his last; he got zapped doing it. The wounds were sufficient for him to be flown to the U.S. to recover and be discharged.

Sergeant Grassburg offered me an experimental backpack called a rucksack. The Army was testing its effectiveness with line personnel in infantry units. These packs weren't fastened to pistol belts as regular issue backpacks. If a rucksack became hung up on a vine, or had to be taken off prior to entering a narrow trench or tunnel, fording a stream, or climbing a tree, it could be easily removed by popping straps off the shoulders. This allowed exclusive mobility with only ammo pouches, grenades, bayonet, and canteens hanging from the pistol belt.

This pack also carried the weight higher on the shoulders, was lighter, and had a greater payload.

Three days of C rations was 27 cans, all bulky items to store. Men stuffed cans and onions in socks, tying them on top their backpack harnesses.

The medics had light green cloth for wrapping wounds. Troops began wrapping them around their necks like a scarf, keeping scorpions and leeches from sliding inside. It also made an excellent face cloth and towel for the streams.

The tunnels we encountered presented a problem until Army Research developed a few answers: C-4 plastic explosives, tear gas and concussion grenades, and repelling lines.

I reviewed my pictures taken when we arrived eight months prior and compared them to recent ones, noticing a change in our physical appearance because of new equipment. Subtler was our psychological attitude. Most had been involved in jungle operations and experienced danger, resulting in an indifferent, almost invincible attitude. Bombs, bullets, grenades, and traps used to snuff their lives had failed. The natural elements were nearly as critical: rains, swamps, mosquitoes, flies, scorpions, leeches, red ants, and snakes. So many life-threatening situations prevailed that if the soldier was alive after this, it meant more than simple luck or fortune. God was on his side. When a soldier imagines he is invincible, he is finally on the threshold of being combat ready.

Saigon Harbor was impractical for war. It was on a river delta, 50 miles inside the South China Sea. The port couldn't handle all the equipment. Also, the VC began paddling out of mangrove swamps of the Rung Sat Special Zone at night, attaching mines to freighters.

Vung Tau was on the coast, north of the Saigon River Delta, with ample space for docking and unloading. Supply depot facilities were being constructed at Long Binh next to Brigade at Tan Heip. This would be an ideal location for a depot because it was at the end of Highway #1. This expressway stretched 17 miles from Saigon and free from VC activity. Highway #15 connected Long Binh to Vung Tau only 17 miles away; unfortunately it was only two narrow lanes and the VC were active.

Brigade would eventually move base camps halfway up #15 to Vung Tau, securing it.

The next mission was "Operation Mallet" scheduled to be in the Iron Triangle. It was also designed to keep the VC off balance, find out where their camps were, and destroy them so the infiltrating North Vietnamese would not have bases.

I flew to the operation with Bravo; the men gleefully exclaiming they were anxious to try their new toys. The main complaint from many was our units were still too large and ponderous. The American Army had always depended on size and depth, rather then stealth and flexibility; our units were too cumbersome for guerrilla warfare. The men said they were confident of their ability and should be broken into smaller, more mobile units. I began to sweat at 0600 hours when the sun first shone. By the time we arrived at the LZ at 0700, I was jungle ready, clothes drenched. The blast of chopper blades during our flight did nothing to cool me off.

The infantrymen proudly displayed their new toys to door gunners, inviting them to the jungle; couldn't find volunteers. Most of the service people in Vietnam were in constant danger, some more often than others; absolutely no one, except us, cared to venture into the jungle and remain overnight.

Four days passed with no enemy, only two small, smelly camps.

Brigade began receiving a flood of replacements. Most were younger than we, 18 and 19, and immature, looking and acting like kids. The new "cruits" were escorted through overrun camps, familiarized with and prepared for what to expect each time a camp was attacked.

I scratched my hooch next to the CO and his staff the fifth night out. The CO told me the point squad was ambush on both sides of the trail and wondering if I cared to join them. The sky was twilight, rapidly enveloped by night; also, too late to move my camp. Again I was feeling run down and tired, weak from either insufficient sleep, the deficiency in calories due to eliminating rations to lessen my load, or the nine months of constant pressure; most likely it was a combination of all.

At sunrise the next day, everybody broke camp, their objective a clearing half a day away. There was no schedule for this mission, consequently the troops casually broke camp. I planned on joining the point squad but got into a conversation with the RTO.

The point squad had two new men who were excited with the new method preparing heated cans of chow with onion and Tabasco Sauce. Instead of heating the rations inside the concealment of jungle, they sat on their steel pots at the edge of the trail, heating in a C ration can stove.

Six North Vietnamese soldiers rounded the corner on bikes and almost knocked them off the helmets. The startled enemy jumped off and ran into the jungle. The new men were stunned; by the time they regained their composure, found their rifles, aimed, and began firing, their targets had disappeared. Regardless, they continued to spray lead into the jungle. Fortunately no one was in their line of fire.

Initially I ran toward the shooting but wisely returned to the CP. The indiscriminate fire from new troops showed no preference. Five of the enemy found their way back to the trail and continued running the opposite direction. The sixth floundered about the jungle, crashed through the bush, and busted out in front of an infantryman with a new M-16. One second and six bullets later we had another KIA.

The commanding officer didn't want to remain here since announcing our presence. He moved the company on file into the jungle, searching adjacent to the trail, thinking we might find a camp belonging to the intercepted enemy.

The North Vietnamese had dropped their bikes, crammed with supplies, which had to be evacuated for Intelligence. This might offer clues to their buildup in the Iron Triangle.

There weren't any clearings large enough to accommodate a chopper LZ. Six new arrivals were assigned to push a captured bike along the trail while the remainder of the company swept the jungle. SSgt. Ernest Taylor was in charge of the 'cruits. I joined them because walking the dirt road was easier than the half-crouch, half-crawl, pull and tug I would do in the jungle.

Sergeant Taylor cautioned the men several times to stop bunching up and whispering. During their first time in combat, they acted appropriately.

These enemy soldiers had prearranged plans to reassemble 200 meters to the rear if and when they made contact. They weren't aware of the size of our force, thinking it a patrol because they saw only two. They recognized Americans, but didn't recognize the gun firing because they had never heard anything fire as rapidly before.

They were surprised also because Americans weren't supposed to be here. Badly needed medical and combat supplies were strapped to the bikes; recovery was compulsory.

These Commies reassembled in the small clearing they passed earlier, immediately before the road traced over a rise. They didn't know what happened to their sixth comrade, assumed him dead, and proceeded to set an ambush here.

Each had his weapon, a few hand grenades, and two rocket-propelled grenades. They lay waiting in five different spots on the backside of the rise, creating deadly crossfire taught in their minimal training.

The green troops with bikes, Sergeant Taylor, and I approached them on the trail. They assumed we were the patrol that ambushed them earlier.

Two of the Communists waited at the bottom of the crest of the trail, each with a rocket grenade, waiting for us to come into range. The moment they saw the top of the helmets of the first three men reach the crest, they hastily fired both rockets, which signaled the others to commence firing.

Sergeant Taylor just separated the two leading men again when they reached the top. I was next to the third man with the remaining two directly behind.

I heard two explosions, saw two brilliant white flashes, and watched one of the men spin backward and slowly crumble to the ground, extending his arm to break his fall. The other buckled forward like a fighter receiving a blow to the abdomen, slowly staggering to the side and faced Sergeant Taylor who held him as he collapsed.

In that fraction of a second, three rifles began firing. I lunged to the right of the trail toward the adjacent trench. These trenches are convenient places for mines with trip wires. I swept my hand inside the trench for wires as I fell in.

The man with a bike behind me flopped into the trench by my side.

During an ambush, you must instantly hit the ground; next you defend yourself. When firing back, do so as quickly and accurately as possible. If you don't how where the enemy is, or if you're not in a secure location, find cover. I had cover from my trench and was trying to determine, from the shots, exactly where my targets were. I stuck my head up and was prepared to return fire directly.

Sergeant Taylor helped both wounded below the crest. I glanced at the trooper next to me with both hands on top of his helmet crying, "They shot Johnny, they shot Johnny!"

I banged the top of his helmet, "I don't care about Johnny. I care about myself and I want to live. Keep your eyes open and watch the flank!"

He cried more.

I asked God why I should be here with this replacement.

He continued squawking about his pal getting zapped.

Captain Richards put a platoon on line laying down a base of fire. G.I. grenades exploded on the enemy at the bottom of the hill. A trooper with an M-79 was called to the right flank. He popped a round that exploded in the trees and sprayed shrapnel above the trail, killing the two men who shot grenades.

There was so much firing, I couldn't keep track of who was what; wisely I kept my head inside and below the trench.

I glanced behind and saw Sergeant Jefferson's squad run out of the jungle, cross the trail, and lope into the trees on top of a small hill to my left. They were being fired at the entire time; fortunately nobody was hit.

Each found the cover of a tree and sighted on their targets still firing at them. A five-second burst of energy from their 12-gauge, M-79, M-16, and auto M-14 immediately curtailed the remaining enemy fire.

"The enemy is such a poor shot; too bad for him," I thought as I comprehended this situation from my ditch while lighting a cigarette.

The small clearing the VC used wasn't the one we planned on using as LZ, yet the CO decided to use it for evacuating the two wounded. I felt it time to leave because I hadn't submitted any news material for two weeks. We left the enemy bodies to rot.

I arrived at base camp an hour before sunset. Headquarters mess was still open; the hot chow lacked the symphony of fine tastes I formerly associated with eating. The guys in my tent had iced beer. The water in the 50-gallon barrel was still at the day's temperature, dispensing a comfortable shower. Rick and Lansen claimed they found another new whorehouse with the nicest women in the entire country, and that I could have first radio watch to allow a solid night's sleep later. They were buttering me up so I would choose one or all to accompany me during my visit to the Air Force photo lab the next day.

In the morning I wrote three articles and drove HQ 1 to Bien Hoa. Sarge would not let Rick and Lansen go because they had work to complete; I had a Commo man as shotgun. I left him at a bar to wait until I finished. Unfortunately I arrived too late to have lunch with the Air Force and was stuck with having to buy a stale sandwich and another carton of Winstons at the PX. I was smoking three, sometimes four packs a day now. I had one lit for almost every minute of daylight. Another bonus of being back at camp was I could smoke at night in the tent. Every photo I have of myself shows me with a Winston between two fingers.

They were a crutch for me. I believe they helped keep my sanity, not knowing which I liked better, the cigarettes or M-16.

Later that afternoon Hans returned from a mail pick-up at Division. His truck was muddy and had to be washed before he delivered to the CP the next day. He asked me to be shotgun. The water point was Brigade Headquarters, next to the supply depot of Long Binh, the village of Tan Heip, and a cement bridge adjacent to the Widow's Village. I didn't feel like making the 10-minute drive in the day's 130° heat, but was persuaded by the promise of a few iced brews. Beer cooler and weapons loaded, we headed to the stream.

Several men were washing their vehicles when we drove down the bank to the chugging water pump. I reminded Hans I was "shotgun," not "car wash," lit another Winston, sat on a rock under a tree at the bank, cracked open a cold brew, and watched.

Several Vietnamese women were there with reed baskets supported from a shouldered bamboo spit, selling local beer. One approached me; she was about 28 and looked simple in typical peasant garb of dark silk trousers and light fabric jersey top with the traditional large straw circular hat. Regardless that I was drinking a cold Bud just yanked out of the cooler, she tried to sell me one of her warm local beers. I shooed her away.

Five minutes later she walked to me again. This time she squatted down, looked directly into my eyes, leaned closer, and whispered, "You buy me Salem," which meant, "Go to the PX at Brigade next door and get her a pack of Salems" the Vietnamese favorite.

"Nah, I don't want to buy you anything, just get out of here now, di-di-mau!" We had to be cautious of any Vietnamese man, woman, or kid who initiated goodwill; the VC had zapped some of the guys lately under that gesture.

"You buy me Salem," she waved $2 in front of my face.

"No! I said I'm not going to buy you anything," I said now slightly annoyed.

"Here, you buy me Salem, you sleep with me. Come, me show you chop-chop," she said as she walked to the stream away from the water point.

Now she began to talk my language.

My mind began racing: "Is she setting me for an ambush, does she have chow (chop-chop) for me, does she need to get away from the 'chugging' water pump sound to work out a deal on black marketing Salems?"

I waved to Hans I'd be back shortly, grabbed another beer, made it obvious I insured a round was in my chamber, and flicked the selector to full. My eyes scrutinized bushes lining the stream ahead for enemy movement.

She stopped in the bushes by the stream, turned to me, and locked her green eyes on mine.

I was still very much into my combat mode, scouring the other side, the bank ahead, and crest of the bank where the tops of Brigade's tents were visible. The "chugging" water pump was still audible.

She lay her hat and baskets by stream's edge, smiled, and said, "Me chop-chop you."

"Me chop-chop you?" I asked. "Oh," I giggled when I realized what she was getting at, "you chop-chop me. You want to eat me!"

The delicate features of her face thrilled me after she removed the obscuring large hat. Her shiny black hair pulled into a bun revealed a face of perfection, sheathed in a coating of velvet-smooth skin.

Her dark, penetrating eyes burned deep into my heart. She slowly raised the right hand to her neck, delicately undoing the first button, the second, and third.

I could no longer hear the water pump; instead, I began to hear Johnny Mathis singing. My heart thumped. I felt heat and throbbing between my legs, swept from the jungles of Vietnam to a beach party in Cape Cod.

Button four and finally five at the tiny waistline. Her hand drifted to her left collar. I thought she was going to scratch because I was feeling hot, excited, and itchy.

Her index finger and thumb pinched the neck of her top and gradually slipped it down her shoulder revealing the most perfect left breast I had ever imagined, looking like breasts are supposed to look, as they are depicted in statues. It was a funnel resting on a table of velvet.

The music playing in my head fleeted from a trio, to a choir, to a symphony; I got hotter and began to tremble because an extreme pain developed in my groin caused by the swelling in my snug, tailored fatigues.

"Me chop-chop," she hissed, kneeling at my feet while sliding the right index finger down the middle of my chest, ultimately ending at the top of my fly, directly under the pistol belt.

My crotch was in severe pain as I stood at parade rest: legs apart, rifle butt at my left foot, right hand holding the Bud along the seam of my pants, and glossy eyes staring directly ahead.

She popped the top fly button, number two, and finally at button three my penis shot directly out of its entrapment. The pain was gone; then four and five. Ah-h-h, I was pounding, ready to explode. That wonderful thing of mine was standing up directly, a soldier at attention.

Her right hand tenderly took my trooper by the thumb and forefinger and, ever so gently, eased it down so she was looking directly at it. She leaned forward, nimbly kissed the head after gliding back the foreskin, then gradually eased it back.

I was trembling; actually shaking in nervous premonition for the union of her sensuous lips with my pulsating peter.

"Me beer," she breathed as she removed the brew from my hand, lifted it to her mouth, poured some inside, and returned it. She closed her eyes, bending forward like a monk in suspended animation.

My now-frayed mind was still articulate enough to realize she didn't swallow the beer. The reason was obvious after she kissed the head again and gingerly opened her mouth so it sealed around my joint entering completely inside. She sloshed the cold beer back and forth in her mouth, masturbating me with currents of hot and cold pleasure. The beer became hot after a dozen of these sloshes—she slurped it down.

I didn't know where I was.

The tongue slid around the bottom of my tool, like a sausage into a bun, while she began emitting hot saliva and furiously sucking it down. Next she placed her first two fingers and thumb of her left hand between her mouth and the root in my groin while gracefully gliding back and forth with the dexterity of a surgeon. Shakes, trembles, moans, sweat, and excruciating pleasure; I exploded into the cosmos.

"Oh-h-h-h," I moaned. "My God, help me, arhh-r-r-r!"

A gush of pleasure permeated me as I had never felt before.

"Ray, is that you; are you OK?" Hans heard my groans, thinking I got zapped. Welcome back to reality, I heard the water pump again.

"Yeah, I'll be right there." I tucked myself in and returned.

He wanted to know happened and if I was with that broad, noticing the sweat and face beet red, concluding I just had sex.

I said I was looking for the PX.

We were about to leave. She came over with both knees wet, smiled warmly, stuffed $2 into my top pocket, and whispered, "Salem."

I smiled, gave thumbs up, pointed to the pump, and said, "Seven o'clock," showing seven fingers.

"You hot shit, Pezzoli, what've you been doing? Did you get head from her?"

"Yaaa!"

We pulled into the PX for Salems.

Hans wondered why I bought Salem instead of Winston.

I told him the story.

He called me a dumb shit, that I should keep the money and forget the cigarettes. She paid me 200 P for head.

I called him a dummy, saying I would shack up tonight and get it free again.

"You'll never get away with it."

I would tell Sarge I had to turn a story at Saigon and imagined I would stay at her pad, one of those shacks in the Widow's Village.

He started yucking his goofy laugh, like one of Disney's Seven Dwarfs in *Snow White,* and his big ears flopped back and forth.

I told Sarge I had stories at AP and UPI and had a ride there from Brigade.

My charade was almost blown by Hans whispering to Rick and Lansen, about what transpired. The three were giggling and punching each other so obviously, I was afraid Sergeant Grassburg would become suspicious. He must have had an idea we were involved with improper activities. Preaching in his righteous Baptist vocabulary, "If you get any diseases from those dad gum whoores [he didn't like to say that word so he slurred it] you're going to get an incurable disease and they'll have to cut that thing of yours off."

"It's combat strain, Sarge."

I had chow, clipped two more grenades on my pistol belt, dusted my weapon off, and went to the tent next door to discuss my intentions with our Vietnamese interpreter, Fung. He thought I wouldn't have any Viet Cong problems with the women from the Widow's Village, if that was where I was going; they all hated the VC.

Hans returned me to Brigade Headquarters at dusk.

She was at the water point exactly where we planned. I hesitated to give her the Salems because I was afraid she would thank me and leave; instead, I was pleasantly surprised when she smiled and motioned, "Come with me."

It was 1930 hours and dark now. I didn't have a pass for Tan Heip and was obvious with full combat gear. Supply troops from Long Bien were allowed in Tan Heip on pass, dressed in civvies. I had neither and would have been conspicuous walking through the village.

The woman was aware of my predicament so she bypassed Tan Heip's main street of bars and shops. We followed the stream under the bridge and traversed the bank through darkness to the jungle behind the village. I recognized we weren't going into the Widow's Village.

"Dung lat," Vietnamese for "halt," then a series of excited words.

I had forgotten the Vietnamese checkpoint on the road above.

"Hey, me numba one American G.I.," I shouted, "me no VC!"

I sensed this nervous soldier was close to shooting me. All he could see were two dark figures creeping along the edge of the stream at night, one with a rifle, the other carrying something, possibly VC trying to blow the bridge. Very slowly and deliberately I raised my rifle above my head with both hands while climbing the bank directly to him.

When I neared the road, lights illuminated me. He immediately recognized an American soldier and took the gun off me while I walked to the gun that almost shot me. The soldier was glad I was American; he nervously laughed when I got next to him, lowering his weapon, "Number one GI," he laughed apologetically.

I laughed with him, shook his hand, gave him a Winston, and pointed to the woman by the edge of the stream: "Boom-boom girl."

"Oh, boom-boom? OK."

I slid back to the woman, as military vehicles were about to pass.

We took a trail that led from the stream between sparse mud huts into the jungle. I didn't know if I was going to like this so much now; this wasn't the Widow's Village. I was alone in the jungle at night, a few hundred yards from town and civilization.

She lived next to the stream in a 12-foot mud hut with its single door covered by burlap cloth.

A kerosene lantern provided lighting. The bed was a six-inch tall bamboo cot with teak slats resting on a frame supported by short, stubby legs. I assumed the pillow was the rectangular woven reed object at the head.

She motioned to go outside to the patio of hard clay next to the gurgling stream, removed her hat, and sat me on the end of a two-foot bench.

I placed the M-16 in my lap, made sure it was on full, took off then snapped closed my pistol belt, and hung it around my shoulder.

This lithe creature turned to me, untied and removed a boot, placed it on the ground next to us, took my sock by the toe, gradually slid it off. She repeated the same with the other foot before she tenderly massaged each. I could hear the orchestra beginning to tune up while Mathis cleared his throat.

Aside from this activity, I was still in the combat mode, trying to figure out what was going to happen next, aware I was in a jungle with guys—and women—that would love to kill Americans. My thoughts were disrupted when my dream stood up in front of me and looked directly inside me again with those eyes. They glowed reflection from the kerosene lantern, penetrating the pitch-black jungle night.

She released something along her waist and the slacks slid down her legs.

I didn't notice she wasn't wearing panties because I was palpitating from the sight of her smooth flesh and flowing shape. She turned to the stream as she unbuttoned the waist. Peaking from the bottom of its flap were two of the most symmetrical buns ever been created; most in Vietnam had less meat.

The top disappeared—who ever said a back wasn't beautiful? She released her bun of hair, cascading a gush of straight, silky black hair, embracing her back to the top of her buttocks as she waded into the stream.

She turned and faced me. I slipped into a spellbound trance when I saw her with everything au naturel, a dream I could never have perceived while savoring it with my limited persona. She splashed herself with stream water; the velvet skin reflected lantern light, appearing as a tasty golden hue.

This creature was more attractive than I conceived initially. She was tall, about five feet, six inches, with a narrow, flat, well-defined waist and concave line running from her navel to the base of her conspicuous rib cage.

Her piercing eyes called me to the stream's edge to wait while she waded to me. I laid the rifle and pistol belt on the bench to join her. The stream became louder, its melody flowing through my head.

One hand unbuttoned my top shirt button, while the other began to remove my shirt. When she reached the third button, she slowly squirted a stream of water from her mouth onto the middle of my now bare chest. After the bottom button was released, she walked behind me, put both hands on the collar, eased the shirt down my back, folded it, and placed it on the bench.

I wasn't wearing a belt; consequently the top three buttons of my pants were easy to release. I wasn't wearing undershorts either. After she slid my pants down, I became to her pleasure au naturel also, so involved observing her beauty, sex never occurred. Passed by my limp dick, she gave it an affectionate flick.

She poured on ladles of water from a crock, lathered me, and fastidiously, methodically, and erotically washed me. After I was thoroughly washed and rinsed, we went inside the hut where she signaled me to stretch out on the bed face down. My dream knelt on the floor and spread a scented, tingly oil over my body: kneading sore back muscles, plucking the skin between the vertebrae, massaging calves, and folding her fingers inside my toes. While she stroked inside my upper thigh, her hand casually stroked my testicles, stimulating heart and hormones.

She rolled me over and applied oil to my face, neck, armpits, navel, and almost perpendicular penis. One hand embraced it while the other took the vial of oil to her lips parted by that talented tongue with sides folded up, forming a scoop again. She poured some oil inside, carefully bent down, and lapped it around my foreskin. I began quivering, not knowing if it was from pain, pleasure, or promise. My erratic, erotic mind wandered: had I been captured and was being tortured in a prison?

The next thing I became cognizant of was her climbing on top of my prone body. She faced and straddled me, gently uniting cock with cunt. A quixotic union. We were completely molded and bonded together, fused as one.

I don't remember what happened next, my memory is completely blank. I sincerely think I went to Heaven for there is nothing on Earth spreading the pleasure mainlined through my body. Now I know why I want to go to Heaven when I die. I don't expect more than I experienced here.

The next thing I remember was entwined by legs and arms on the mat. The hue from golden brown lamplight was reflected from her skin by my oils rubbed off during lovemaking. My hand stroked her long hair while it caressed her back where its lower bend was attached to her compact derriere. I had one butt in my hand, playfully pinching it. The other hand randomly played with my rifle sling next to the cot.

I glanced at my watch, 2300. I would like to spend tomorrow night with her, but didn't think I could pull it off.

We dozed; awaken shortly by voices of young men talking outside.

I had spent most of my time in the jungles during combat operations. Normally people don't walk in jungles at night after returning from the local bowling alley or PTA meeting, as you find in middle America. I realized they weren't Vietnamese Rangers on patrol. My suspicions were confirmed by her look of terror, understanding what they said. She held up five fingers, somehow being aware of their number. These were VC, stopping at our sacred patio, taking a break on patrol!

My left hand discreetly slid down the side of the cot to the rifle barrel, gliding over the breach to the small of the stock. I raised it to my lap; silently releasing the safety while insuring the selector was on full. There was always a round in my chamber, so I didn't have to check. I rested the rifle on top of my knee, held the pistol grip with my left hand and aimed the weapon at the middle of the burlap-covered door by adjusting my leg.

Fortunately my pistol belt was closed, facilitating lifting it as I draped it around my shoulder, a bandoleer. Meticulously I removed a grenade from the belt and slid the pin out, holding the lever back. "If any of them come through that burlap," I reasoned, "I'll release the lever of the grenade starting a cook-off." By then, hopefully, there would be more than one VC looking down the muzzle of my rifle, enjoying a serving of M-16. At the same time I'll throw the cooked-off grenade outside, and with luck, blow away the rest.

I realized I didn't have boots on and motioned my friend to slip my boots on and wrap the shoestrings around my ankles.

The VC was still talking outside while her eyes remained frozen wide. I began shaking now, probably from fear, until realizing I was still naked except for boots. If the VC came inside, they probably would die from laughing rather than bullets.

I began to grasp how foolish I looked and wondered how to get back to my camp if I was in a firefight, managing to get out alive. I couldn't sneak back down the road to my camp because there wasn't enough cover and concealment along the way. Even if I managed to get back, I probably would get shot by one of the troops in an OP because I didn't know the password. Also there was this deal about not having clothes. I couldn't very well low crawl through the grass around the camp, secluding myself until I reached my tent because the grass wasn't tall enough.

Fortunately, the VC left in a half hour. I remained awake another hour before catnapping the rest of the night—with my clothes on.

I said good-bye at sunrise and went to the brigade information office, wasting time as I lined up an alibi before returning to camp so the "trip into Saigon" would look authentic.

I arrived in time to grab my camera, pack C rations, fill canteens, procure extra ammo, and jump on the supply convoy leaving for the mission. This was perfect timing because I wouldn't have to explain my whereabouts to anybody—how the enemy caught me with my pants down.

We arrived at Forward CP at 1100. There wasn't transportation to the boonies for two days. The CP was on alert status because the other two battalions in this brigade operation were finding indications of a strong enemy presence.

Over 24 base camps had been discovered so far. One was of regimental size that had a provincial hospital with records dating back to 1960. Next to it were 10 freshly dug graves of VC killed earlier during this operation.

Our other battalion, the 2nd Battalion, 18th Infantry, ran into a heavily fortified village complex with bunkers on its flanks. An air strike was called; when it was lifted, they assaulted the tree line backed by two tanks. There was too much resistance inside the tree line; they withdrew in order to saturate it with artillery and gunships. The following morning the troops entered the tree line and discovered everything devastated and abandoned.

My battalion made minor contact earlier that day, accomplishing nothing more than a few ambushes. I joined them two days after 2/18's contact, hoping we would find the remnants of that camp.

We couldn't find anything and assumed the VC and North Vietnamese were so chopped up they were either in seclusion or returned to Cambodia. The battalion returned to the base camp February 15.

"Operation Mastiff" began in four days, leaving insufficient time to clean equipment, read and write letters, go on pass and R&R, get drunk and laid, and prepare to go to Dau Tieng, 50 miles southwest of Saigon and five miles from Cambodia.

I wrote releases and did what everyone else did, except go on pass. My parents were concerned about my spirit because the media made sure we were aware of protests, no matter how small and insignificant. I assured them the most important thing to me was my life and refused to let anything interfere with it.

My work made me feel positive, in addition to the availability of cheap sex.

Winston cigarettes helped, as did a good drunk once in a while. Saying mass with the chaplain without all the trappings and grandiose splendor of a magnificent edifice like a cathedral brought me closer to God. There weren't any of these accouterments in the jungle during mass to intoxicate my senses with God; I wasn't befuddled by the church's golden grandeur.

Captain Million attended an officers' party in Bien Hoa the third night back. This area was so secure now that traffic was allowed at night without escort or convoy. His driver, Jimmy O'Riley, asked if I felt like going. We could have a few drinks in a bar or get laid while the captain was doing his thing, which sounded fine.

The hamlet of Tan Heip became a happening place with the development of Long Binh. The personnel had regular 9:00–5:00 jobs with free time to fill at night.

The village was bustling like a vacation resort as we drove through at dusk. These troops were in their civvies, resembling college students on spring break, scouting the bars in their relentless quest to find the nicest girl at the cheapest price. Most of them were drunk by now.

Jim had to slow down and finally stop because pedestrian traffic jammed both sides of the road.

We piercingly heard an Army .45 fired on the left bank of the road. The normal commotion of traffic, bars, drunks, and jukeboxes stopped immediately.

The three of us jumped outside and used it as cover. I could tell the gun wasn't fired directly at us because its shots didn't have the "crack" it normally makes when the barrel is pointed at you.

I saw a Vietnamese Ranger from the local post behind the stump of a tree on the bank opposite me, waving the .45 into the air, and squeezing off a few rounds. It was obvious he was mad about something, but not aiming to kill.

One of the drunks crouching behind our jeep, demanded my M-16 so he could shoot.

"I'll shoot you first if you touch this!"

The thought of a clerk with an M-16 in his drunken hands was mind boggling, considering the carnage he would produce.

"Let's get him," Captain Million shouted.

I moved out, my rifle pointing directly at the man, his heart in my sights. I didn't want to kill him because he wasn't threatening anyone but was merely, as it seemed apparent to me, letting off steam.

"Kill him—kill him," the men shouted.

He stopped firing his .45, looking into my devastating M-16.

I didn't flinch and stared at him down my barrel, waiting for him to make the wrong move.

He wisely decided against anything but turning and retreating between two beer stands.

We chased him down the narrow alley into a larger, perpendicular one, with Million yelling, "dung lat—halt," as if he really would have halted.

A building was directly behind the man at a fork. He hesitated a second to decide left or right. A squeeze of my trigger would have placed six M-16 rounds into him. I made two squeezes, spraying 12 rounds around him, creating a semicircular halo in the tin-walled building behind.

This guy must have thought he experienced a miracle not getting hit and made a hasty decision on the way to run.

So here I am, chasing a guy down an alley with my weapon at port arms while Captain Million is puffing next to me, giving me a tongue lashing, "I told you guys to fire these semi-automatic—you don't hit anything on full."

"I'm not trying to kill him; if I wanted to kill him I would have. I'm just trying to scare him," I argued back, resembling the Keystone Cops.

This complex of huts was adjacent to the jungle. By the time we reached the end of the alley, he had disappeared down a jungle trail and decided against following farther.

MPs were at our jeep when we returned and wanted to know the status of our chase. They claimed the alleged girlfriend of the guy was working in a beer stand, prostituting on the side. He didn't like it and killed her in the bar before firing into the air.

I cleaned and oiled the breach of my gun, clicked in a full magazine, flamed a cigarette, and enjoyed the scenery en route to our destination in Bien Hoa where Jim and I had a few beers, pinched a couple of whores, and waited for Captain Million to finish his thing.

Chapter 15

Malaria Tablets Today—
It Must Be Friday

The Black Virgin Mountain kept vigilant eyes guarding the countryside to Cambodia. At her base was the extensive Michelin Rubber Plantation, still owned by that French company. The VC would periodically launch mortar attacks from the 1,500-foot summit, dissolving into Cambodia's jungles where the South Vietnamese were prohibited from pursuing.

Three American advisors were killed when VC in the plantation ambushed their Viet unit six months previously, their bodies carelessly buried by plantation workers. One of our duties was locate, excavate, and return their remains.

Our Forward CP was on the Dau Tieng airstrip. French civilians would help locate the bodies. They landed a small aircraft, taxied between rows of C-130 four-engine turboprops, Huey troop carriers, and Cobra gunships, to our Battalion Operations tent. We drove them to the French villa 2nd Brigade used as a tactical operation center and medical clearing station.

This would be the first time in Vietnam 2nd Brigade's Medical personnel had an opportunity to work in a permanent structure rather than in tents.

The French took troops to the graves with the workers who made the burial. I elected not to go; it would have been too depressing seeing these beautiful men's remains unceremoniously excavated. Their soul is now resting at the Wall.

We heard shots about the perimeter that night. Another case of trigger-happy support troops firing at a monkey or frog.

I returned from chow in the morning and was cleaning my weapon when an NCO walked into Personnel with papers, claiming to have a story.

One of the guys from Communications guarded their installation the previous night. A VC crawled in front and fired three shots, all into his helmet but missing his head.

SSgt. Franklin Strong was an unlikely looking soldier: delicate features, round physique, mild mannered, and soft spoken. This Commo man never saw combat and remained shaking six hours after.

The generator shut off for refueling. In that quiet, Strong heard movement in the night air and alerted his squad. A moment later the generator was restarted and three shots rang out. The first round pierced the top of his helmet, heaving it up. The second ripped it at midcenter, lifting it more, while the third took it off, piercing the visor.

I reneged on a photo because he still appeared terrified.

"Pezzoli, got a supply chopper going to Alpha, wanta go?"

"Be right there."

Alpha held a junction of jungle, field, stream, and marshes, an infiltration point for North Vietnamese. Alpha monitored activities there, ambushed whomever they found, and was reserve for Bravo or Charlie if needed.

They had been in the jungle three days. There, two days was like an R&R: relax with loose security, minimum patrolling, and advantage of the only cool, clear spring water in Vietnam. The water was free of bugs a foot of its exit, being too cold there for insects and the like.

Iced soft drinks were included. I chatted with the men retrieving supplies and treats. A NCO familiarized me with the perimeter, including this spring with men taking turns washing. An outpost was established where an oxcart trail crossed a small stream before traversing a wide field.

Major Weeks was here; I hung my hammock from a tree near him. Our location had protection from that raised trail. Also, the spring and its fresh, cool water were on the other side.

I was helping with supplies when I heard shouts in Vietnamese inside the jungle adjacent to us. The CO shouted, "Where's Tom?!" our interpreter.

Tom joined us running to the commotion. Scattered in the shouting was a G.I. ordering, "Dung lat!" Halt!

Tom demanded what they wanted.

The VC surrendered.

By the time we arrived, men had collected their guns.

One was in his teens, the other his late 20s. They saw our chopper, indicating Americans were there, also indicative of how vulnerable we were. VC were watching the same chopper I arrived on. Chilling.

Tom interrogated them; the CO still reluctant to bring them inside perimeter, fearing a trick to expose defenses. A man gave each VC an iced Pepsi, relaxing each to the extent they laughed during interrogation.

The young VC was forced into service two years earlier to "help free his country from capitalists." He thought he was free before and escaped but was recaptured, disciplined, and sent into the jungle to manage a rancid relay station for infiltrating North Viets.

The other had been a VC for five years, believed the Communist line of Utopia with everyone owning everything, and the State and Big Brother always protecting you. He became disillusioned with the totalitarian system over the years. After American troops arrived, it became obvious how we helped Vietnam. Both were isolated from Americans next to Cambodia, but made plans to surrender at any opportunity.

I wedged into the tiny clearing where they were being questioned, taking a classic snapshot of two of the enemy, smiles on their faces, drinking Pepsis, and one pointing to where VC were concealed.

Later, after developing this shot at the Air Force photo lab, the technicians almost banned me. It had been impossible for them to purchase soft drinks at their PX, yet the Army treated the enemy to Pepsi.

A chopper evacuated them to Division.

Later I noticed two men drinking from the spring, one opposite the other. The heavy one was drinking from his helmet, while the skinny guy nursed a canteen. What a great photo, a real paradox.

The Army wouldn't accept this because the men weren't using water purification tablets for the cleanest natural water in Vietnam. Men didn't use tablets when water looked and tasted this clean. Maybe if we had, fewer would have had the runs.

Persistence and patience did pay off; later in the day I managed to take another great photo permitted for release. Two guys were washing each other in the spring. One was bent down, leaning forward on his toes, with his hands on the ground and butt in the air as the other washed soap off his back with a helmet of water.

At 1500 that afternoon I heard rounds next to the OP where the road crossed the stream, 30 yards from me. I was sitting shirtless at the time, resting against a tree. I slapped on my pistol belt and grabbed the M-16 with one hand and the camera with the other.

The OP relaxed along the bank of the river crossing. VC snuck along the bank so stealthy that our guys weren't aware; they were pinned so acutely they were unable to raise their rifles to return fire. One was isolated behind a tree on the left, while the other two "proned" behind a one-foot mound on the opposite side.

This spring offered us something unique to the jungles of Vietnam: good-tasting water. It was cool, clean, and moving. Consequently the bugs which can be seen in front, were kept from the base where we gathered our water.

I zigged along the road toward them. The VC fired at me with his automatic weapon; I dove into the trench on the side. He stopped firing, probably to sight on me again. I zagged down the road another five feet before diving into the opposite side before I was in the crosshairs.

While running, I noticed a foxhole 10 feet from me in the center of the road between the pinned men and a short distance from the stream where the VC where hiding. I figured the guy shooting didn't have many rounds left in his magazine and had to take a chance: I didn't know how deep the foxhole was. If I managed to get there without getting shot and found it too shallow or small, I would be a sitting duck.

I noticed Major Weeks hopscotching behind, motioning the other side so he wouldn't arrive at that spot the same time I did. The VC began firing at me when I reached halfway across the road and continued until I disappeared into the trench. After I landed, I heard the dull sound of the last round fired from his magazine, the sound I had been waiting for. Immediately I ran to the foxhole which fortunately was large enough to accommodate me.

VC crept across the stream in the center and hid behind the bushes, center left, where their auto fire kept the man (1) by the tree, left, and the two men (2 and 3), at right, pinned down so they couldn't fire back. I was being fired at while I lifted the camera above the foxhole for this photo before cooking off and throwing a grenade behind the bushes on the left.

The VC reloaded and fired after I raised my camera outside the hole, capturing "The Great Vietnamese War Photo." Three G.I.s pinned while a machine gun was firing at the photographer from the stream, eight feet away.

Major Weeks was adjacent to me on the left.

"Anybody in front?" I yelled.

"VC!"

I yanked a grenade off my ammo pack, cooked it off, and threw it forward like a baseball into the grass along the stream. If I lobbed it, like the grenade is typically thrown, it might have hit low branches on the tree the man on the left was hiding behind.

After my grenade exploded, I poked my head up, spraying a base of fire.

"What'cha got there, Ray?" Major Weeks yelled from his side. I laughed when I noticed him for the first time. He was shirtless, helmetless, weaponless, sweaty, and very excited. His red handlebar mustache was quivering in the wind and his adrenaline was obviously flowing. This was the real thing, the combat he had trained for and loved.

"I think I scared them away."

"Gimme artillery, FO up here now," he bellowed.

The FO saw two guys running a thousand meters away.

"Well, dissolve them," snarled the major.

Artillery bracketed them with marker rounds in front, behind, left, then right, finally barraging the middle of the box, obliterating them—a cat playing with a mouse before killing it.

"Good shooting; put two marks on your barrels," the FO called to his gunners.

"Hold it," I protested. "That's an Infantry kill isn't it, sir?" I called to Major Weeks.

He said to let it go; Artillery needed credit for doing something.

The Army wouldn't accept this "great war photo" also; the men don't have shirts on, looking unprepared.

"That is usually what happens during an ambush," I replied to no avail.

The next day Alpha broke into platoon-sized units of 45 men and departed on three separate long-range patrols. I chose 3rd Platoon; they were patrolling that field adjacent to Cambodia, 500 yards away and looking ominous. Even though nature knows no political boundaries, we knew it was loaded with thousands of enemy waiting to cut our throats.

Hours later, small-arms fire was heard from these trees. Our patrol slipped into the jungle, blended with the foliage, and remained out of sight, protected by cover.

The platoon leader took out his map to orient our location. He noticed the firing came from Cambodia and we couldn't return it. Jane Fonda should be able to rest more easily now, knowing we did not shoot at the enemy while in Cambodia, even though he was in violation of international law.

The RTO called Brigade Headquarters; they said to keep our rifles locked and that the Air Force couldn't help us either, suggesting we continue to patrol inside the tree line shielding us from being shot at.

Later our patrol entered a village by a stream adjacent to the field. They had heard about Americans but had never seen one. The children cautiously approached us during a break. The stream didn't smell bad; we filled up and splashed our faces. It was noon; the men began to eat.

Six curious boys approached us as we sat on our helmets in the center of their hamlet. We showed them our C rations and P-38 can opener, amazing them with its operation.

One of the men thought they looked hungry and waved a can. They were famished!

We took rations out of packs, gave each a box, and described its contents.

The kids delicately opened each like a gourmet meal, completely amazed by the intricacy of its three cans: the meat, bread, and dessert. Also, the plastic bag—including a spoon, toilet paper, salt, pepper, instant coffee, cream, and matches—was unique.

The C's tasted best at midday after being heated by 120° temperature. We demonstrated how the minute P-38 opened cans, folding the lid back and forming a handle. The meals were foods they had never seen before. They cautiously placed the spoon in their mouths. After tasting it, they obviously relished the meal, devouring everything in the box.

Other men joined us and began playing with the kids. Two had boys their ages—these kids reminded everyone of home.

The platoon sergeant stopped by to remind us we were in "Charlie's" back yard and to use caution with kids; they could be bait for a trap. It was difficult to believe, but realistic.

"Saddle up, we're moving out."

We said good-bye to the boys; each wiped their mouths with C ration toilet paper and grabbed our fingers with both hands, chanting, "G.I. America OK."

We felt positive about being there—unfortunately this doesn't last long in combat. Later in the afternoon men were noticed emerging from the jungle and about to cross our field. The point reacted by crouching, then creeping forward. These armed VC detected them and darted back to the trail. The squad pursued them while we waited by the field as security.

The first man doing the chasing rounded a corner and was met with three shots from a gun behind a bush by the trail, five feet away. He threw himself to the ground and fired two lethal M-16 bursts of 12 rounds.

Sergeant Taylor was behind him and dropped after this shot also, simultaneously holding the trigger on his 12 gauge, pumping four loads of 00 buck into the bush.

I came up behind as he rolled the body over.

"It's a kid," Taylor stammered. The VC had told him to stay put with a rusty bolt-action rifle, holding us back while they escaped. This is the type of people the VC are.

The second man said they were not people, just animals. They didn't have any concept about the phenomenally efficient killing machine they dealt with—the American soldier.

Sergeant Taylor was furious. The VC had the boy conned into ambushing us, probably saying Americans were cowards, would run whenever they were shot at and never fire back. Sarge felt he had murdered someone when he noticed he killed a boy.

I told him he wasn't the murderer; the VC were.

A defensive perimeter was established for the night in a clearing by a stream. The platoon leader's intuition cautioned him that the VC might have another ambush ahead. He felt it best establishing defenses with the advantage of time, surprise, and location. We were five miles from the support of our company and desirous not to become involved with forces too large to handle.

The clearing of our objective was only a few hundred yards from our small field. In case a superior group was encountered, this clearing could be reached in a few minutes by running down the trail. Once here, the platoon would be in a more beneficial position for protection from chopper and air strikes.

I was surprised our OPs didn't make contact with any patrols that night; I was certain we would find many. They might have realized we had a perimeter and decided against tempting fate.

Morning orders were to change course, taking a 160-degree heading into the jungle. This would parallel us to Cambodia and intersect streams at several locations ideal for enemy camps. If we didn't make contact, the patrol should reach a clearing and make camp by midafternoon.

The course reached a trail and stream intersection with many footprints crossing it. The time was 1100, a good time for rest, chow, wash, and ambush. Each of the four squads fixed an ambush while offering the men an opportunity to wash.

The medic passed out our week's malaria tablets. "Must be Friday," mumbled one of the men. None of the enemy passed; we left at 1300.

Our heading kept intersecting this well-worn trail. The point man discovered a large anthill next to a bend where vines behind it appeared to have been trampled over. He apprehensively motioned the rest of his squad to come on line before creeping forward.

They heard male and female voices laughing inside and crawled to a typical VC base camp.

Twenty men and nine women were eating and drinking sake at two tables with three others guarding the camp. They discovered a VC R&R center.

Word was passed back to the platoon leader who joined. The VC appeared to be having a "good ol' time," completely oblivious. The lieutenant instructed his patrol to cautiously crawl around the camp, forming a semicircle.

Spying on the VC partying while they were completely unaware of us was like fishing in a crystal clear mountain stream. The fish swims toward your bait at the end of a bob, ignorant of the hook, line, and sinker, seeing only the meal.

This would be easy; we would probably kill most of them without receiving injuries. I sighted three sitting at a table; two short bursts from my M-16 would kill them. I lay, apprehensively watching and waiting for the fire signal, while the rest of the platoon maneuvered around.

The difference between a fisherman and a novice is that the fisherman is proficient enough to let the fish nibble, then yank the line when he gulps the hook, snaring him. Several replacements had watched too many combat movies and had not yet acquired the patience and perseverance required of a hunter and killer. We planned to cook off and throw grenades, then spray the whole area fully automatic. One of the young bucks impatiently began to spray his M-16 before the signal, scaring many into trenches and tunnels.

Most of us had the pin out of our grenades, waiting for the signal to fire. After the premature shots we ran into the compound, dropping grenades into the now-occupied trenches and tunnel shafts. Many of the VC didn't flee far enough into the tunnels to escape grenade blasts; consequently parts of their bodies were blown off. The troops also had our latest toy, the concussion grenade, designed for tunnels and trenches where it would blow sand and rock through tunnels like bird-shot from a shotgun.

The campground trembled from explosions. After the grenades were dispensed, C-4 plastic explosives were next. When the camouflaged exit to a tunnel was found, its cover was ripped off and more explosives thrown in.

The platoon leader called cease-fire, checking our status. He called the Vietnamese interpreter, Sergeant Loc, to question if anything was alive down there. To our surprise, he got replies saying they were hurt very badly and asking to give up.

He told them to come out with nothing in their hands and we had a doctor. Also they were cautioned there had better not be booby traps, snakes, glass, or stakes inside. If troops were hurt, all would be killed.

The men were instructed not to help or touch them, keeping rifles on them. If it turned out to be a trick, all were to be wasted.

Six women and 18 men came out of the tunnels in a daze, basically whole but with pieces missing.

Author Ray Pezzoli, left, and Vietnamese interpreter Sgt. Loc.

All appeared to have been rubbed over sandpaper because of the sand blasted from the explosions. Most had lost their hearing and much of their equilibrium because of blown-out inner ears.

Troops explored the tunnels and found a vast amount of supplies and military documents. Fortunately for "Charlie," he paid heed and left no surprises underground.

I walked the clearing escorting wounded VC and guarding a chopper before we were flown to the Brigade Med facility at the chalet in Dau Tieng. The women were so fat, unattractive, and dirty it was inconceivable how anyone would want to make love to anything like that. I felt sorry for the medics who had to bathe them before treating their wounds.

Each was absolutely docile, a shark out of water, completely out of its environment and helpless. An hour before, they tried to kill us. Now they were glad it was over.

A supply chopper later dropped bootie off in Bien Hoa. I hitched a lift for my latest photos. The Air Force had seen me only once when I

Me after four days in the boonies by Cambodia.

emerged directly out of the jungle before being civilized by a shower and change of clothes at base camp. They insisted on photos of me now because I looked "so authentic."

I still had the taste of jungle in my lungs and took an impressive picture, a legitimate-looking combat G.I.

I returned to base camp, changed clothes, and scribbled two stories and captions. The guys at Personnel volunteered to edit, type, and submit them. The chopper returned to Dau Tieng at 1800 hours.

"Pezzoli, *Look Magazine* is here doing a special on Father."

Father Confroy felt compelled to take mass to the troops whenever possible, even if it meant inside the jungles. Frequently he accompanied convoys to hostile forward areas for troops returning for a break.

"Church is in His Combat Pack" appeared in the July 1966 issue of *Look*.

Crow, the colonel's driver, returned to the States; his replacement was Pfc. Henry Shadrick. Crow was forceful, dominating, and macho, while Shad was a quiet, subtle perfectionist.

Rick wanted to christen Shad at a local whorehouse. I was against it because, although there was a Vietnamese army unit in town, the proximity to Cambodia and local presence of enemy was dangerous. We probably would have been court-martialed if we had gotten the colonel's new driver killed or a dose.

Jimmy O'Riley received a "Dear John" letter from his girl in New York City, tossing him for a guy who had been chasing her. His boss, Captain Million, tried to console him, but the little Irishman wouldn't listen. His pale white face was red from anguish; his stutter had improved, but now he could hardly communicate. She could have waited another month until he returned instead of breaking it off with a guy in combat. Jimmy was sincere to her, rarely whoring with us.

"Operation Hattiesburg" would begin the next day, February 26. When Alpha was extracted in the morning, the entire 1st of the 18th would be together at Dau Tieng for decorations. In the afternoon, troops would mount choppers and assault another jungle near Cambodia, Tay Ninh province, in the town of Phuoc Vinh.

Chapter 16

My Life Changes Forever

A large North Viet unit assembled in Tay Ninh Province, awaiting a challenge. The Communists wanted to absorb this area, placing them within striking distance of Saigon.

A Viet Ranger unit tried to keep Phuoc Vinh and its airport under control, but the force was not adequate to assert sufficient influence in the countryside. Many vacant, grand old villas dotted the area. This was indicative of Communist terrorism where prosperous people of commerce were forced to leave their businesses and villas for safer areas. The net result was that a thriving economy was snuffed out, paradoxically hindering the living standards of the masses instead of helping them.

When each company landed at the city's dirt strip, they broke into platoon-sized patrols and searched the surrounding jungles. Local hamlets were ghost towns; their inhabitants captured, killed, or driven out.

The dirt road my patrol scouted was one lane. We noticed recent oxcart marks in the soft dirt, but didn't see people. I was the first man in the column, flanked by a man on each soft sand shoulder, walking through knee-high elephant grass; the rest of the patrol stretched a quarter mile behind.

"Mines," the man on my right casually said, withdrawing his foot from the mine he almost stepped on. Alertness and concentration again saved me from injury. It was extraordinary how someone could see those minute three prongs through the tall grass, protruding only an inch above the ground. He placed a sheet of toilet paper on top of them, signaled the rear, and continued walking.

Summer was coming to Vietnam, meaning more heat and fewer refreshing monsoon rains. The sun reflected off the golden sand road while the air was still. The heat, especially with full packs, was intolerable. Fortunately we entered the jungle and its relief of 97-degree temperatures and 97-percent humidity.

An inexperienced point man confronted two VC on the trail and fired a few wild shots, scaring each away. We chased them a short distance then stopped.

Fearing ambushes, the patrol moved off the trail, continuing inside the jungle. The jungle was quiet, a condition with humans present, prevalent in the proximity of a VC camp.

Several shots were fired ahead of me, followed by rapid bursts of M-16 fire. The point had found a base camp of enemy neatly clad in sandy brown attire. I was with the squad behind point. We swung to the left flank, jumping the perimeter trench. The point kept the enemy busy with a base of fire, which appeared to confuse them by our crossfire. Several were hit and dropped immediately with none of the dying dramatics frequently seen on the tube. There were a dozen; rather than fire back, most looked for a place to hide.

Some leaped into tunnels while others dropped weapons and ran.

The rest of the platoon secured the camp and collected equipment while dropping grenades down shafts. When the enemy was dead or dying, neutralized, or no longer a threat, volunteers looked for remainders and equipment in tunnels.

Normally whenever a VC was discovered, he surrendered immediately and peacefully. They had rifles in the tunnels, but couldn't swing around to shoot. One of these Commies didn't play the game and grabbed a G.I.'s pistol from an adjacent tunnel. The soldier did what we were taught in Ranger School: neutralize the enemy in whatever way possible. Before the enemy figured how to shoot an Army .45, the infantryman snatched his mouth with both hands and pulled his lips and cheeks apart.

The VC wasn't a pleasant sight when I saw him at the top of the tunnel. Six others were found hiding in the tunnels and immediately surrendered; none got away. We killed seven, wounded two, and captured seven.

This was a story but I didn't take a photo of the Communist with his mouth ripped open. Some "do-gooder" would have protested we were brutal to the enemy, while we, and the spirits of the Wall, insured this freedom.

The closest clearing for prisoner evacuation was too far for that day. Camp was made for the night; the following morning two choppers would meet us there at 0800 hours.

I arrived at Phuoc Vinh's adequate, manicured dirt strip with the prisoners in time for a supply ship to another patrol. They were searching a field 17 miles long and three miles wide, running adjacent to Cambodia with an excellent chance finding action there.

We were airborne for five minutes, climbed to cruise altitude, and headed west to our destination. I enjoyed the cooler air, gazing out the door and reflecting.

An innocuous "whiss-ss" sound outside startled me, emphasized by the door gunner bumping me as he jumped back.

"They're shooting at us!" he shouted as he whipped his weapon around firing bursts and the chopper made evasive maneuvers. Fortunately none of the rounds found their mark.

The gunner told me later that in most cases, gunners couldn't hear rifle fire from the ground because of chopper noise. On the ground our ears could tell us exactly where the shot was placed. In the air, gunners depended upon sounds made by the trajectory of the bullet passing their heads—unnerving.

The patrol secured the LZ at the top of this large field. Goosebumps popped up on my arms discerning the jungles of Cambodia inside the west tree line with North Vietnamese troops waiting.

The temperature was hotter than normal and light reflected off pale grass, amplifying the intensity. Fortunately the day had a breeze. The elephant grass was manageable: waist high but not thick, impeding movement.

We patrolled the center of the field; if the enemy attacked from either side, we wouldn't have protection from the jungle a mile away; lucky though, anthills that would provide protection in a gunfight punctuated the field.

By midday we hadn't made contact and prepared for lunch. I was third from point and noticed the man next to me run to point. Both stopped, aimed their rifles, and then ran forward again. Two Vietnamese were 500 feet in front without weapons. Their reluctance to fire allowed them to disappear behind clumps of bushes a quarter of a mile away.

"Don't have them go chasing those people," the platoon leader called, "could be an ambush."

They didn't pursue any further, returning to our patrol line.

The patrol had an hour for chow after semicircling, with eyes open for these two men.

I could prepare something special from the mundane C rations.

An anthill next to me was ideal for a table: three feet in diameter and flat on top. And, equally important, not many ants.

Canned ham and eggs tastes only marginal if cold. Heated with chopped onions and Tabasco sauce it's a delight during patrols.

I took crackers and Cheez Whiz out of their can and ventilated a stove for heat tablets. The ham and eggs were simmering nicely while I prepared the rest of lunch. Cheeze Whiz on crackers melts in 130-degree sun, creating imitation pizzas. Our sleeves usually sufficed as napkins. Today we had sufficient time; I dined first class, using toilet paper.

My canteen water was still refreshingly cool from the night.

There was a grove of trees 1,000 yards away near the middle of the field, with a growth of dense, lush vegetation; an ocean in the middle of a sea of tan straw.

"How magnificent," I fantasized, scanning the area. I held the can of ham and eggs next to my nose, sniffing it before the first bite. Birds played on top of the anthill next to me, making a few sweeps overhead, seemingly interested in my meal.

I rested my butt on the edge, my right foot cocked against it, the first spoonful on the way to my mouth.

"Crack," stunned by a bullet fired from the grove of trees.

"Whap," a fraction of a second later the bullet splattered the damp, jelly-like clay under my foot, quivering it.

"Yallow-w," I howled falling backward, tossing both hands up, and the lunch over my head. My feet lifted up, continuing over my head; I reverse somersaulted.

I fruitlessly fired a whole magazine of M-16 .223 rounds where the bullet was fired, aware my bullets would be accurate only half that distance.

In spite of this, I felt better.

"Pezzoli," the RTO yelled, "the CO heard the shooting and wants to know what it's all about."

I told him I was shooting at someone that tried to kill me and upset my meal.

A gunship was in the air and I would take a strike.

I identified myself on his frequency; the chopper was aware of our location and would arrive in five, describing the target as the southeast corner of the clump of trees.

I almost immediately heard the "Wapp, wapp, clack, clack" telltale sound a Huey. Next I saw it, a black speck in the bright blue sky, barely visible above the field of weaving grass. At first it appeared to be suspended like a mobile. When it neared, the shape became distinctive and I could discern movement.

The chopper was a Cobra with two rocket pods, each housing 12 rockets with a 7.62-mm Gatling gun on each side, capable of firing five rounds a second.

I radioed the chopper, instructing him of his proximity to the target.

The crew maneuvered around the back of this grove spoiling the VC's opportunity for a lucky shot. By the time they aligned with the target, they were 3,000 yards away, outside rifle range.

I vectored the chopper into position like a boy playing a video game.

A rocket was fired; the contrail marked its path, exploding above the mark. I still saw the exact spot the bullet was fired.

"Down a hundred, left two hundred."

The next rocket was fired exactly a hundred down and two left of the first. "Bull's-eye! Fire for effect."

The remaining 22 rockets and hundreds of 7.62-mm rounds obliterated everything. After the smoke cleared the vegetation was completely dissolved. The only thing added was a black hole in the vegetation.

I congratulated the crew, guaranteeing they got their target, told them to go back, clean their magnificent equipment, and have a couple of cool ones on us.

I pulled another can out of my pack and began to rapidly prepare it. Unfortunately, I heard, "OK, saddle up; we got to move out now!"

Whenever I'm disturbed while eating now, I remind people the last time someone upset my meal I had them dissolved in an air strike.

The field started narrowing by the south end, swinging close to Cambodia. Late in the afternoon, we arrived at its end, establishing ambush sites.

The patrol leader and top sergeant oriented the men, many of whom were recent replacements, with their situation along the edge of the field. Most of the jungle bordering the opposite side was in Cambodia. A VC could not be fired at until he left that jungle completely behind and was unquestionably in Vietnam. There was one possibility for ambush, a portion of the jungle bulged into the field belonging in Vietnam. Any ignorant VC who strayed into it would qualify as a "target of opportunity."

The infantrymen experienced President Lyndon Johnson's idea of fighting a war: if the bad guys weren't in the right place at the right time, they weren't bad guys anymore.

I was behind the squad lying prone inside the trees, reconnoitering the field. This quiet was an opportunity to open a can of spaghetti and meatballs, liberally dose it with Tabasco sauce, and stir in a chopped onion to eat while I waited for the picture show to commence. The wait wasn't long; I wished I had a box of hot buttered popcorn and iced Coke for this action flick.

Two VC emerged from Cambodian jungle, clinging to the edge while stalking toward our direction. The men in front acted as they were new "in country," excited like kids, jabbering while waving their weapons about. I wiped my mouth on my sleeve, put my chow away, and lay the M-16 against a tree. The VC were out of effective range; all I could do was watch.

"Let's get them!"

The top sergeant heard this commotion and crawled past to investigate. "Wait one dad gum minute, you young bucks," the seasoned old warrior cautioned his new warriors. "I'll take care of 'em."

I asked one of the troops about him.

"Oh, Sarge's an ol' Tennessee squirrel hunter; he's supposed to be a fantastic shot. Watch, he'll get 'em both."

I edged closer for a better view.

He growled to me about my movement; they might see flashes.

The soldiers' M-16, 12 gauge, and M-79 wouldn't reach the VC over 800 meters away. He told them to watch and learn as it might save their lives sometime.

We couldn't shoot them until they reached the bunch of bushes sticking into Vietnam, then they were fair game. Be patient and don't scare them away. When they reached the outstretch of bushes Sarge would "git 'em."

Kentucky windage; wetting his finger, he held it for wind direction and speed. Next he wiped it on the gun sight, preventing shine. The maximum effective range of Sarge's M-14 was 850 meters, the distance to his targets.

The "ol' Tennessee squirrel hunter" laid his barrel in the crotch of a bush. His eyes squinted, watching the targets across this field of sun, 10 football fields away—following and waiting for his prey to wander into Vietnam.

His finger slowly curled, tightening the trigger while removing slack in the mechanism.

The troops were dead silent.

A slight breeze rocked the Sarge, he lost his concentration.

The VC reached the clump.

"Get them, get them now," urged one of the men.

Someone cautioned him quiet. They were next to each other; he had to wait until they were apart so he could get both.

A fly landed on Sarge's cheek and began skittering about until it reached beads of perspiration on his forehead for a drink.

Sarge was a statue. The only thing moving were his eyes, squinting tighter now that the men moved apart and stopped, facing our direction. This was a dream: the enemy seemed to sense we were scouting them. They stopped, split apart, turned, and looked directly toward us—displaying a magnificent view of their chests.

"CRACK, CRACK!" Two rapid shots. Two seconds later they fell like bowling pins.

"Strike," the ol' Tennessee squirrel hunter muttered, shooing away the fly. "Got 'em rascals."

He scanned that area with binoculars and didn't notice movement. "Nobody retrieve 'em." They weren't going anywhere.

"Bang, bang—you're dead!"

The platoon remained for two days; hopefully they might be able to ambush a few more while resting. First Platoon patrolled the jungle by the border, two miles away, for camps.

A Supply chopper deposited water for 1st Platoon; I took the lift. Lt. Col. Staples, our battalion commander, was there.

They captured a base camp earlier, killed a few infiltrators, and captured important papers and medical supplies. I took pictures before evacuation.

The next two days yielded nothing. As we established a perimeter for Supply, it arrived.

Sergeant Major Rocks called me.

"Got someone for you here," he said as the chopper lifted off. Father Confroy, our chaplain, arrived.

I couldn't imagine what he was doing here. I explained we had rowdies next door and that the chopper wouldn't return until morning.

He thanked me for my concern, reminding me it was Sunday, we hadn't had mass in a while, and he could take the chopper in the morning. He asked for a place for mass to say before dusk and to spread the word.

There wasn't room in the jungle and mass couldn't be celebrated in the LZ. Also we had to be quiet so the VC wouldn't know we were there. In addition, it was pretty late and Father couldn't stay for the night.

He asked the sergeant major for men to hack a hole in the jungle. In addition, that chopper wouldn't return until the morning. I was stuck with him that night. He reminded me about voices; if the VC didn't hear the chopper, they couldn't hear a thing.

The sergeant major growled to three soldiers, "Get machetes and cut a hole for the Father."

He grabbed two others: "Spread the word the Father's going to say mass at 1700 hours. Take three C rations cases and stack as an altar. A.S.A.P."

I took Father to my six- by three-foot hooch: VC hammock between two trees and hacked out jungle. I cut another spot next to me for his poncho, folding it in half to slide into. One of the trees my hammock was strung on had a short stubby branch, ideal for his pistol belt and pack.

Fortunately he had a minimum of infantry training and didn't require much jungle living orientation except, in the advent of hostile firing, I told him to "keep your head down and sit right here in my back pocket."

I offered to prepare one of my jungle specialties of heated C- Rations. He declined my invite, rationalizing he had chow before leaving.

The men did an excellent job clearing a spot for mass, completely eliminating all shrubs, vines, and branches. Even the tall elephant grass was stamped down during the process. Unfortunately stamping caused water to secrete out of the sponge-like mat of the jungle floor, creating a potpourri of yellow mud and green vegetation.

Men squeezed into our tiny sanctum; even Sergeant Major Rocks joined. Curiously, no one had taken his weapon. Their shifting from foot to foot while waiting for mass formed a quagmire below.

Father unfurled a white altar cloth and draped it across the top of the stacked muddy C ration cases. "A seemingly sacrilegious act for an altar," I mused. The rations become consecrated by the cloth, holy vessels, and hosts.

His yellow, clay-coated boots immediately rubbed onto his immaculate white cassock.

Everything else was turning muddy. He lifted the golden chalice, Communion tray, and host vessel out of their transport case and placed them on the altar next to cruets of water and wine.

The jungle turned quiet; I didn't hear the constant working of birds. Was the enemy was near, or was it God? I didn't notice the mud while the men stopped perspiring.

"Pez, are all the men here? Are we ready to start?"

I cautioned him to whisper. Also, it might be a good idea we didn't use the chime to signal raising the host and wine.

"Oh, thank you, Pez."

I was afraid flies and mosquitoes would crowd into the hosts and red wine, but was surprised to see that for the first time in Vietnam there weren't any.

The wind painted a melodic sound whispering through entanglements of vines and teakwood. Silence, except for the soft prayers of Father; the entire world appeared put on hold. This stagnant jungle felt fresh.

Jesus' Last Supper was conducted in Jerusalem in an inauspicious room of a nondescript clay structure, celebrating his imminent death on a simple table barely large enough to accommodate 13 people, possibly covered by a tablecloth.

Father held the large host above his head, looked into the heavens and said, "Take this and eat, for this is my body." Sun filtered through the opaque jungle canopy, creating shafts of light sifting between the trees and dancing about the altar.

"Take this and drink" he said raising the chalice with wine. Trees swayed in the breeze, causing shafts of light to blend together on the chalice.

When Father said, "For this is my blood ..." everything appeared to slow down, not exactly slow motion, but in another dimension where everything is slow. I was removed from our world, watching life from a different perspective—a TV screen.

That beacon of sun concentrating on the chalice now reflected brilliance, dazzling my eyes. Warm air caressed the back of my ears; troops became captivated, time halted, feeling neither hot nor cold, wet nor dry.

He lowered the chalice and events began to ensue at an increasing pace, like a phonograph wound up. "This is how Christ's disciples felt during the last supper when Christ broke the bread and served the wine."

The men experienced the real thing, not dwarfed by colossal edifices contaminating our view of God, or dazzled by gold, silver, and ivory obscuring His beauty.

We had found God.

Father left in the morning chopper.

The patrol remained there several days but nothing else was found. The 1st of the 18th went home several days later on March 6.

Chapter 17

At Least the Vietnamese People Appreciate Us

Marty said it was good to hear I sounded positive, which was difficult with all the news about war protesters. They were only the minority and the media blows everything out of proportion. Sensible Americans realized we were doing a great job.

The girl I had met at Cape Cod had recently moved to San Francisco and invited me to visit her.

The media fell into a rut, a skipping record; continuous dialog about KIAs or WIAs became a boring redundancy. Anything decent was tame, not warranting circulation.

My material appeared in military publications; unfortunately none of my caring, human-interest stories appeared in civilian publications. The Army lifted its cap on using photos of wounded troops, and that became about all the national news digested.

There's nothing glorious about being wounded; a WIA is a heart's beat from death. If I, or any of my troops, had seen a camera team photographing our men badly wounded or dying, we would have not thought lightly about it.

In 1992 Ginger Casey condensed a version of his article, appearing in *Image,* to reappear in *Reader's Digest.* It was called, "Have They No Shame?" It disclosed reporters' lack of discretion for a story, the bottom line being money.

He wrote: "A kind of frenzy takes place over a highly charged event and reporters don't necessarily act, they react.

"And we journalists rarely consider the consequences of our presence at an event."

In another article from the *Digest,* William K. Lane Jr. shared a condensed version of his *Wall Street Journal* story, "American Vets: Ambushed in Hollywood," noting hundreds of Americans fighting in Vietnam deserve better than to be caricatured as a legion of losers.

He said few of us needed a support group. That rarely was there a need to indulge in "prattle about 'post-traumatic-stress disorder.'" That some of the bravest and best men who ever wore an American uniform fought in that war.

Len Morgan, a journalist for *Flying Magazine,* wrote in June 1991: "The news media's primary objective is money. The media's professed aims are to report events, record history, and present both sides of an important issue but the bottom line is none of the above. This media primarily exists to earn profits for its stockholders. Success is measured by circulation and ratings, which in turn determines advertising rates. A thrill-a-minute approach is the result." If nothing exciting happens, ratings slip, and profits drop.

I found a ride to the photo lab to print photos. By early afternoon I hitched to the four corners at 2nd Brigade Headquarters and the bustling village of Tan Heip. While walking through, I saw the girl I was with when the VC caught me with my pants off.

She smiled, took my hand, and led me to her new house. It had been recently constructed out of whitewashed clay and was covered with a thatched tin roof. The floor was poured clay with drainage ditches. The only furnishings were a cot, small dresser, curtains over the windows, and straw mats hanging from the front and rear doors.

She served a beer she had soaking in the creek behind. I began calculations: "What to do, lay her now and leave, or shack up tonight?"

My decision was interrupted by the noise of two Vietnamese boys running through the rear door, shouting as they came. She called something back, like a warning. The two boys, both about 14, stumbled to a stop and stared at me with surprised expressions on their faces. One, the girl's brother, began laughing with her like a typical kid. I couldn't understand what they were saying, but their conversation didn't appear significant.

What alarmed me was her brother's friend, who stared at me with the look of Hollywood's vicious World War II Jap.

The kid glared at me exactly like that now, obviously not enjoying my presence! He had to be a VC. Several captured ones looked at us the same way, the old, hard-core types who dug tunnels for a decade. I was surprised seeing this young kid with that same penetrating glare.

I obviously moved my M-16 to auto, then conspicuously pulled the bolt back reassuring for all that a round was chambered. The metal flap covering the breech clicked open; I gradually tilted the weapon sideward and glanced in.

Gradually I rearranged my back against the wall so the muzzle rested on my boot, pointed directly at him. My left hand grasped the pistol grip, middle finger caressed the trigger, and eyes looked directly into his. I had the advantage of wearing dark glasses, scanning the woman and brother without them realizing I was looking.

"Hm-m-m," I thought, "What do I do if more people come in?" The cottage was on the main street; still, Communists had never been shy about provoking a gunfight in public. I was aware the advantage was mine, for the time being, and thought it best to leave while it was still practical.

The guys back at Headquarters vowed I would be zapped yet.

I had pictures and stories to turn into Division Headquarters the next day. HQ 2 would be available at noon; I asked Communications for a shotgun. The NCO said Tobey was available.

He was glad to break the monotony and thrilled when I said we had time for women after—if he wanted.

We had chow together and drove to Division, stopping at whorehouses along the way to review the selection for our return.

I didn't speak much with the people from the division information office because we needed time with the ladies.

We left and got only a mile away before seeing five trucks stopped.

"Let's see what the problem is, Tobey."

Men hid behind trucks with an MP running about, waving his weapon, and looking threatening. He wore a military baseball cap, flak vest with two grenades hanging, and buck knife with bone handle on his pistol belt. His dark sunglasses, plus Grease Gun with three taped magazines, gave the impression of Hollywood's version of a G.I. He continued to wave his rifle toward us yelling something like, "Stop, they're out there. VC shooting."

"Let's go, Tobey."

I asked what the deal was.

Someone was out there, he puffed, pointing to a cluster of clay huts along the right the side of the road. They sniped.

I looked at Tobey, he looked back at me and we laughed, "Well, let's go get them."

"Huh?"

We needed someone else. Tobey grabbed a driver hiding behind his truck, looking ineffective.

Tobey laughed that we had to give him a try; there was nobody else.

I told him to get behind Tobey and me, next to the MP. I figured the firing probably came from the second hut and told the MP to run around the right side, the driver the opposite. I cautioned all to beware of someone coming out the back door, not to shoot each other, and watch where they aimed first. As Tobey and I advanced, I told him the window and me the door before lighting another, then glanced at him on the opposite side of the road. He wore a combat experienced infantryman's look of confidence. His eyes intensely scanned the front, his M-14 held in the ready, finger snug against the trigger. I felt secure until I glanced behind at the driver and MP.

The driver's eyes were at half-mast, looking like he was sleepwalking while the MP crouched, still waving his rifle.

"Oh, my God," I prayed, "help me now!"

Fifteen feet from the hut, we charged. The MP and driver split, running around each side. The door and window had burlap hanging. Tobey leaped up and dove through the window, landing on his elbows and legs in the prone. I plunged through the door and went prone also, each rifle searching for a target.

Nobody inside!

An M-14 fired a burst behind the hut.

I gasped at the sound; the driver shot the MP. We sprang up and continued through the hut, discovering, to our surprise, the driver had drilled the VC when he ran out the back without hitting the MP.

We left the hut with the MP handling the details of this shooting.

The time was getting late; it was essential to return before dusk, without stopping for talent. In addition, Tobey and I were still wound up from the shooting and didn't feel like sex. We had done something better; we just killed a VC.

Work began on our new base camp at Bear Cat on Highway #15, the highway leading from the coastal town of Vung Tau to Bien Hoa. Engineers bulldozed a mile clearing out of the jungle, constructed a protective wall of sand 20 feet tall and 10 feet wide, and laid roads with drainage ditches. The defensive perimeter was hollowed out at different locations for situating gun emplacements. They were guarded by the Vietnamese Ranger unit at the beginning of our dirt road on Highway #15, two miles away.

A local VC unit had been acting frisky lately, sniping and planting mines as the engineers worked. "Operation Salem" began March 13, its objective multipurpose: kill or disrupt these VC, find their camps, and introduce the Viet Rangers to their new neighbors.

This six-day mission united us with the Sat Cong (Kill Cong), an elite Vietnamese Special Forces unit attached to the outpost. These men specialized in long-range patrols; the Brass felt we might gain patrolling techniques from them.

The location was 15 miles from our current camp and 20 miles northeast of Saigon. My battalion, the 1st of the 18th, was on this long-range patrol with no other Big Red One unit. We convoyed here where Charlie Company met our patrol partners, the Sat Cong.

All 10 seemed taller than average Vietnamese, wearing camouflaged fatigues and floppy hats, carrying a Swedish K. The K fired .45-caliber bullets and was more accurate and reliable than our .45 calibers, the Thompson and Grease Gun. They looked at us cautiously at first, as did we. The only Vietnamese we knew prior to them were our interpreters, prostitutes, and pimps. These men had met a few U.S. advisors previously, but association with Americans had been brief. We would be patrolling with soldiers from the country we were helping to defend.

Intelligence learned of a VC training camp near Bear Cat. Arrivals from the North were familiarized with the area. It was compulsory locating this facility, disrupting enemy activities against our new base. Also, Highway #15 to Vung Tau was opening for supplies to Long Binh Supply Depot but not considered secure yet.

The leader of the Sat Cong was a lieutenant of Chinese extraction, a little taller than his group. He spoke some English, discussing the patrol route with the battalion commander, Lieutenant Colonel Staples before departing. He wanted point, but the colonel told him to restrain for a few days until troops familiarized with each other.

We found the VC camp the third day out, vacated for two weeks. There were black pajamas, personal letters, and a propaganda poster printed in English. It capitalized on social unrest in the U.S., exemplified by the protest marches the previous October. Someone maintained this camp because we found two beautiful, healthy, fat pigs on leashes.

The CO didn't think the VC knew we were there, deciding to stay for the night, establishing ambushes. We knifed the pigs and prepared to discard them in a stagnant swamp. One of the Vietnamese troops stopped us; he wanted to cook ham for dinner. The CO OKed it under the stipulation that all cooking apparatus would away and out by sunset. He put the Vietnamese soldiers in the center of the perimeter because of language and identification problems.

A couple of men assisted the Vietnamese preparing the ham. One had been a butcher in the States and advised the ham would take too long to cook as it was. He suggested carving slices, placing them inside banana leaves, and saturating them with onion and Tabasco sauce while cooking over an open flame. One of the Vietnamese offered rice, which was cooked in fish-smelling oil. The cuisine was ready by nightfall. Gourmet dining in the jungle; the G.I.s and Sat Cong stuffed themselves.

The butcher and the man with the rice immediately hit it off, developing an amiable relationship in the short time left to the patrol. This feeling spread to the rest of the troops and in two days the Sat Cong knew the typical favorite American clichés. We learned something valuable from them: pointers on long-range patrols.

Our patrol found 10 hooches the next day with 50 pounds of Chinese TNT, a Claymore-type antipersonnel mine, and a new 20-pound mine. They were preparing to blow the mines when four "civilians" wandered into camp on an oxcart. The Viet soldiers questioned them, learning they were woodcutters with no tools, had never seen this hut with TNT and mines before, and had forgotten their IDs at home, 10 miles of jungle away. A supply chopper evacuated them to Army Republic of Vietnam (ARVN) Headquarters for interrogation.

The operation terminated less than half a day's walk to Bear Cat. The CO granted the Sat Cong permission to take point.

Shortly after, a VC casually sauntered along the trail with his carbine slung over his shoulder. A short burst from a Swedish K ended his life.

Intelligence told us when we returned that the four captured VC "volunteered" helpful information about their unit and intentions when Highway #15 opened to transport supplies.

Unfortunately, this information was too late; the VC ambushed a three-truck convoy from Vung Tau on the last day of our operation, March 18.

When we arrived at camp, it also became the first day of our next operation, "Wheaton." The accompanying platoon patrol was immediately shuttled to the ambush site to assist with the wounded, search for enemy stragglers, and recover supplies. We were surprised when we arrived; all the trucks and supplies remained intact. The reason was obvious when we discovered they were—C rations.

Two of the six men in the ambush were killed and the rest wounded. There was no idea how many VC were killed. After a while the truck drivers noticed the VC stopped firing, probably because most had been killed.

All trucks had damage to their engines and had to be towed. While a chopper removed the casualties, we searched, unsuccessfully, for wounded enemy before establishing a perimeter for the night. A clean stream nearby offered an opportunity to wash. We also had the "honorarium" of access to three truckloads of C rations.

I returned to my old base camp the next day, wrote stories, ate chow, and assisted with packing Headquarters' equipment. In two days, March 21, we moved from camp at Ho Nai to the new one at Bear Cat.

The movement was well organized; we went by unit, at different times on different days, with the infantry first. The units felt they were moving into a land development area, each established in their designated spot; it was more decent than the crude base camps we had had before.

Our camp was two miles down a straight two-lane dirt road directly behind the Ranger camp on Highway #15. The Sat Cong said they would be able to rest securely at nights with their with new neighbors.

The 2nd Brigade of the Big Red One would be together for the first time in Vietnam, all 5,000 plus "under one roof."

After the equipment was moved, most of the infantry took passes before "Operation Bend" at Cambodia in two days, the Red infiltration route. General Westmoreland's Staff MAC-V wasn't as concerned with killing the enemy as they were with knowing his disposition.

This was "Charlie's" neighborhood from the air: all jungle and a few small fields, but no farms, streams, swamps, huts, or trails.

The choppers with Bravo landed in a field and patrolled a trail through the jungle to the next clearing, two hours away. I was with them because they were closest to Cambodia's border. Large units of North Vietnamese were expected, compelling companies to be kept whole.

It became obvious a large force was prevalent. The trail was well worn with recent footprints and bicycle tracks. Although this trail was wide enough for an oxcart, there were no such tracks. We speculated it was an infiltration route for personnel rather than supplies.

The company stopped in the shade for lunch, a time to seek enemy movement. I ate chow at the ambush position, hoping to capture some action.

We left in two hours after no contact. As we crossed the field, I moved up two from point before entering a jungle trail.

An hour later this widened, following adjacent to a long, narrow field. Several bunched together, surveying this field before following the trail along the edge. I unbuttoned the top pocket of my shirt to look at my small camera, making sure perspiration from my chest wasn't leaking into its plastic bag.

I was always in a quandary if I saw someone whether to shoot him with my camera or my M-16. Normally I was in front, wisely electing to use the rifle.

Most of Bravo was out of the jungle and along the trail winding the edge of the field. While nonchalantly walking next to point, I tried to button the flap on my camera pocket. The button was wet from perspiration and kept slipping.

I stopped, but instinctively looked ahead before lowering my eyes to fasten it. A young Vietnamese wearing a tan shirt, pants, and pistol belt almost bumped into me from the other way. He immediately turned and fled across the field like a spooked deer.

"Do I shoot him with the camera or rifle?" I was perplexed during this moment of truth.

My pocket flap was still open; I thrust my hand in, grabbing the camera. The protection bag and my shirt were drenched while the straps of my rucksack pulled my shirt back, gripping the camera.

One try—it could not come out!

"Dong lat," the point called to this VC kid.

I focused my M-16 on the fleeing enemy, 30 feet away, firing two six-round bursts while the point pumped his 12 gauge. A trooper had just turned the corner and fired an M-79, exploding wide.

I pulled my muzzle away after the second burst, dragging the gun's smoke. My target dropped abruptly, as if swallowed by a hole. I saw his shirt in the tall grass, observed him moving, popped the rucksack off, and ran after him holding the M-16 by the pistol grip while attempting to pull the camera out with the other hand. It came out easily because the ruck-sack straps weren't restricting it. The camera was out of the plastic bag by the time I reached my victim.

He was still alive and panting heavily on his stomach.

"He's still alive, lying on his hands. Got him covered!"

I held my rifle with one hand, tried to focus with the other, and pushed the grass down around him with my feet squeezing him into the picture.

"Pant, pant"—and finally "gasp." His breath stopped as two men reached his body. I finally got a great photo—an enemy the moment he died!

The point man and our interpreter cautiously turned him. My neat little .223 mm hole was visible through his shirt in the center of his back, and I congratulated myself on the nice shot.

The point man argued he had shot him.

I explained it was not a 12-gauge hole.

He insisted it was a slug hole from 00 Buck.

I didn't care what he claimed. My concern was that I finally took the great picture, which could not be denied. I also knew I was the one who killed that VC.

We patrolled the rest of the day and set ambushes at night, but didn't make any more contact.

The next day we scouted three more fields and waited in ambush for several hours but didn't find any activity. This surprised us because we had seen indications of many VC.

"Bend" terminated the next day, March 27. The next operation, "Abilene," would begin March 30. On March 28 we spent the morning searching for a location to establish the Forward CP. We found a clearing in the early afternoon and secured the perimeter for the other companies which

The moment the VC that I just shot stopped breathing. Two troopers are "fetching" him. The VC's shoulder is barely visible in the lower right-hand corner of the photograph.

were to arrive shortly. I helped several men prepare the Headquarters tents. I took my shirt off but it did nothing to ease the heat. I felt weak and swallowed three salt tablets, hoping to restore my energy while realizing I should have taken them earlier.

The water trailer arrived with water that must have been in the sun all day. It was pumped from local streams, then somehow purified before we got it. When this stuff was cool it tasted marginal; after it got hot it was barely palatable regardless how thirsty you were. I managed to force down a cup anyway.

The next few days kept me busy with duties associated with Headquarters; I was obliged to help them in addition to reporting.

It was March 29, and the new operation was to begin that next day. Major Weeks suggested I join Alpha and told Sergeant Grassburg to let me get some rest; I didn't look good. Hans said he was holding mail for me at our base camp in Bear Cat. Rick screamed that a new whorehouse opened up with "Numba ten thou boom-boom girls."

I didn't really care.

They wondered what was wrong with me, that I must be "getting short."

Most of us classified as "old timers or short timers" had less than two months. I felt exhausted, tired, and sick from heat, moisture, subhuman living conditions, lack of rest, mosquitoes, flies that bite, exhaustion, and constant danger. I did not feel like accompanying the troops but it was expected. If I had to go on this operation, I was determined to make it as easy as possible.

The troops normally carried double the basic load of ammo; I took half that, 100 rounds. I carried two, sometimes three grenades—this time I took only one. There were supposed to be streams with clean water; only one canteen would by needed, I fantasized. I felt I had been force-feeding myself C rations. Each box consisted of three cans; I selected only one or two cans per meal and didn't take onions or Tabasco. I felt I didn't need a bayonet; if necessary, to stab someone, I'd use my sharper machete, hacking off a piece.

I departed with Alpha at sunrise, melting into the jungle behind our camp. Intelligence heard sounds of groups of people moving and talking from listening devices. Our assignment was investigating them.

The heat made life intolerable. We weren't blessed with winter monsoons in the afternoon. I was thirsty but didn't want to drink my limited amount of water. Unfortunately I had a headache and couldn't sleep between radio watches. "A splash of cool water on my face in the morning with a clean towel to wipe it off," I fantasized.

Captain Barrell marked our location with smoke grenades the second day. Major Weeks, flying in an observation chopper, identified this as where sounds were transmitted.

Two squads reconned while the rest remained in the bush. There were shots from their guns.

The men radioed they had captured a small village with women, kids, and men with crossbows.

"Crossbows?" Captain Barrell queried.

They suspected poison arrows also.

The village was almost completely secluded inside trees draped with vines. A wide trail wound down the center while a clean stream snuggled outside. There were 12 huts, some chickens, a pig, plus several patches of garden.

Six captured VC with a Viet national policeman questioning them while a GI examines one of their crossbows that shot poison arrows.

"Where are all the men?" we asked.

"Out in the jungle hunting," the typical reply from a VC village.

The four men carrying crossbows were sitting in a group at the center of the village with the bows and arrows lying next to them. Nobody watched them; each was concerned with looking for war souvenirs of arms and equipment in the village. I positioned my weapon on these four from a discrete distance. They appeared to be cooperating with us; I didn't want to upset the situation by being too aggressive.

One of the G.I.s walked by, picked up a crossbow and began examining it. I snapped a photo. He took an arrow out of the quiver, placed it in the weapon, and attempted to cock it by placing the stock against his belt, struggled as he eased back on the bowstring, yet failed to pull it back far enough to cock.

One of the Viet Cong laughed at his struggle and volunteered to show how to arm it. He sat on the ground with his feet against the inside of the bow and bent forward, taking the string in his hands, leaning back, and pulling at the same time. Now that it was cocked, he placed an arrow into the breach, aiming into the brush.

"OK, great!" The infantryman thanked him and walked away.

The Viet Cong kept the bow in his hands, looking for another American to show how he fully armed his weapon but everyone was too busy to notice.

"Who is watching these prisoners?" demanded Captain Barrell as he passed the captives. "We've got armed prisoners here and nobody's watching them. Get someone here!"

The captain didn't notice I had them covered. In any case, they were cooperating amicably.

This road passed into a small field, eventually meandering to the Forward CP. A convoy would arrive in an hour to take the villagers to a Vietnamese army post. I had taken some good pictures and contemplated going back to print them. Still, there was enemy activity here, so I decided to stay a few more days so as not to miss something. The troops rambunctiously explored the camp and tunnels for spoils and souvenirs until we moved out.

I had another difficult time sleeping this night; my scalp was painfully itchy. Regardless how much I scratched, it still persisted. I was afraid I had crabs or lice.

I didn't want to eat in the morning. Also, I didn't feel like being up front with the point; fighting the branches and vines wasn't appealing anymore. I had no energy. My scalp was still itchy at noon; I scratched so hard I expected hair to come out.

The company spent several hours having lunch while waiting in ambush. I lay in the sun at the edge of the field with a squad. The sun blasted down relentlessly with no air circulating. My clothes were drenched with sweat and canteen water tasted foul.

The company moved out later in the afternoon, continuing its sweep. I was faint, waiting until almost everyone passed before I joined.

I ate only one can of chow that evening because I had given most of my rations away and suffered through another sleepless night, leaving me completely exhausted.

I knew the fourth day of this sweep was Friday because malaria tablets were distributed. I asked the medic if he thought I had malaria. He couldn't tell what was wrong, but said my eyes were yellow and I didn't look healthy.

The Supply chopper arrived at noon; I returned to base camp Bear Cat.

"What's wrong?" Sergeant Grassburg queried while he removed camouflage branches from my helmet.

I said I'd go to the Med tent to check for malaria.

He supposed I got something from them "dad gum whoores."

My blood was clear; the medics speculated I was exhausted.

Grassburg said no radio watch for me that night; the colonel wanted me resting.

I wrote three stories, tried to eat hot chow out of my greasy mess kit, and drank two iced soft drinks. When I crawled into my sleeping bag and mosquito net at 2100 I was exhausted, but I couldn't sleep most of the night.

Sergeant Grassburg was going to Bien Hoa and asked if I had pictures to print.

I looked so bad the Air Force technicians volunteered to print the photos, and they asked me to have chow with them.

I didn't feel hungry.

They suggested I go anyway; I might find something I liked.

Their mess hall was a restaurant: air conditioned, tables covered with cloth, porcelain plates, silverware, glasses, and linen napkins. Vietnamese worked the tables as waiters.

The serving line was set up like an exclusive cafeteria in New York City with a selection of carved roast beef, fried chicken, and filet of sole. I could take part of each selection if I wanted. Iced butter for hot rolls. White and chocolate milk. They even had ice cream! I took seconds on everything, eating so much my stomach ached and skin tingled. I was content now, realizing what was wrong on the operation—I almost cracked up again, starving myself.

I was in the boonies with the troops in a day, feeling more like my old self: anticipating combat.

The three companies had killed a dozen North Vietnamese and captured all their equipment. They had found two more base camps, ambushed three groups, and Bravo was ambushed with casualties. There was still enemy activity when I joined them.

The VC had an ambush waiting for Bravo the day before when they crossed a field. "A hundred were stretched out inside a field we crossed," Captain Richards told me. They had mines inside the tree line when his company entered the jungle. The troops didn't stand a chance; one man was killed and two others wounded. He was going to do something different crossing the large field ahead.

I joined four sent up the flank to destroy anything ahead before the company crossed.

We began almost casually walking together in a group. The field was three miles wide with no cover and only a partial concealment by the tall grass. Bravo's destination was trees on the other side; trails had been noticed.

The company looked obvious stretched out crossing the field. We definitely were not fooling anyone.

Our squad was a half-mile off their left flank, now crouching as we hustled. The trees at our destination turned out to be a small grove of rubber trees. Sergeant Berry called Captain Richards and reported we were flanking a rubber plantation and we had him covered.

One of our men noticed someone by the edge of the trees. A Vietnamese with black clothes and a rifle hid behind the bank framing them.

We stalked him, noticing he surveyed Bravo as they traverse the field. We snuck 25 feet from him before hiding behind shrubbery, ensuring he wasn't ambush bait for us.

He sensed our presence and whipped around, looking directly in our eyes.

"Dung lat!"

More decisions: do I shoot him with my camera or rifle?

I flipped my rucksack off and unbuttoned my jacket pocket. The VC began escaping along a trail traversing a seven-foot bank. I ran after him along the top while the squad fired four weapons at him, an auto M-14, M-16, an auto carbine, and M-79 grenade launcher, directly behind and next to me. I had the utmost confidence in their fire discipline, knowing they were aiming directly at the target and I wasn't in danger of being hit by stray shots.

I was running 10 feet from the VC when I slipped against the side of the bank, gun in one hand, camera the other, and eyes still on him. At that moment he disappeared from the trail like a fly whisked off your arm.

I scrambled to my feet and noticed he had fallen down the opposite side of the bank and was lying at its base, panting heavily on his back. I slid down the bank with my rifle and camera on him simultaneously.

"He's down and alive. Have him covered!"

Two men ran along the trail to him; I got that photo.

He was breathing heavily as we examined him. An M-16 round entered his arm at the wrist and tumbled up his forearm to the elbow, splitting his arm open in two places. These two gashes along his forearm

Opposite: Two U.S. soldiers crouch over the badly wounded VC (barely discernible in photograph) I had been chasing. Even though his head had been enlarged by a M-16 round in the roof of his mouth and right arm split up the middle by another, he continued panting another 45 minutes until the medic put three bullets into his head.

appeared severed by a scalpel. The other round entered his open mouth, plunging into the roof, causing his cheeks to puff like he had mumps. Both his mouth and forearm were void of any blood. If I hadn't known a bullet had gone into his mouth, I would have suspected a toothache or mumps. None of the spray of blood seen in movies coated him.

The rest of the company joined us from the field. Three VC ambushed a squad sent to secure the right flank where the grove bordered the jungle. One was hit; the others saturated the jungle with lead and a few grenades. The squad didn't know if they hit anyone, but incoming rounds terminated.

I heard these shots and joined to help. The guy shot in the leg wrapped it with a first aid pad and was assisted through the plantation by buddies.

"This is my opportunity for a photo of a wounded G.I."

As I lined him up for another "Great War Photo," he started laughing.

"Stop laughing," I pleaded. I wanted a photo of pain after being shot. He laughed even harder.

This was a million-dollar wound and it would take him home because he was short.

A chopper evacuated him, but not the brain-dead VC still panting.

The company entered the jungle behind the grove after an hour. The CO didn't want to stay in the open rubber trees which made a good target for artillery.

"Move out."

A burst rang out from the medic's carbine. The man was brain dead and would have died eventually; the medic sped up the process.

The CO split Bravo into platoon-sized patrols with 3rd Platoon assigned a route adjacent to Cambodia, bait for the fish while the other two platoons were the net. I joined the bait.

We reconned the edge of a clearing wandering parallel to Cambodia while other patrols looked for camps in the jungles behind us.

After searching during the morning and part of the afternoon, Brigade terminated this operation. They had us alter our route and move to an LZ in the jungle for a flight and rest at Forward CP.

Our new route led us into the jungle, traversing a clean, shallow stream where the point halted us. He sniffed the familiar foul human aroma of an enemy base camp emanating inside.

I joined him and two squads crawling toward that smell, leading to the trench parameter around a camp. We gingerly crawled over roots and vines encircling the compound. Peeking through the tall grass next to the trench perimeter, we saw four men sitting at a crude table. The inside was void of vegetation.

A VC lifted a camouflaged tunnel cover and called to someone below. We thought he might have sensed our presence and was signaling others. The point, two men on his right and one the left instantly fired, striking the VC down like wheat before the reaper. The four were dead and the camp was immediately secured. Three others began exploring the tunnel complex with flashlights and .45-caliber pistols.

One crawled 35 feet along a narrow shaft when his flashlight beam illuminated black pajamas ahead. He fired four times and saw the figure collapse. Cautiously he snaked to the moaning figure, disarmed it, and pulled the person with him squirming backward.

After the troops managed to lift the victim to the surface, they saw an 18-year-old girl.

The medic did his best to plug the three wounds in her legs, one pumping blood from an artery. She required immediate hospital treatment, but dense jungle prohibited a copter from landing. The patrol had announced its presence and had to leave immediately by disappearing into the jungle toward the closest clearing a mile away.

The medic devised a makeshift stretcher out of his poncho draped over two legs of the enemy's conference table. Four men carried the stretcher while two others hacked a three-foot swath through the jungle.

Moving through the jungle was difficult for infantrymen doing the carrying and hacking. In addition to their 65 pounds of equipment and 105-degree temperature and 99-percent humidity, they had to contend with hauling her. The urgency to arrive at the LZ before sunset and danger of enemy contact increased their ordeal. They endangered lives by noisily hacking a path in enemy territory, which could easily be followed. I was amazed no one complained that someone who tried to kill them earlier was responsible for their hardships.

Frequently one of the men asked the medic about her condition. Others volunteered to carry the stretcher or chop ahead.

After three hours of struggling, they realized the clearing could not be made before sunset so a night perimeter was drawn; everyone was alert for the attack we thought was imminent. The men had their hopes: if there was no enemy contact that night, it would be a short distance in the morning.

The medic hacked a spot, erecting a shelter over the girl with his poncho. Another trooper donated his poncho to spread on the ground. During the night, practically each of the 45 men left his position, minding her condition.

They inquired about making her more comfortable, water, chow, or bedding.

Unfortunately her pulse became weak, irregular, and her face cooled. The wounds in her legs appeared to have stopped bleeding, but the medic suspected internal bleeding.

At 0130 her pulse stopped, her breathing ceased, and her face got cold. A grave was dug in the morning and buried where she died. Each of the men paid their respects, some tossing wild flowers on the grave.

This was a great story the men asked me not to write. They felt responsible for her death, not shooting to neutralize an armed enemy, but because of their slow portage. If security relaxed, they might have reached the clearing before dark. I couldn't see how this was possible.

I would have questioned its credibility had I not been there. This is one of many instances where the men in Vietnam went out of their way to aid their captives, an enemy who was trying to kill them moments before.

This war was one gigantic paradox, part of the soul of the Wall.

Bravo remained in a blocking, ambush status at another field for two days. Alpha joined them for the night, both patrolling the next day.

We noticed enemy signs, but didn't see him or his equipment. Alpha had made contact with a squad while Bravo ambushed two different groups, one at night and the other in early morning. By midafternoon the second day, the trail passed the bottom of a bald hill standing above the thinly vegetated field. Alpha would be exposed while crossing; Captain Barrell needed to survey the route ahead.

I noticed him climbing the hill with his RTO, Billy Day, and decided to join them. Barrell was cresting the hill while I was halfway up and a little forward. The hill was difficult to climb because of stumps, roots, rocks, and gullies.

Billy reached the top first; in front was a rock with someone hiding behind it. A VC with a rifle behind that rock hadn't seen me. He was too far to get a sharp photo; I decided to kill him instead.

The gully I was in had loose rocks. In my haste, I slipped and fell on my face, rifle clanking the helmet. The VC saw me, turned, and ran down the hill away from me. I flung off my rucksack and ran after him while we scrambled over the rocky surface. I positioned myself directly behind him and tried to remain on his tail down the hill toward the jungle.

I lost sight of him when he disappeared into another gully, but continued, not knowing what I'd do when and if I caught him. Moments later he surfaced and half of Alpha opened fire.

He switched to the left and disappeared into a third gully, obscuring him from everyone but me.

I couldn't stop for a picture now; he would disappear before I focused. There was a grove of six-foot reeds at the bottom. If I took the time to aim and shoot my weapon, he would be into the reeds. I could throw a grenade into them, but I didn't know where he was. I hoped the troops would hit him. If they wounded him, I would finish him off.

The VC headed into the reeds. While running, I held the M-16 up to sight and tripped over a rock. I lay momentarily, getting my bearings. So many bullets buzzed my head I would be zapped if I sprang up. Their firing stopped after the VC entered the reeds. I struggled to my feet and continued to pursue but stopped immediately after entering the reeds. I was in his territory now; he held the upper hand.

"Hey PIO, here's your pack." The troops firing had caught up with me.

"Oh, thanks, man."

Captain Barrell told me this hill was identification for enemy artillery strikes and we should leave.

After another day, the three rifle companies were called to CP for a day and night of rest, wash, chow, mail, God, decorations, and to meet the new 1st Division CO, Maj. Gen. William E. DePuy. This short, bantam rooster-type person had sharp, penetrating eyes. He passed out a few medals, bestowed a few promotions, and spoke about professionalism in soldiering. The most important factor of soldiering, he asserted, was a physical and mental well-being. We could begin that right now by making sure we were always clean-shaven.

Since troops were always near water, they could shave at least every other day. There also was conjecture that if they shaved their mustaches, they would look more freshly shaven.

"I don't think Charlie cares what I look like when I finish with him," one of the men suggested.

Condolences were offered to Major Weeks whose red handlebar mustache was magnificent.

"It's an order," he grumbled.

I would have been furious over such a senseless directive, but I was not the man Major Weeks was. Even though this order seemed chicken-shit, in a short time everyone respected General DePuy, recognizing him as a vast improvement over his predecessor.

I found a chopper back to Bear Cat the next day. Our new base camp was to be occupied shortly.

PIO Lt. Philip Angle asked for good pictures with captions. He was making a yearbook about our year in Vietnam and wanted me to scrutinize my negatives and prints.

The men would return in two days, I was to find out how many wanted a copy. Also he asked if I had heard about C Company, 2nd Battalion, 16th Infantry who ran into heavy resistance.

They were involved in our operation. We didn't find concentrations of enemy because they prepared to assault C Company

Charlie assembled for lunch in a field close to the jungle. Enemy artillery fired at them, forcing them into the jungle where a battalion-sized unit lurked. They were surrounded until well after midnight. Each time they beat off an attack, they tightened their perimeter, removing many enemy bodies.

Artillery supported Charlie, firing over 1,100 rounds. At times, artillery FO called projectiles within 30 yards of their perimeter. They found over 100 bodies outside the perimeter in the morning while many of their wounded had crawled away.

The operation terminated April 14, with infantrymen returning to their new base camp. It was the most successful operation for the Big Red One to date, although my battalion didn't find much. It produced the greatest amount of enemy supplies and equipment; most of it was materiel for North Vietnamese regulars found in staging areas. Tractors, trailers, bombs, rockets, grenades, and thousands of rounds of ammunition were found along with communications equipment, clothing, and medical supplies. Over 30 weapons were recovered from Chinese automatic weapons and hand-thrown antitank grenades, to Alpha's crossbows and knives with pearl handles. Thirty-three base camps were found and burned with nearly 850 tons of rice recovered. Nobody had any idea how many wounded died or how many were killed by bombs and artillery and never discovered.

A nice Vietnamese family opened up several laundries on Highway #15 outside camp. They were Buddhist and had three kids. The father had been in the military and was discharged a short time before, saying he hoped this stuff would end soon so his people could move on with their lives.

I told him to pray also. The way things had been going lately, I thought we'd be out of Vietnam shortly—man, was I wrong.

Chapter 18

I Can Finally See the End of the Tunnel

If I had stories done I could go on pass to Vung Tau. The next operation began April 17; I had time.

An R&R center opened there, which was supposed to be a "happening place." The girls from Saigon went there on vacation looking for action.

It was 17 miles north on Highway #15, still a great distance, with VC hiding between here and there. Troops would convoy to Saigon and fly to Vung Tau, the French Riviera of Southeast Asia.

I told Major Weeks about it. He mentioned looking outside the plane; I'd be flying directly over our next operation, "Wildwood I & II." The mangrove, saltwater swamps of the Rung Sat Special Zone and Saigon River winding inland were a haven for the VC. The Marines combed it two months ago, ambushing 52. The VC blew up freighters then hid there. Vung Tau would be the CP. The impenetrable swamps were connected by a maze of waterways. The operation would consist of small-unit ambushes, which should be fun.

The Marines would brief us about the swamps before we entered.

Ten of us went on pass together; most were short-timers like me. One was the medic who ran through the jungle into the guns in November, helping a guy next to me. Another was Tobey, the Commo man with me when we neutralized the sniper blocking the MP. The third was a company commander's RTO I had assisted with radio watch many times. The fourth was the S-4 Personnel three-quarter-ton truck driver from my tent.

We convoyed to the International Airport in Saigon, boarded a twin turboprop Caribou, and cruised at 2,000 feet. I lay on the open rear flap during the 20-minute flight, taking photos from the air, a different perspective to an infantryman. The Saigon River meandered its muddy 50 miles to the coast 20 miles away. Guarding the bay at the river's mouth

The Rung Sat Special Zone next to the Saigon River, the site of our next operation. Maybe I might get shot there.

was the hump of Vung Tau. These saltwater swamps were laced with numerous waterways, many only several feet wide but six or eight feet deep.

The Saigon River spits its yellow silt into the South China Sea opposite Vung Tau. Freighters waited by the mouth for their turn to squeeze up the narrow channel to congested Saigon. Whenever Highway #15 was secured, freighters would unload here, eliminating this bottleneck.

Vung Tau was a fantasy world that didn't belong with the grime of jungles, reminding me of home in Cape Cod, a hub of activity. We checked into a newly constructed structure complete with cafeteria, swimming pool, private rooms, and pool tables.

Everybody explored the town individually. It was a novelty with no weapons, while wearing shorts, T-shirt, and sneaks. Many houses were freshly painted and charming with tiny yards and flowerbeds.

Beach #2 or "French Beach" was on the ocean side with rock cliffs and Buddhist graves visible at low tide.

Japanese gun emplacements had been carved into the cliffs. A number of small islands offshore had emplacements also. Vung Tau had been a major supply facility for the Japanese during World War II, with emplace-

Bermuda, Cape Cod, Santa Barbara? No, our forward command post for this operation—the Vietnamese village of Vung Tau on the South China Sea.

ments protecting it. Looking out to sea, I imagined I was Japanese, scanning the sea, searching for American ships with Marines.

Beach #3 was past a bluff forming the boundary for Beach #2, a mile-long sandy beach 100 yards wide with sparkling, crystal clear water reflecting a tan bottom. It halted against a tall, craggy hill joined by a string of gray, mist-covered hills behind town, perpendicular to the beach. This could have been the Caribbean or Hawaii, apropos for soldiers experiencing the worst of Vietnam, now enjoying its best.

Lining the first quarter of a mile was a Pandora's box of goodies: beer stands with women in two-piece bikinis, shorts, and knee-length printed T-shirts and football jerseys.

I stopped at the first bar, finding what I was looking for: American rock & roll music, girls, and a few G.I.s in civvies drinking Ba Muoi Ba "33," "numba one beer." The same happened in the next place, as it was in the next. The men told me the nightlife included cheap beer and Saigon ladies on hiatus.

Later in the day, I met the guys. We bought fifths of booze at the PX, planted ourselves at a beer stand, and proceeded to get drunk.

"Take a photo of me, Pezzoli; you never got one," the drunken medic babbled.

Beach #3 lined with beer stands and occupied by families playing together.

"Help that lady, Doc."

An elderly lady carried two baskets suspended from a splint across her shoulders. Mumbling scant Vietnamese, I managed to convey my wish to place the baskets across Doc's shoulders. He wove at the edge of the beach in a drunken stupor, face forward, ashen in color, dark glasses slipping down his nose, open shirt exposing his larger than infantry-sized waistline with the bottoms of his shorts ending at the knees of his short stubby legs.

Friends later questioned whether this was the one who had saved so many soldiers under fire.

This R&R was over before it started.

The drive and desire to leave this combat area in one piece was strong, permeating everything we said. Most of the talk was, "Where is your replacement?"

I still had two more months and was afraid to think about leaving—too much can happen in a short time. I was thinking more rationally now about surviving and the law of averages. Vung Tau with its good-looking girls, cold beer, T-shirts, rock and roll, no curfew, and beach sand, prompted me to reassess my priorities, cooling it not to get zapped.

I was still a long-timer, but definitely getting short.

April 17–21: Marine officers divided Battalion into groups and indoctrinated about their experiences in the Rung Sat. Their operation had

A Marine officer briefing our troops on what to expect in the coming operation in the Rung Sat Special Zone.

The Rung Sat at high tide.

Typical movement there at high tide.

been four months earlier; Brass felt whatever insight passed on to our troops would be beneficial. Marine assistance was no ego problem; the men appreciated it because we had the same goal—kill as many as we could. This not only helped us kill more than the Marines, it also saved lives.

Battalion procured 450 VC hammocks, similar to mine, for the troops in the swamps covered by six feet of water at high tide. Also, when the tide was out, the ground was flats of mud.

We spent three days in swamps with the Marines, becoming acclimated to chest-high salt water; narrow, fast-moving streams six feet deep; and bamboo twigs with pricks as hard as steel that ripped equipment and punctured flesh.

The equipment used during each of their company's 36 hour sweeps was optional. Steel pots if wanted, basic load of ammo, one day's rations, one canteen of water, no flak vests or entrenching tools, and fewer grenades and mines. Ropes and rappelling clips were necessary in river crossings. This light load made troops more flexible crossing streams and sloshing through mud at low tide. The VC laid logs across streams, then tightroped across narrow, deep streams. The wider streams were crossed holding the side of an air mattress piled with equipment.

The point man crossing a stream.

Our "ferry" pulls into port.

We were experienced jungle veterans, most with a year of combat. Unfortunately, guys from the cities found it as difficult in swamps as they did with the trees, bushes, and vines of jungles. They were uncomfortable around water or walking logs above the water. In the same respect, southerners, guys from the Great Lakes, or New England raised in woods and around water were comfortable.

The VC weren't here, that's why this location was selected for training.

On April 22, Lt. Col. Bill Staples said good-bye, departing for a new assignment. He said he would miss the men; they felt the same. He rejuvenated our organization into a substantial fighting force; his presence was an inspiration for all.

He addressed the men during his last reveille, saying this is the one we've been waiting for; we had finally been assigned a turkey shoot. Headquarters let us fight "Charles" on our terms, tapering into patrol units. Many had been with the Big Red One since June, met the enemy, seen action, and knew how to handle themselves. Our experiences taught and benefited replacements.

Only one company was in the swamps at a time; the other was in reserve, while the third went on pass in Vung Tau, drying feet and bodies from salt-water swamps. They were there for 36 hours before being replaced by another company.

He described how "Charles" got around on boats; there were no roads or trails in the mud. We would slosh through, occasionally in water up to our chests. Troops would ambush every stream. Many camps had docks. If occupied, they were at camp; if empty, we would wait.

The Marines killed 52. When he returned to the States, the colonel said, he wanted to read where the Big Red One outshot the Marines.

He asked the old veterans to take replacements and show them the ropes, giving each the benefit we didn't have; it might save someone's life.

Major Weeks called me the next day. This operation was in two parts, the first really unique. In "Wildwood I" the Vietnamese "Junk Navy" would block and support us. Their LST landing craft would load a platoon then deposit them in the swamp. Four from Recon Platoon were on the LST also, liaison for troops. If I decided to join, I couldn't be supplied.

Adjustments were made for Recon; I attached myself.

I printed yearbook photos and bought cigarettes, driving HQ 4 with Hans, our "vicious kraut," shotgun.

After the photo lab, we stopped at the PX, meeting the supply sergeant, SSgt. Rick Herberts, whose obesity was obvious.

He suggested we convoy back; the VC had been shooting at trucks today.

He was so big I doubted he could shoulder a weapon over his stomach while sitting in a jeep. Neither he, the driver, nor their shotgun had ever fired at the enemy; they were probably looking for our protection.

Sarge sat in the back of the jeep; he couldn't fit in the front. I drove slowly, only 50 mph, while following them. This was an appropriate speed for the two-lane tar road but slow for contested roads with the enemy ambushing vehicles.

Ten miles outside Bien Hoa, I heard a machine gun firing on my right at Sgt. Herberts's jeep. The most absurd thing I saw here was beefy Sgt. Herberts bending forward, attempting to squash himself to hide from bullets, like folding a medicine ball in half. This was another episode that explained why the VC always lost more men then we did. If they couldn't hit Sgt. Herberts in the back of an open, slow-moving jeep with a machine gun, whom could they hit?

Seconds later, my jeep was in the line of fire. On the right was a small field with a clump of bushes in the middle with a red, serpent-like tongue flashing at me from a machine gun muzzle.

The road was in the first stage of being widened with a bank of dirt lining the left side. While watching the flashes I noticed bullets walking that dirt, bracketing my jeep, and keeping abreast with me. Another scene from movies where the hero is shot at with bullets skipping after his heels. Fortunately, we were the heroes because nobody was hit.

During this, my protection, the shotgun, our great Nazi soldier, screamed, "They're shooting at us!" He dropped his M-16 and grabbed the jeep's panic bar with both hands.

"Shoot back, dummy!"

"They're firing!"

I downshifted, put the pedal to the metal, and disappeared down the road.

Approaching the opposite direction was a three-quarter-ton Vietnamese Recon truck. A mounted machine gun in its body fired over our heads into the ambush.

I didn't speak to Hans again or tell the men how he choked under fire. He left for the States a week later.

The next day, April 26, Operation "Wildwood I" began. I drove to the swamps with a convoy protected by Recon. Charlie Company loaded three platoons into three small Vietnamese landing craft docked at the Saigon River.

Alpha Company was in reserve, while Bravo was at the Forward CP in Vung Tau. I had never noticed this assortment of gear and uniforms before. Everyone dressed and carried whatever they wanted, looking

A more stable stream bottom surrounded by a cover of bamboo.

more like mercenaries than American troops. They were wearing scarves, soft hats, socks stuffed with rations and grenades, and ammo bandoleers hanging cross-shouldered like banditos. Each had spare socks tied to harnesses for night, hopefully drying their feet in soaked boots. Insect repellent was carried, as were knives, a few machetes, air mattresses, ropes, and clips carried somewhere on their persons.

The Vietnamese junk commander was in my craft with four men from Recon. The platoon we ferried departed when the stream became too small for our craft. I was glad I elected to cover the war from this vantage point for a change. I could sit and watch without having to enter the swamps.

The Recon Sergeant reminded me we going to have to eat whatever food they made. I gave him a litany of crud I had digested, feeling I shouldn't have a problem eating their food.

These sailors were congenial and honored that I, a reporter, would be accompanying them. The boat's kitchen consisted of a two-gallon steel pot, fire pit, indigenous vegetables stacked in the corner with live ducks, chickens, and a goose tied together by their feet.

Guaranteed fresh meat; I couldn't go wrong.

After Infantry embarked, the pit was lit and the steel pot was filled with the water of the Saigon River, a murky, silt-saturated brown.

Departing one of the small Vietnamese landing craft.

Our first meal was duck.

When the "spiced" Saigon River boiled, the duck's throat was cut and its blood collected in a cup. The fowl was thrown into the pot for an hour. Next the "chef" carefully removed our meal from its savory roux, cut off the head, and plucked the bird clean. Finally he chopped the feet off with a cleaver, plunging them into a strong, Oriental-smelling marinade. Finally he hacked up the rest of the bird—bones, intestines, and tail. With a flourish he placed this concoction into four bowls of miscellaneous pot-boiled vegetables and placed a crock of rice in the middle. Each person put a scoop of sticky rice on his plate, surrounded it with the contents of each of the bowls, and topped it with a sprinkling of flavored duck's blood.

I attempted to show courage and bravado by helping myself to the rice and vegetables only. These sailors noticed this. After a brief discussion they smiled and plopped the neck, supposedly the choice part, onto my plate.

I returned their smiles, warily tweaking it with chopsticks, and strategically placed it in the side of my mouth, making off I was chewing it. After their attention returned to the meal, I discretely placed my hand next to my mouth, spit the neck into it, and dropped it overboard.

I began to enjoy the unique taste of the vegetables, rice, and sauces until I realized this mission would last a week and eventually I would have to begin eating the game and drinking river water.

We finished eating; the men of Recon ate more comfortably than I, probably because they didn't see the meal prepared. The Vietnamese commanding officer brought out a porcelain tea set with hot sake and poured a cup for his staff and the Americans. I felt neglected until the cook approached me with a large glass filled with something faintly more transparent than the river water: sake.

The sailors toasted me, "chin chin," "toast toast."

"Chin chin," everybody chanted until I finished the glass in 10 minutes. You don't consume a glass of heated sake in 10 minutes and remain sober long.

The boat pulled into a pier and we questioned fishermen about the VC. The craft tied up and sailors walked onto the pier. I struggled up and tried to follow, putting one foot on the bench by the side of the boat and the other on the pier. I swung my weight forward to raise myself. My brain spun inside my skull. The sailors found this entertaining and, grabbing my arms, escorted me into the lower cabin where I passed out for several hours.

I was hungry before the next meal and gulped down the chicken, prepared the same way as the duck. The following day I ate goose cooked in a similar manner. The last day we had shrimp purchased from river fishermen and barbecued teriyaki style. My bowel movement the second day reminded me I had done something wrong the previous day, like drinking from the polluted Saigon River.

Platoons departed their landing craft; initially the water was waist high. After an agonizing half hour, the land rose sufficiently to allow walking on top of the snarls. Simultaneously two platoons intersected walks, fashioned with trimmed twigs fastened across parallel runners of small branches carved through the undergrowth. The meticulous attention to detail of this primitive walkway was phenomenal.

Each designated a point squad to prowl the walk leading down slope to a stream, the logical location for a camp, with the remainder of men discretely behind.

Wind was an ally, murmuring and whistling through the overhead cover, drowning incriminating sounds.

Ten minutes later both points discovered camps constructed on these ramps of branches and twigs. Six enemy were sitting on logs in the center of one while eight lounged in hammocks and beds fashioned in bushes in the other. Their complacency was absurd; neither camp had rudimentary defenses.

The points signaled their situation. They flashed six and eight fingers, indicating the number of VC, and extended a hand, palm out, meaning to stop and they had the situation under control. Both patrol leaders coordinated so attacks would be simultaneous, not permitting a warning to the other camp. The platoons radioed Recon, positioning the LSTs in blocking positions, thwarting escape.

The five points of each patrol assembled on line, surveying the enemy's inner sanctum 15 meters away. Each man selected two targets close to each other, signaled the rear when ready, and fired. A moment later the point from the other patrol fired. The vegetation was so dense; the patrols thought they were miles apart. Each was astonished by their proximity after hearing each other's firing, virtually next door.

In a few seconds, both disciplined squads firing M-14s, M-16s, shotguns, and M-79s decimated targets of opportunity. The Big Red One announced its presence in the Rung Sat to the Communists.

Both point squads gingerly entered the camps, ensuring their targets were dead before signaling the others. Each camp was a holding station for new troops. Beds, military equipment, putrid food, and cooking facilities were elevated above daily tides.

Much of their facilities had roofs of leaf-laden branches to splash off the perpetual monsoons. The men from both groups curiously inspected the camps, seeing the enemy's living quarters above ground for the first time—the novelty of being invited into his home.

This gunfire alerted the VC within a five-mile radius of something obscene; Americans stalking them in their back yard. For the remainder of the operation, the troops realized their element of surprise was lost, yet they would find the pickings great.

Both patrols found weapons and material, lifted out by chopper. Bodies were dumped into streams, boats ignited, and putrid food left.

By 1300, the third patrol found a stream next to a camp, sans boat and residents, and established a homecoming. Its location, above sea level, afforded the men a golden opportunity to lie on dry ground, resting from an exhausting day battling the swamps.

At 1600, the platoon leader prepared to move to another location when the men were alerted by a splashing sound. Immediately after, four armed VC nonchalantly poled their flat-bottomed boat around the corner of a waterway, erect sitting ducks. Two M-16s, one 12 gauge, and an M-79 lifted two off their feet and blew them into the drink while the others collapsed inside.

This war was finally becoming fun while frustration reared it ugly head. Throughout Wildwood I & II, the Communists were frequently blasted out of their boats during an ambush and sunk, yet they could not be claimed as kills because the evidence sank.

After 36 hours, the LSTs rendezvoused with their platoon and returned to the dock where duties were rotated.

There was sporadic gunfire from patrols. In two cases, they found base camps and positioned LSTs to block retreats, most of the time ambushing sitting ducks.

On the fifth day, as a platoon overran a camp, the VC escaped in the direction of our LSTs. Two of the Vietnamese boats formed a pincer movement on the small peninsula and trapped them, killing all six in a smooth, coordinated effort. Meanwhile the infantry racked up four more inside the camp. I was surprised and impressed by how professional Vietnamese sailors were. We wished Americans at home knew the same. Unfortunately, this aspect of the war was never deemed newsworthy, but the Wall knows it.

"Wildwood I" terminated May 2 and "Wildwood II" began the next day. Twenty-three of the enemy had been killed, according to the body count, without a G.I. injured. This operation had become a piece of cake, almost boring and redundant.

The operation was transferred to the Forward CP at Vung Tau, with the Vietnamese Navy released. The patrols were delivered to the swamps by truck and begin fording a river, tandem clutching a rubber raft. The first two men were point, paddling across. The remainder of the troops kept weapons trained on the opposite bank until the point crossed and secured it. Now the patrol would comfortably launch other rafts.

This operation was on a higher, drier, and more sparsely vegetated swamp, punctuated with trails. This more human-friendly portion of the Rung Sat would, naturally, be more abundant with enemy. Also the terrain would facilitate ground travel between base camps above sea level; the infantry would have to work harder for their kills now. His enemy would not be traveling exclusively in boats; many would be discovered in camps and walking their maze of hidden trails.

I met Hans's replacement, Doc, at the CP. The new mail clerk was big and affable. He wore bifocals and was a scholarly appearing guy who looked as though he may not have accomplished many long-range patrols. His physical condition was about as poor as his equipment. His salvation was a great personality and sense of humor; we were happy to have him as a member of Headquarters Staff

On my first night at the CP, Rick, Lansen, and I took Doc on the town to show him the ropes: what beer to drink, the type of girls to use a rubber with, how to watch out for VC, the price of pussy, and how to negotiate for it.

There was so much traffic between Vung Tau and our base camp at Bear Cat that the VC kept their heads down along Highway #15. I convoyed to the camp, then drove to Bien Hoa for photos. By the time I returned to Vung Tau, there had been a switch of troops; the ones out in the swamps were drying out at beer stands. Interviewing troops for stories there seemed a practical way to accomplish my job; I couldn't be in the swamps all the time.

In several days I had become a regular at the stands; all the bartenders and female customers knew me. The men always sat with me, related what happened during their patrol, and bought beer so I would mention their name.

SSgt. Roland Spengemann was getting short like me with only six weeks left. He noticed me and brought over a round of beers.

"Look what happened," he said, pointing to a bandage just below the bottom of his bathing suit. His squad had been in a dry spot in the swamp, next to a camp, when a sniper hit the ammo pouch of the guy next to him, causing cartridges to explode. No one was hit. The VC shot again and hit the RTO's radio. It ricocheted; Spengemann felt something bang his leg. Running his hand down the back he "felt this sucker sticking out," pulling a gnarled bullet out of his pocket. He said he was so surprised and insulted getting zapped, especially being shot, he didn't call a medic to give the bastard satisfaction he shot anyone. He pulled it out by the end and gave it to the medic for antiseptic and cover. It was a million-dollar wound that should not heal until after discharge.

The heat on the VC had been turned up. They turned themselves in to the South Vietnamese out of disappointment with their organization and new dangers. Alpha conducted the first sweep with a patrol escorted to a base camp by a rallier. This enemy lieutenant, a Viet Cong since 1954, escorted one of Alpha's patrols to a base camp.

The point squad saw barbed wire with punji traps in front and a machine gun bunker inside. They were about to climb over the barbed wire when the machine gun opened up. Their lives were actually saved by the punji traps surrounding the camp. They knocked the poisonous stakes over with their boots and slid inside, using them as foxholes to fire from.

Five grenades were strapped to the trees. A string was attached to the pins; fortunately, only two worked when tripped, injuring no one. The two men in the traps threw grenades like baseballs, directly into two gun slits of the bunker, killing everyone inside. After the explosions, they received heavy supporting fire from behind, providing time to climb over the barbed wire and scramble into the trench surrounding the camp. It sounded like Infiltration Course at Basic Training with guns and grenades all going off at once.

Alpha didn't have time to completely encircle the whole camp and lost several VC who escaped out a rear tunnel. When the camp was secured, several men went into the tunnels and found two other VC hiding next to a large amount of Chinese 7.62-mm ammo and carbines, grenades, and mines.

By the end of two weeks, Battalion had 35 killed by body count with only two men slightly injured. The operation had been highly successful so far, a satisfactory going-away present!

Being stationed at Vung Tau was a paid vacation in Wonderland. Staff didn't have reveille in the morning or bed check at night, though we had to monitor the radio nights. These were divided into shifts: drinking in the bars, return for watch, then back to the bars to continue where we left off.

Every day more camps were attacked and destroyed while the VC continued to be ambushed in boats. The entire operation ran as smoothly as clockwork; everybody accomplished their duties with an air of professionals. Then the tragedy struck—something we always dreaded—we killed one of our own. If they could have they would have been content to return to life the 43 Communists snuffed out so far in exchange for the lost soldier.

This euphoria in the Rung Sat had been short lived.

The Vanguards were deflated by this disaster, now offering a different perspective: this was still war, not a kid's game, and should be treated appropriately.

The platoon was silent during their ride to the CP an hour later. Normally they would have been laughing about the prospects of 36 hours of fun and games during their break at the resort. They had nothing to laugh about now with the body of a good soldier wrapped in his OD poncho, bouncing in the dust by their feet, in the body of a truck.

The Reds were instructed to keep away because too many were getting zapped. Many from North Vietnam trapped inside these 30 square miles of swamps were ordered to ambush G.I.s. They hauled their equipment from small camps and consolidated into large units at camps with the best fortifications.

Six enemy ambushed a trail crossing a field neighboring the edge of the Rung Sat. It was isolated; the infantry was in the swamps, leaving a slim chance patrols would advance here.

They brought hash, making their stay tolerable; it was not produced in South Vietnam, but was a staple of Communists' shipments.

They carved positions inside the tree line. An ocean breeze blowing across the field cut the humidity, keeping them cool and comfortable. This, and the hash, removed them from the new danger terrifying the swamps.

The morning of the second day, Operations, S-3, directed a Charlie Company patrol to leave the swamps and probe the hard ground leading to Vung Tau. They headed to a field rising and climbing to a dirt road for a convoy.

A trail crossed this field where the land began its transition from mucky saltwater marsh to a ground mixture of fresh water and clay. Sparse brown grass grew in the football field-sized area, barely enough to satisfy a small herd of goats.

The VC rested, scarcely secluded by grass and lightly foliated bushes. They observed the patrol spread out upon entering the field and expand into a 50-yard area from their thin patrol line, dispersing cautiously forward.

"Crack," then "crack," and "crack and crack."

Incoming rounds!

The G.I.s dove to the damp ground astonished; bullets were splattering the mud about them in a random manner. Also, the guns fired slowly, leaving the impression they weren't targets. They saw six VC shooting only 30 meters away, standing along the field, aiming their weapons, weaving from side to side, squeezing rounds—one at a time.

Much happens in one second of a firefight with Americans in combat: an M-16 spews forth six .223-mm magnum rounds, pellets spray 360-degrees from an M-79, and eight 00 buck pellets leap from the muzzle of a pump.

It took a second for these 45 men to dive prone and one more second to realize who was firing and sight in.

During the third and forth seconds, all weapons fired together, unleashing a dynamic display of firepower. The VC were riddled before they hit the ground.

When the firing stopped the men walked to the bodies, casually because there was no question all were dead—around a tube of hash.

"Man, will you look at this; these guys were all screwed up!" They felt like murderers. The VC didn't stand a fighting chance stoned. That euphoria received when a Viet Cong was killed did not stimulate them as usual. Also Charlie Company didn't want this publicized; they were afraid "do-gooders" might claim war crimes again. This is another story from the Wall.

By mid-May, Jimmy O'Riley and Sergeant Grassburg returned to the States, leaving me the "old vet" in Personnel. I had no supervisor familiar with my many stories; consequently I slacked off.

Lt. Philip Angle returned from Japan assembling the brigade yearbook, "First Year, Pictorial History, 2nd Brigade." Brigade CO asked him why there weren't more photos of troops in the swamps. Lt. Angle thought I might have been shot, but periodically noticed stories. He drove to Vung

Tau with a convoy that afternoon and was left at Personnel, who said I was at Beach #3.

He demanded a ride.

When Angle arrived at my beach bar, I was sitting at a table with two guys drying out from Charlie Company in the fellowship of three bikinis.

Granted, I looked casual with shorts, T-shirt, and beers, but assured him I was interviewing the troops, holding up my pad with scribbled notes.

He questioned my sincerity, pleading more great photos.

My insistence I was getting short had no effect, and he ordered me back.

I asked Headquarters if I should start looking for my replacement. They told me I had a month left.

I continued interviewing soldiers at Beach #3, making runs down Highway #15 to Bear Cat, Bien Hoa, Division at Di An, and having a fantastic time at Vung Tau's bars.

One day I was told to look through personnel files for my replacement. I was to find him, break him in one day out there, and be careful not to get him shot. After training, he would return to his unit until I was ready to rotate.

I found a guy, Nestler, in Communications, who had been in Vietnam only three weeks, described the job including the boonies, and discovered he was still interested. He had not seen action yet, which may be why he accepted. I felt Nestler was Infantry and should not have a problem adjusting to the jungle.

I told him he had the job and to join me at Alpha, the last patrol of this operation, June 7.

Nestler looked like a typical replacement, excited like a dog anticipating a romp in the woods with his master.

I cautioned him about being too anxious taking pictures; I had almost been zapped several times, while Woods of the 16th got it.

Alpha divided the company into two squad patrols of 12 men. Each was 15 minutes apart, assisting each other if resistance became too difficult.

We crossed a five-foot wide, six-foot deep stream by walking across a log the VC had laid below the surface. The point man noticed a stick on each side of the stream, designating a crossing point.

Immediately inside the jungle was a base camp next to the crossing. Walkways were built for six elevated sleeping platforms with canopies of twigs. Underneath one sat three crock-pots of contaminated beans. It's amazing, for all we know about Vietnam, no one ever discovered how many VC died from dysentery.

A grimy, weathered shirt hung from one. A short-timer snatched it. "This is gonna be a nightshirt for my kid brother."

A VC trail. The submerged crossing log rests above the six foot deep stream and is identified by stakes at each end.

"What's this, a grinder?" They discovered a stone wheel that revolved around an axle on a stone table crushing rice into flour. This was a mess hall for the VC.

Troops spotted a well and examined its water. It was covered with green scum and bugs. The guys couldn't imagine anyone drinking this stuff. Several men felt brave and stuck their finger inside for a taste; it had a hint of salt, which wasn't surprising considering they were at sea level in salt-water swamps.

An aluminum auxiliary fuel tank for U.S. fighters lay next to it, intact and unscathed. It had been jettisoned during flight but was surprisingly undamaged.

Behind it were 200 spoons in a box pounded out of another fuel tank. Next to them was its wooden mold. Wire cutters sliced the shape from a tank, placed into the form, pounded the shape, and finally filed its edges. Everybody helped himself to souvenirs.

Troops hacked a hole so a chopper could evacuate the mill and supplies, getting the tank and spoons on a second trip.

The beds, part of the walk, and well were destroyed, leaving the food.

Destroying the well there.

After the evacuation, we followed a trail to another camp. It was empty. An adjacent patrol radioed that four VC were poling along a waterway and to ambush them. The men took advantage of this wait for lunch. I was still searching for the "Great Vietnam War Photo" and thought I would show Nestler how to do it.

The three ambush men were lying on the ground next to the stream, looking across at the VC camp.

I told Nestler he must learn to trust the professionalism of troops, that they would not shoot him if they knew his intentions.

The rest of the patrol was behind us with security; we were safe. "Come here and watch," I said as I stepped in front of the men. The other patrol saw the VC coming this way, probably returning to their camp by us.

I secured my right foot into the perpendicular bank of the stream, rifle slung over my shoulder grasping a small tree with my left hand and pushing the camera out from the leaves for an unobstructed photo when VC rounded the creek.

Stay put when firing starts; if you move, the bullets would zap you passing just inches on either side, I informed him.

An ambush site with soldiers waiting for the VC to return to their camp on the stream in front.

I hid my camera inside the leaves until the VC came, then I would stick it out and snap as fast as I could.

I turned to glance at him and saw a pathetic sight. This six-foot, two-inch soldier was crouched between two ambush men, so scared his legs were visibly shaking. Let me rephrase it: they were knocking, in a slow, deliberate, wide, one "clunk" per second knock. His helmet was tilted back at an angle with perspiration gushing like a waterfall. The steamed glasses slid forward and rested on the tip of his nose while his eyes, magnified by the thick, almost opaque glasses, resembled goggles. He held his rifle more tightly than a trapeze artist holds the bar. Yet the rifle's muzzle was sticking in the mud.

"What's wrong with you?"

He was so scared he couldn't respond. The men lying in ambush glanced up and chuckled.

"That's my replacement," I confessed.

I told him he was making me nervous; take the barrel out of the mud and clean it.

I waited another 15 minutes, then moved because I was tired of hanging. We waited two more hours but the VC never showed up.

The patrol moved out again. I took second from point so Nestler could experience being up front. We crossed an area of sparse vegetation on a yellow, hard clay bottom with a thin film of water collecting. I looked for Nestler; he had dropped two behind. The point bumped a skinny, 10-foot bush crowned by a bee's nest. He ran left and I to the right because of less vegetation.

I was fast enough and wasn't stung. In doing so, I managed to lose the patrol that ran left. I tried to be cool and backtrack my footsteps in the mud like the Weweantic Indians of Cape Cod.

Five feet after I began, my prints had been dissolved by the incoming tide. Every bush, tree, and limb was identical. I tried dead reckoning where I thought the rest ran.

Two M-16s were fired from a different direction then the one in which I thought my patrol had escaped. "Possibly the other patrol. Bad guys are here and I'm probably in the middle of a firefight."

A few more bursts, then silence. I became nervous, realizing it best to admit a goof-up. Confess I was lost and remain alive.

"Oh, 3rd Platoon," I whispered, "3rd Platoon, where are you? This is Pezzoli, the PIO. I'm lost."

"We're over here," was a loud whisper from a direction I wasn't expecting.

They weren't more then 20 feet, but I didn't have any idea where.

The objective was reached, a junction of two streams. Ambushes were formed and camp established for the night. I introduced Nestler to the platoon leader, medic, and RTO, and told him he would be assisting with radio watch. I hung my hammock between two trees and crawled inside for my first full, uninterrupted, night's sleep in my last combat patrol.

"Pezzoli," whispered my replacement later in the evening, "you're snoring."

I was so mellow and seemingly invincible to danger, I relaxed significantly to snore as I slept.

We returned to Vung Tau the next day, packed everything, and returned to Bear Cat. I assured my superiors I had thoroughly trained my replacement and was ready to return to the States; it fell on deaf ears. I printed pictures and wrote stories.

This operation had been highly successful looking at the box score: 58 VC confirmed dead, outshooting the Marines, in addition to unsubstantiated VC who sank after being zapped. One G.I. was killed by his own man while several received minor injuries, not including the two bee stings. I hope his family never finds out how he lost his life; yet the Wall knows.

The chapter closed on the 1st of the 18th Vanguards first year in Vietnam.

Personnel was busy rotating people to the States and processing replacements.

June 14: "Pezzoli, have your replacement move in today. Take him to the Air Force lab. The operation starts tomorrow; get him squared away."

Nestler was such a nerd; I didn't show him the best whorehouses. He babbled incessantly like a kindergarten kid preparing for his first zoo visit.

I introduced my replacement to the Air Force.

Martin and the Sarge wouldn't acknowledge him; the Pfc. grunted.

They thanked me for the VC toys, blustering how they would return and show everyone how rough it was.

When we returned in the afternoon, I strolled through rifle companies A, B, and C. There were strangers, staring at me peculiarly after noticing I had been watching. I felt I was left behind because I wasn't needed anymore. All of the men must have felt the same way when they left, that they should still be helping in the boonies.

I was awakened the next morning at 0400 by the commotion of troops preparing for combat. I had chow at the same time, but by myself; nobody knew me. Choppers arrived at 0600 and left with the troops.

There was a Brigade operation in some jungle; most of Bear Cat was empty. The tents were bare; nobody around. I felt drained.

My orders arrived; separation was June 19.

In four days I would leave for the Replacement Center in Saigon and wait for a flight.

Personnel was sufficiently staffed and didn't need help. Rick and Lansen had me ride shotgun during trips to Division.

June 17, 1966: We had killed 178 VC by body count and lost 21 men this year. Nothing to be jubilant about because 21 men were lost to their families, the world, and us. Unfortunately, many never respected their sacrifices.

We discovered and destroyed tons of equipment, documented and overran over 125 VC base camps, and thoroughly upset plans for infiltration into the jungles between Saigon and Cambodia.

Also, and equally important, we gave the Vietnamese a relief and hope from Communist terror.

The next day I would go to Bien Hoa, say good-bye to the bar ladies, and get Winstons at the PX.

"Twenty-four hours and a wake-up Ray, you're there."

"You're right, almost there."

Chapter 19

It's Not Over Till It's Over

"Dear Marty, I'll be arriving in Oakland the 23rd and take you up on your offer for dinner."

The guys let me have early radio watch; I was having chow at 0400 before hitching to Bien Hoa on the first truck leaving camp.

I lay down at 2200, the end of my watch, as the rest of the tent returned from a movie. The guys babbled about the flick; I stared into the darkness at the top of our tent.

When Brigade moved into the new base camp at Bear Cat, they had to literally move the Viet Cong out first. Their big regimental headquarters, five miles up the road, was discovered and destroyed in November. Enlargement of the road between Bear Cat and Long Binh Supply Depot was almost complete, accommodating the increase in traffic. After we moved into the camp, the VC tried ambushing traffic but in most cases they ended up being snuffed out.

The Viet Cong felt a frontal assault on Bear Cat would be disastrous because of the superior defensive perimeter. It was impossible for them to situate artillery pieces in the jungle adequate for an assault because it was too dense. About the only way they would be successful inflicting injuries was by mining the two-mile dirt road to Highway #15. This road ran straight two miles from the camp to the Ranger Outpost, making a right and left S turn to Highway #15. Engineers had superbly constructed it: packed clay on top of gravel with drainage ditches on the sides.

A local VC unit had nine mines. If they tried to bury them halfway between the two camps, a mile from both, it might be accomplished on a moonless night. Rather than having one or two men take several hours planting mines, nine men could plant one in a ninth of the time or 20 minutes.

Their biggest danger was discovery by sentries scanning the perimeter. They were out of the effective range of the sentry's rifles. Also, if patrols were sent out, VC scouts would warn of this.

These men wore orange and tan clothes, closely matching the color of the road.

By midnight most of the camp was asleep. They would crawl through the scrub on either side of the road and wait by the edge of the ditch for their signal, after which they could slide into the ditch. At another signal, they would crawl to a spot on the road and dig a hole for their mine. It would be difficult for sentries to see them if they moved slowly; at night the eye notices movement before recognizing anything. The mines were submerged directly under the surface. When exploded, energy releases through the thin top layer, blasting shrapnel and energy upward. The most conspicuous problem would be restoring clay over the top to look packed and worn.

Several days before, the VC dug a sample of dirt similar to the road and practiced packing it around a mine. Their camp was almost discovered by a Vietnamese Ranger patrol.

"Twenty-four and a wake-up, get up short-timer, it's 0400 hrs."

The camp was quiet. After showering I walked to chow at 0430; the only others eating were KPs, three replacements, and another guy leaving today.

I returned to my tent, clipped on the pistol belt, and glanced at my M-16 as I checked the round in the chamber for the last time. At 0545, while the sun began its torrid ascent, I walked to the main gate for a ride on the first vehicle. I took photos showing folks home the "real thing."

The first truck left at 0600. While we drove out to Highway #15, I took pictures of the perimeter behind, the dirt road, and the Vietnamese outpost, documenting my "home" in Vietnam.

The driver couldn't wait while I said good-bye to the family of the laundry; another truck would arrive shortly.

I told them I would leave for America tomorrow. They wished me well. The Communists got this family in April 1975 when they overran the country.

While talking with them I noticed no traffic leaving camp.

I walked across the street by the stream at our water point and took a picture of where my cleaner drinking water came from. While walking back to the laundry, I noticed four ox and wagons, loaded with wood and driven by men dressed in tan peasant-type clothes; they were the infamous "woodcutters" we saw frequently in the jungle.

I would loved to have blasted them; they would have been the last VC I killed. Instead of my rifle, I shot them with my camera, catching a mean snarl from the guy in front. He definitely was a VC. Friends later asked why I didn't zap them.

On top of the machine gun bunker at the entrance to my base camp at Bear Cat.

VC, I surmised, disguised as woodchoppers. I received a nasty glare from the first one.

You couldn't go killing someone for looking at you the wrong way.

I became impatient; it was strange that there was no traffic. Finally a jeep meandered along Highway #15 from Vung Tau.

"What are you doing driving without a shotgun?"

He said he had to get tents at Long Binh Supply Depot.

I reminded him the road wasn't secure, he didn't have a shotgun, the roof was on, and the windshield was not lying down.

He said they couldn't spare anyone.

I began a dissertation about the dangers ahead, stimulating his speed to a more prudent 70 mph.

I pointed out the dirt shoulder where bullets had kicked up the sand.

He pushed the speed to 80. The jeep bounced so violently it literally floated along the road. Unfortunately the photo of the last place I almost lost my life by enemy fire showed part of the jeep's roof.

Opposite: The Viet Ranger camp two miles down the dirt road from my base camp, Bear Cat. At that spot we fortunately had missed nine mines planted in the two-mile dirt road.

At the Long Binh four corners I got an immediate ride the rest of the way. I said good-bye at the photo lab again, had lunch at a Vietnamese restaurant, and made a final stop at the PX for transportation.

Guys from CP were there, asking if I was OK; they thought I got blown up.

"What are you talking about?"

The VC had planted nine mines in the road. The first two trucks that left in the morning were blown up; they wondered why I didn't get hurt.

I did leave first; we missed all the mines while the second and third trucks were blown up—a traumatic realization.

I rode back with this trooper, who claimed Brass thought the VC were going to ambush today. I was lucky for an APC leading four trucks in the convoy.

Unfortunately this time, at a time we were prepared, the VC didn't challenge.

I took photos of the two holes blown by the mines while driving past; one still had pieces of tire around it. "My God, you're still watching me," I thanked Him.

Midafternoon and everyone was involved with duties. I turned my combat gear in to Supply, especially hating to part with my M-16.

Meager belongings were squeezed into a duffel bag. All of my negatives and most of my clippings, rough story drafts, and photos remained. I wanted to leave and think how to pack them.

Nobody seemed to notice me in the tent; I sat on a locker in the corner and watched men do their duties. The Headquarters Company First sergeant walked inside, searching for a KP. He glanced at me and said with trepidation,

"Arrh, Pezzoli, you're not doing anything. Mind doing KP the rest of the day?"

How degrading. The last duty in Vietnam—KP!

I was barely a memory now, hardly existing to anyone.

For the second time in Vietnam, I slipped into my dress Class-A uniform in the morning and waved to somebody in Personnel tent driving by.

We were taken to a nondescript room in 1st Division Headquarters for processing. I received a minor physical and I was astonished by my weight. When I arrived, I weighed a solid 205, but now I was 175—I had lost 30 pounds. I was in good shape all my life. In Vietnam, I became lean and mean.

At the Replacement Center, Ton Se Nhut Airport, Saigon, everyone was herded into an empty room to hold.

Troops from the Big Red One and the 173rd Airborne were given duties requiring a rifle. Some guarded the grounds, while others, including me, rode shotgun running errands. We never knew when a flight would be available; consequently our bags remained packed. The Infantry was fortunate though; the remainder were given menial chores like KP and policing the area.

The M-14 I was issued had been neglected, receiving absolutely no maintenance, leaving it dry and dusty with specks of rust. I asked for gun oil and patches. Replacements didn't know what I was talking about.

On the afternoon of June 22, 1966, my name was called on the PA system; a plane was available. "Personnel, be at Gate #3 in 15 minutes, at 1500 hours—as you are."

At Gate #3 we were placed in the manifest order of sequence, with Infantry first and Support next. Most of Support and Logistics were in Class-A's, while we, the Infantry, still wore jungle fatigues.

"We need 26 spaces. The last 26 men fall out; you're rescheduled," boomed the PA.

The men behind grumbled somebody with clout needs this flight.

A staff sergeant aggressively approached from the rear, gruffly counting, "24, 25, 26."

"You men," he barked, "fall out. Return to the barracks."

A man complained he had been waiting for three days.

The sergeant growled that these men spent many three-day periods in considerably more demanding situations than he.

"Get those men out of here. Come here, troop," he said in an almost apologetic tone leading a man by the arm to the end of the line. "Each of you will board this plane for home."

Twenty-six soldiers came forward slowly, methodically, silently, to their places at the end of the line. All walked with a panther's air of determination and assurance stalking his game, completely confident, growling not needed to assert who they were. They were tall and lean, looking like zombies: large eyes fixed on expressionless, hollow faces. Each wore fatigues out of a Supply crate lacking nametags, patches, and insignia. Their clothes were ill fitting with packing creases, not tainted by sweat.

Each had boots caked with plastered yellow clay and three days' growth of beard, sweat, and insect repellent, the look of jungle etched across their faces.

They were Infantry: each man looked tall and lean, with that look of confidence a man has when he knows he is a man. A look that never can be imitated. Whenever Hollywood depicts a man, it is usually unsuccessful because first they need a man, not a mere actor, playing the role. Secondly, the director must know a real man to portray one.

I asked Sarge who they were.

They were the 173rd Airborne, just pulled out from rescuing a trapped platoon. The 26 were cleared for rotation and waiting at Personnel for convoying to Saigon. One of their units discovered a large North Vietnamese unit and was on the verge of being overrun—troops were needed for rescue.

All 26 instantly volunteered to leave the security and safety of home to venture into the uncertainties of combat to save men from their unit. Each was reissued equipment and lifted to the jungle. Their assistance was instrumental in destroying the North Vietnamese unit, turning a potential defeat into victory, and saving many American lives. The sergeant said they "really kicked ass."

These men, who were in the jungle three days, returned to camp long enough to slip into new fatigues, splash water on their faces, and load onto a truck with priority orders for placement on the first airliner available.

I have never written about these men before and doubt if anybody ever heard of them. These are the real heroes of Vietnam. They turned their boat around in a secure harbor and ventured into the storm to save their buddies. These paratroopers were made up of that genuine, everyday, all-American grit seldom found on screens or contaminating families through TV or the Internet.

I saw and had been around real heroes during this year. They didn't cuss, chew tobacco, smoke marijuana, wear patches over their eye, bandannas around their head, or cut the sleeves off their shirts. They were the mundane, unpretentious person seen on any street in any town.

These men were heroes then. Later, after landing on the other side of the big pond, they would become butchers, bakers, and candlestick makers.

They probably didn't get decorations for this because they were discharged 24 hours later. Each received a distinction which never could be pinned on his chest: that they returned home as men.

Hanging in the closet at home will be a stained and tattered jungle fatigue jacket. The son will ask, "What did you do in the war, Daddy? Did you kill anyone?"

"Son, you never glorify killing people, even though they were bad."

There are fewer names on the Wall because of their heroism while the souls there understand their glory.

I sat next to someone on the plane, but didn't notice him. I was by myself.

This beautiful Boeing 707 finally moved, commencing its taxi.

"About time they started moving this piece of shit!"

A major with a support organization pin on his lapel was obviously drunk, and definitely out of place.

"I can't wait to get out of this sewer with these fuckin,' slant-eyed gooks."

His friend tried to soothe him but agitated him more. I felt like most of the other guys; willing to shut him up any way necessary.

"Better shut him up, or else!" A growl from the rear by the 173rd. I would never question the ability of that man to back his words. The friend attempted to calm him again and it worked.

We took off in the direction of the ocean. Outside my window was the Rung Sat Special Zone, the site of my last operation. Immediately above it was the resort of Vung Tau, my playground. The plane began to turn north before reaching the coast, giving me an opportunity to look west and see those innocuous jungles of the Iron Triangle and Cambodia where we spent so much time. They seemed innocent from 10,000, 11,000, and 12,000 feet. It was difficult to imagine, at this altitude, what was occurring under those jungle canopies.

The major had hushed now; maybe he passed out. As I stared at him, wondering what kind of person he was, I noticed a little guy sitting in front of him, a Pfc. about 20, median height, and wiry build. I'm calling him a "little guy" because he was smaller and younger than most infantrymen there, in their middle 20s.

I was surprised I had not noticed him earlier with a Chinese 7.62-mm carbine between his legs and barrel and retracted bayonet resting on his shoulder. Of course I never noticed him, he was sitting quietly, probably reflecting on what he had been involved in. The foul mouth woke up and started whispering, this being the only time I had heard foul language in Vietnam. I know Oliver Stone and Hollywood deems this necessary to depict masculinity.

I had been around real men and heroes. That little guy sitting in front of the big mouth and 26 paratroopers were twice the hero you would find on the screen. Movies would be apropos illustrating how men who did the fighting actually looked; they would be better portraying the soul of these heroes rather than the kaleidoscope of goofs shoved into our faces.

The troops left the plane on the tarmac at Oakland Army Terminal and walked to the Processing Center next door. Waiting outside the gate was fresh meat waiting to fly to Vietnam. The difference between the replacements and troops of the Big Red One and 173rd Airborne was phenomenal. The green troops sat on duffel bags wearing Class-A's with almost no metal. Each with the innocent expressions of lambs on the way to slaughter gawked at real combat soldiers walking in their slow, deliberate pace at what appeared hundreds of feet above. None of these arriving soldiers moved his eyes; each looked and walked in a straight, deliberate manner. Their jaws were set squarely, and they walked like cougars.

The replacements couldn't have asked for a better example of what real warriors looked like.

I called my parents, saying I had arrived in San Francisco and would be taking a train across the U.S., wanting to see this country I almost lost my life for. My next call was to Marty saying I would be finished processing the next day. She gave me the bus schedule and directions to her home in Burlingame.

All our papers were in order. Before discharge, the officer addressing us wanted to bring it to our attention that if we were to reenlist, we would be eligible for an attractive bonus.

He spoke to deaf ears.

June 23, 1966, I walked out of Oakland Army Terminal in Class-A's, a discharged U.S. soldier. I found a water cooler by the main gate and took a drink, washing down a malaria tablet, which I would have to continue taking for the next three Fridays.

I walked a quarter mile to the bus station with my duffel bag over my shoulder and was amazed I wasn't sweating. The temperature at the bus station was 71-degrees with the low humidity typical of California. There were no mosquitoes humming in my ears or flies drinking perspiration from my face. I had been in Vietnam for 11 months, 28 days.

Everything looked new, clean, and perfect. I absorbed the scene while the bus meandered through the streets of Oakland, across a bridge, onto a freeway, and eventually arrived at a taxi in Burlingame, California; I was a blind man seeing again.

The taxi drive left me at Marty's condo and I burst upon her scene like gangbusters, demanding the bedroom to leave my gear and change.

Marty was a nurse at the local hospital. Two male coworkers were visiting when I banged in and were not used to aggressive behavior; they were quite startled.

I opened a refrigerator for a drink, changed the radio station, grabbed a towel and took a hot shower, enjoying my first hot shower at a home for a year.

I blasted upon this domestic scene like taking control of a VC ambush—still out there.

Her friends left by the time I finished cleaning.

She offered me Italian food.

Anything fresh satisfied me.

She suggested chicken cacciatore.

I had forgotten what a chicken looked like.

I didn't feel like talking and was glad she didn't ask about Vietnam. She prepared the meal in the kitchen while I played with the novelty of a TV remote control, finding it fascinating and continued channel surfing while she made small talk.

She offered me some wine.

Anything would be OK.

She shut the air conditioner off so we could talk and asked me to open the window, cautioning me to be careful and not knock out the loose screen.

Fresh, cool Pacific air blew in. Residents were barbecuing on the patio; I smelled the charcoal-singed meat. I couldn't understand what one of the guys said; whatever it was, everybody laughed. This was the first time in over a year I was able to deeply inhale fresh air not saturated with bugs into my nostrils.

The charcoal smelled like a charred body; the human body smells sweeter than steak.

No more hungry red ants or thirsty leeches. No impossible vines, thorns, bamboo shoots, and impenetrable brush impeding my movement. 100-degree temperatures and 100-humidity—all gone.

"Ray, let's say grace before we start eating. Bless us, O Lord."

Those words Father said that day in the jungle by Cambodia, "Eat, for this is my body. Drink, for this is my blood."

"Please open the Chablis."

I forget what she said; she did it.

Our salad was enhanced by crisp lettuce, local tomatoes, sliced red onion, and topped with freshly grated parmesan cheese garnished with extra virgin olive oil on chilled plates.

She mumbled it was too bright inside and would lower the lights.

I didn't know what she was talking about.

Clean, designed cotton tablecloth with plates, silverware, and even linen napkins. The last time I had a meal in a family like atmosphere was with the Vietnamese Junk Navy on the river patrol boat. They were close to each other, a family using wooden plates and chopsticks. This meal smelled much better.

She put Johnny Mathis on, asking if I had heard current music.

There was that "Good Morning, Vietnam" guy.

Americans were generous to you over Christmas?

I wished she'd shut up. In Can Ranh Bay, we never had anything cool in two and a half months.

The chicken cacciatore was her grandmother's recipe, which her non-Italian mother "bastardized." She claimed to have revived it, tasting like Nonna's again.

I wondered why she had to use language like that, supposing it liberated California talk.

The pasta was covered with red; too much sauce and it's not thick enough, reminding me of blood.

"Did they have Italian food in Vietnam?"

How ridiculous! That guy who bled to death in my poncho looked so peaceful lying next to me that night. He was more comfortable than I. I wondered where he was now, probably in Heaven.

Spumoni was dessert; she was right, we didn't have much ice cream, although I had some once at the Air Force.

I clutched the small bowl, with two scoops, in my left hand while trying to dip the spoon in. It was difficult penetrating it because she had just taken the bowls out of the freezer. I drew the bowl closer to exert more effort. The spoon slipped, sliding between the two scoops and flinging one on the floor under the table. I dove there, clawed after it while it rolled across the hard wood floor, swiped it up with my left hand, held it, and gawked at it.

I didn't know what to do with it, so I knelt up and watched it melt in my hand.

"Ray, what are you doing? It's not going to blow up."

I broke down and cried like a baby.

Marty knelt next to me and massaged my shoulders with both hands.

That whole year had finally left—the men, Viet Cong, bugs, rain, hunger, mud, lack of rest, blood, fear, frustrations, everything—it was finally over. I had made it back alive!

I hoped the people of South Vietnam would make it also. They didn't—we threw in the towel and in 1975 they lost their freedom. An extraordinary accomplishment was achieved through Vietnam though; it marked the end of Communist expansion in the world, leaving only a few regimes left. Even North Vietnam's mentor, the former Soviet Union, enjoys freedoms never dreamed of under former despots.

"It's not over till it's over Marty, and it's finally over."

My soul returned; 36 years later I paid homage to the souls in the Wall—let them be heard.

Appendix

What Is Vietnam?

South Vietnam was on the coast south of China, west of the South China Sea, and east of Thailand on a peninsula once called French Indochina. If superimposed over the U.S., Vietnam would cover half of Virginia, then the Carolinas, and Georgia. The delta in the south is marshy; continuing north it transforms into dense jungles, and finally scrub brush-studded hills and eroded plains in the northern quarter.

Its peoples are a combination of Chinese, Malaya Polynesian, Mon-Khmer, and Indian.

China has influenced much of its culture—the language, religion, and politics—since the 1st century AD. The French priest Alexander de Rhodes transformed the alphabet into Roman in the 17th century.

The European Industrial Revolution and capitalism influenced Vietnamese culture in the early 1900s. This forced science and technology caused dissatisfaction and unrest, giving impetus to Ho Chi Minh's interest in the 1917 Russian Revolution and its socialistic Marxist-Leninist thought while working amidst Boston's intellectual atmosphere in the kitchen of the snooty Parker House.

After France was defeated by Germany in World War II, the French Vichy Government made an agreement with Japan to relinquish control of its Southeast Asian colony but continue administering its government. The U.S. Office of Strategic Services (OSS) aided Vietnamese guerrillas fighting the French and Japanese in 1945. That September Ho Chi Minh declared Vietnam independent and called it the Democratic Republic of Vietnam—Democratic to hide its Communist affiliation. In March 1946, after World War II, the French and Ho signed an agreement designating Vietnam a free state.

In October the French tried to enforce custom controls, resulting in conflict. A month later the French bombed Haiphong, killing, as Ho claimed, over 6,000 people. The French Indochina War resulted with Ho

249

asking the U.S. for military aid, which was promptly denied. This golden opportunity for him to be grateful to America was lost.

In 1947 the United Nations assisted in forming two governments in Vietnam, Ho's Communist regime in the North, and the free enterprise Republic of South Vietnam (RVN) in the South. France approved of limited independence for the state of Vietnam in June 1949. When the Communists took power in China during late 1949, they recognized the North as the legitimate government for Vietnam. The Soviet bloc was quick to back it and began supplying it militarily.

One April 28, 1954, a French-Vietnamese conference at Geneva provided that Vietnam was sovereign and independent. A truce was signed July 20, allowing 300 days for free movement between zones. Nine hundred thousand refugees, mostly Roman Catholics, fled south for freedom of religion and speech, escaping the brutal totalitarian Communist state.

The well-organized Communist Viet Minh organization remained structured underground when the Party of the North left the South in 1955. These forces were directed in 1959 by North Vietnam's Central Executive Committee to start a guerrilla war and capture the South.

The war began.

The South Vietnamese lived in what can be called a typical free society with small enterprises or stands along the streets and in marketplaces.

Theirs was a most diversified culture, a melting pot of peoples from Southeast Asia who migrated to enjoy freedoms not enjoyed in their native cultures.

The U.S. involvement started with a few advisors initially, expanding to 334,600 troops in 1969, finally drizzling down to 50 on December 31, 1973. The American public's conception of the war with its many facets was directed and molded by the news media, each attempting to outscoop the other in sensationalism for profit.

February 20, 1970: Dr. Henry Kissinger began secret peace talks in Paris with North Vietnam.

December 31, 1970: 334,600 troops were left.

April 29, 1971: the 1st Calvary Division left; 156,800 troops were left at year's end.

March 30, 1972: the Vietnam Cease-fire Campaign was reached at the peace talks.

March 31: North Vietnam began the Easter Offensive.

May 1: the province capital of Quang-Tri and I Corps fell.

May 4: indefinite halt to the peace talks.

June 10: peace talks resumed.

December 31, 1972: 24,200 U.S. troops remained in Vietnam.

January 15, 1973: President Nixon halted all U.S. offensive action.

January 27: the South, North Vietnamese, and Viet Cong agreed upon a Paris Peace Agreement.

December 31, 1973: 50 troops left.

August 1974: U.S. military aid cut from $1 billion to $700 million.

December 13: North Vietnam attacked Phuoc Long Province and II Corps.

1975. A country was about to be deserted and thousands of its citizens killed.

January 6: Phuoc Long fell.

January 8: a major invasion by the North.

April 1: the entire northern half of the country was abandoned; the South was completely outnumbered.

April 30: Saigon was captured.

Not one U.S. reporter witnessed the demise and carnage when tanks rolled into Saigon.

Soon news of the "Boat People" escaping the tyranny surfaced; this meant much copy; unfortunately their reasons for leaving were omitted.

The war ended with North Vietnam losing over a million soldiers. Contrary to popular thought, America won: losing only one-half of 1 percent of their soldiers, stimulating the demise of Communism throughout the world, and devising the best army in the world through its expertise there.

That was the Republic of Vietnam—and this is the Soul of the Wall.

Index